INFORMATION SECURITY

INFORMATION SECURITY ESSENTIALS

A Guide for Reporters, Editors, and Newsroom Leaders

Susan E. McGregor

COLUMBIA UNIVERSITY PRESS

NEW YORK

Columbia University Press
Publishers Since 1893
New York   Chichester, West Sussex
cup.columbia.edu

Library of Congress Cataloging-in-Publication Data
Names: McGregor, Susan E., author.
Title: Information security essentials : a guide for reporters, editors, and
newsroom leaders / Susan E. McGregor.
Description: New York : Columbia University Press, 2021. |
Includes bibliographical references and index.
Identifiers: LCCN 2020048115 (print) | LCCN 2020048116 (ebook) |
ISBN 9780231192323 (hardback) | ISBN 9780231192330 (trade paperback) |
ISBN 9780231549776 (ebook)
Subjects: LCSH: Journalism—Political aspects—United States—History—
21st century. | Confidential communication—Press—United States. |
Leaks (Disclosure of information)—United States. | Attribution of news—
United States. | Electronic surveillance—Government policy—United States.
Classification: LCC PN4888.P6 M35 2021 (print) | LCC PN4888.P6 (ebook) |
DDC 071/.3—dc23
LC record available at https://lccn.loc.gov/2020048115
LC ebook record available at https://lccn.loc.gov/2020048116

Columbia University Press books are printed
on permanent and durable acid-free paper.

Printed in the United States of America

Cover design: Noah Arlow
Cover image: 123rf

To the many friends and fellow travelers who work so tirelessly to keep the press secure and therefore free: I hope this book helps lighten the heavy load you carry. I cannot express how much I owe to your support, advice, encouragement, and critiques, which have made this work possible. In thanks, I will not deanonymize you here.

CONTENTS

INFORMATION SECURITY ESSENTIALS

Introduction

Late in the afternoon on Monday, June 5, 2017, the *Intercept*, a national-security-focused news organization, published an exclusive report confirming that Russian military intelligence had executed a hacking campaign in late 2016, targeting that year's U.S. presidential election. Drawing on highly classified National Security Agency documents and interviews with security experts, the article was an early and powerful scoop indicating that the Russian government had been directly involved in meddling with the U.S. election.[1]

Just hours later, however, the spotlight on the *Intercept*'s exclusive was usurped by a Justice Department press release announcing the arrest of Reality Leigh Winner, a twenty-five-year-old NSA contractor who was being charged with "removing classified material from a government facility and mailing it to a news outlet."[2] Although the Justice Department statement did not identify the *Intercept* as the outlet in question, details from an FBI affidavit and a search warrant connected to Winner's arrest quickly linked the two.[3] Within hours, the *Intercept*'s story, despite being the "most detailed U.S. government account of Russian interference in the election" to date,[4] was almost wholly overshadowed by the one that journalists fear most: the story about the *Intercept* and how it had burned its source.

In an industry where information security knowledge was once so rarefied that it took months for sources to successfully contact journalists securely,[5] the *Intercept* was an exception. Founded by the very journalists who had first received the Edward Snowden documents and broken the story of NSA mass surveillance in 2013, the *Intercept* had always made information security a central concern of its newsgathering and reporting processes, and security specialists were among its earliest hires.[6] It makes sense, then, that when Winner, disillusioned with U.S. leadership, encountered a new, classified government report outlining a foreign power's attempt to interfere with a U.S. election, she chose to send a printout of it to the *Intercept*.

A few weeks later, however, the reporter Matthew Cole, seeking to authenticate the leaked materials, confirmed to an NSA source that it had been mailed to the *Intercept* from Fort Gordon, Georgia.[7] A review of internal NSA access logs indicated that only six people had printed the report since its creation and only one had a connection with the reporter's news organization: Reality Leigh Winner.[8] Even more, the scanned documents included "microdots"—visible even on the version of the document that the *Intercept* published online—which can be decoded using a standard rubric to reveal both the model and serial number of the printer, as well as the date and time of printing.[9] While many decried the news outlet's oversight in posting scans of the documents to the web, by the time the *Intercept* had uploaded the report, Winner had already been in custody for two days.

Even with world-class experts on staff, the *Intercept* had managed to undermine its story and its credibility—and possibly even send its source to jail. News of Reality Winner's prompt arrest attracted substantial press coverage of its own, including a spate of "what went wrong" articles and social media shaming; Wikileaks founder Julian Assange even offered a $10,000 bounty for information on the reporter whose actions may have contributed to Winner's arrest.[10] As misguided as Assange's offer was, however, it highlights the fact that in today's journalistic environment, having security specialists on staff is not enough, especially if reporters don't know when to involve them in a story.[11] In precisely the same way that every editor in a newsroom—if not every reporter—is expected to know when a story needs to be "lawyered," the realities of twenty-first-century journalism mean that every reporter, editor, and newsroom leader needs to understand the foundations of information security if they hope to avoid the industry's cardinal sins: outing a source and becoming the story.

Unfortunately, there is no prescription for perfect information security, especially given the diversity of tasks involved in reporting, writing, editing, and publishing journalistic work. Because the relevance of a particular security strategy depends on the context of the story, reporter, and news organization, what a local reporter who is out in the field every day needs to know will in some ways be very different from the security concerns of a managing editor tasked with determining policy and setting security priorities for a news organization as a whole. The goal of this book, then, is to offer a kind of roadmap for journalistic information security by combining key concepts with practical guidance, organized by editorial role. By building each chapter's contents on the last, this book aims to provide journalists at all levels of responsibility and experience with both valuable foundational knowledge and actionable advice.

If the idea of integrating information security into your work seems daunting at first, consider Reality Winner's story in a slightly different light: The very documents Winner sought to expose detail the efforts of Russian government operatives who, despite being part of a well-resourced, highly sophisticated, and deeply experienced operation, relied on simple email "phishing" attacks and "spoofing" campaigns to trick usernames and passwords out of their targets.[12] Their election-interference strategies didn't involve complex computer worms or sophisticated spycraft; they essentially ran a digital marketing scam. This means that the "hacking" efforts of an advanced nation-state—whether against election officials or journalists—could have been largely neutralized by little more than multifactor authentication and a few follow-up calls.

Fortunately for news professionals, good information security practice draws on the same skill set as good journalism: a skeptical nature, a meticulous attention to detail, a tireless commitment to confirmation and fact-checking, an eye for anomalies, and a taste for process. In effect, good information security mostly requires turning one's reporting instincts toward the process of communicating, storing, and retrieving information.

What Is "Security"?

It's every breadcrumb we have. From source protection on a daily basis and your metadata collections, to thinking about things like: If you're out in the field and you're filming, how do you secure that at the end of the day when you're crossing a checkpoint?

—Reg Chua, global managing editor, Reuters

WHAT IS "SECURITY"?, CONTINUED

One of the key challenges of information security is bringing more precision to our thinking about *what* we are secure *from* or protected *against*. For example, most of us know that having a deadbolt on our front door is more "secure" than a knob lock, because it's harder than the latter to pick or physically break. We feel confident that the deadbolt will deter a casual thief, but we *also* know that it will not stop a SWAT team, an experienced lockpicker, or a professional locksmith. In these more "traditional" security contexts, most of us have enough background knowledge and experience to choose among security mechanisms without bothering to specify—even to ourselves—what they are securing us from and how.

In the digital world, however, making security judgments is not always so straightforward. In the first place, most of us are not intimately familiar with the particular security properties of various digital technologies. For example, is an online account password more like a door key or a passport? Is it easier to pick a digital lock or a physical one?

Differences in security properties are also not well embodied in digital tools themselves; "the internet" looks basically the same to us whether we are alone or with others, whether we are in the city or the countryside, and for the most part whether we are in our own home or in a foreign capital. Yet our information security needs may vary dramatically from one context to another, even if the way we interface with our information across them feels very much the same.

What, for example, does it mean for a digital messaging program to be "secure"? For some people, that will mean that no one other than the sender and the recipient can read the messages exchanged. For others, however, it will also be important that the messages cannot be traced back to either of the participants. Still others may want to know if a screenshot of the exchange is taken. While all of these features are technically achievable, there are few messaging programs that do all of these things—and good reasons why some might choose not to. When thinking about how "secure" a given tool or process is, context and expectations are everything. Whether something is "secure" can only really be determined once one has answered the questions "from whom?" and "for how long?"

Because the nuances of the digital context are not intuitive for most of us, any useful discussion of "information security" requires precise

CONTINUED

terminology, especially when describing systems, protocols, and expectations. As such, the word "secure" will not appear by itself very often in the remainder of this book. Instead, more particular terms will be introduced and defined so that you can better interpret whether a tool or process is *actually* "secure" given your particular needs and situation.

WHAT TO EXPECT FROM THIS BOOK

This book is organized into five parts. The first, chapters 1 through 3, provides a high-level history of digital communications technology and U.S. law, whose complex and sometimes surprising interplay has not just facilitated but almost mandated the surveillance capacities that shocked so many Americans after the Snowden revelations in 2013. This section also introduces two of the most important intellectual tools for improved information security: "threat modeling" and "attack trees," or resource maps. Though threat modeling and resource mapping both require little in the way of technical expertise, as analytical methods they are essential for effective reasoning and planning around information security issues, whether one is covering a protest or designing institutional guidelines.

The three subsequent parts are targeted toward particular roles in the current news ecosystem: reporters, editors, and newsroom or organizational leaders. While these categories are by no means mutually exclusive, these sections are designed to address the most substantive information-security-related questions and concerns that individuals in each of these roles are likely to encounter in the course of their work. Thus, the reporter's section (chapters 4 through 6) focuses on essentials for account, device, and source protection, as well as managing the raw materials of journalism, such as interview recordings, transcripts, data files, and drafts, both in the office and in the field. The third part (chapters 7 through 9), directed toward editors, builds on and complements the reporter's section by focusing on issues and systems specific to the commissioning and editing processes, such as communicating with freelancers, setting team policies, and managing the exchange of information among reporters, editors, and producers. This section also contains recommendations for developing coherent team-wide approaches that can minimize both security risk and overhead for an entire group or team. The fourth section (chapters 10 through 12) is designed to provide organizational leaders with institutional strategies for improving information security—from restructuring relationships between IT or security teams and the newsroom to making the hiring, technology, budgeting, and policy decisions that reflect the needs and resources of the organization as a whole.

The fifth and final section (chapters 13 and 14) turns toward the future, identifying imminent areas of concern for the press in an increasingly contentious political and technological environment. In the coming years, attacks on the press are likely to grow both more structural and more insidious as a range of actors seeks to undermine public confidence in journalism while leveraging both legal and technical mechanisms to effectively censor critical reporting. Though in many cases still nascent, these issues will continue to create resource and legitimacy crises that news organizations will be forced to navigate as they attempt to secure both their work and their relevance in the coming decade.

One final note about the approach taken here: while the goal of this book is to support robust and rigorous information security practices within the journalistic profession, its core focus is advancing journalism, not "security." This is far from a semantic distinction: a perfectly secure system is one that does nothing. This book is designed to improve security for working journalists and news publications, individuals and institutions that are driven to undertake important and, to a certain degree, inherently risky work. Thus, while there is no doubt that adopting the strategies presented here may require updating entrenched habits and cultures, they are designed to accommodate the diverse and dynamic needs of journalism as effectively and efficiently as possible. They are necessarily imperfect yet in almost every case offer protections that are orders of magnitude better than typical practices today.

Ultimately, what I hope most readers will take away from this book is that the effort to improve their information security will enhance not just the safety of their sources, stories, and colleagues but also the quality of their reporting and publishing. If anything, information security means being alert and engaged with a different aspect of your work, and this can only benefit your journalism in the long run. For in information security as in journalism, it is as Diane Sawyer once said: "If there is one thing I have learned, it's that there's no substitute for paying attention."

CHAPTER 1

The Essentials of Digital Communications

Let us consider the synthesis of a communication network which will allow several hundred major communications stations to talk with one another after an enemy attack.

—Paul Baran, "On Distributed Communications Networks"

In 1964, the engineer Paul Baran published a brief, ten-page paper summarizing the results of roughly two years of research that the Air Force had commissioned on digital data communications networks. Titled simply "On Distributed Communications Networks," Baran's paper outlines the key features and functions of a resilient, asynchronous communications system that we now know as the internet—the core protocols and technologies of which remain largely unchanged more than half a century later.[1]

Today, the technologies that grew out of Baran's ideas have been so thoroughly integrated into our social, political, and economic lives that they function almost like a digital circulatory system: networked digital devices capture, transform, transmit, and deliver information from and to every part of the world via an ever-increasing variety of devices and platforms. No practitioner or observer of twenty-first-century journalism can fail to recognize the especially dramatic effect that these technologies have had on the media industry. As of 2018, for example, more than half of U.S. adults got most of their news from digital sources, with social media alone outstripping print newspapers as a primary source of news.[2]

It's not just news consumption and delivery that the internet has transformed, however; the processes of reporting, editing, and packaging the news have also evolved dramatically. Social media sourcing, data-driven investigations, and an explosion of new publication formats—from interactive graphics to podcasts—attract both widespread audiences and critical acclaim. The demands of adapting to these technologies, however, has left little bandwidth within the industry for examining the side effects of this digital transformation, which threaten the practical and ethical integrity of both newsgathering and publishing by making sources, readers, and revenues vulnerable in myriad new ways. The process of mitigating those threats, then, requires an understanding of how the character of the internet shapes and gives rise to them in the first place.

HOW THE INTERNET WORKS

In the early 1990s, popular conceptions about the newly available consumer and commercial internet were dominated by narratives about the inherently "democratizing" influence of universal access to communications and publishing technology. Today, however, public perceptions about the internet may be much more aligned with the Cold War mentality that so permeate Baran's worldview that neither the attack he alludes to in his paper's opening nor the antagonist behind it needs introduction. Instead, Baran's paper takes for granted that the United States' communication infrastructure *will* be attacked and then moves straight into a discussion of how it—and therefore our society—might survive.

Securing the integrity, reliability, and resilience of communication systems has always been a central concern of military operations. During the American Revolution, for example, George Washington relied on private couriers rather than postal mail to protect his sensitive communications from interception and corruption.[3] It was also no accident that some of the new republic's most significant and detailed legislation concerned the handling of the mails: the Postal Act of 1792, for example, made the interruption, delay, invasion, or corruption of the mails a federal offense—a counterpoint to the British Crown's frequent interference with the Royal Mail.[4]

By the mid-twentieth century, creating a communications system that offered military-grade integrity and availability meant inverting the paradigm of the popular and widespread telephone system: rather than requiring synchronous, persistent connections, the new communication technology needed to be distributed, redundant, asynchronous, unpredictable, and cheap. To achieve this, the message format had to be discrete and independently routable. And rather than relying on a hub-and-spoke infrastructure that offered adversaries obvious targets for attack, digital messages needed to travel opportunistically across a fully decentralized network. The internet, as originally conceived, was the atomized communications design needed for survivable communications in the atomic age.

A RESILIENT SYSTEM, RIPE FOR SURVEILLANCE

To this day, the primary technological design at the heart of the internet—and all digital communications—is "packet switching," a process by which chunks of data—whether they are parts of a web page, an email message, or a video or document file—are broken into uniformly sized digital "packets." Individually labeled using a standard addressing convention, each packet is then routed to its destination via a web of interconnected "transport" nodes. Each time a node receives a packet, it reads the attached address information and passes it on to whatever adjacent node is closest to that destination, in an iterative process that is repeated until the packet reaches its intended recipient. Once all the packets in a file, webpage, MP3, etc. reach their target, they are reassembled by the recipient's device. If a packet gets lost or destroyed along the way, the receiver's system can use the "return address" on those that arrived successfully to request that any missing or corrupted packets be resent.

The small size of each packet and the opportunistic, nearest-neighbor routing approach of internet routing helps maximize both the capacity and durability of the system. For example, Baran calculated that a truly distributed internet could function even if 40 percent of its nodes were destroyed and the links among them worked only half the time.[5] Because of the high fault tolerance of the network design, node hardware can be made cheaply enough to be plentiful—and the more plentiful the nodes, the more resilient the network.

Baran's innovations transformed communications design and made the scale and robustness of the internet possible. However, that design comes with a built-in privacy cost, because the packet metadata—especially the origin and destination addresses—that the system requires to function is also precisely what makes it such an enormously efficient means of surveillance.

Packet-switching technology doesn't just govern data exchanged over the internet. It also helps stitch together almost all digital device networks, from Bluetooth keyboards to Wi-Fi routers. In order to maximize interoperability, these technologies have been designed to limit expense, with still more privacy and security costs incurred in the process. For journalists, this means that protecting your work while reporting with digital tools is very different from the precautions one had to take in the analog era. Now your tools can report on *you.*

GETTING TO THE WEB

In the days of dialup internet connections, it was arguably obvious what entities could "see" your data as it traveled from your device to the web and back again. Getting online once meant connecting your computer to an external modem with a physical cable and then plugging that modem into a physical jack in the wall, which had at some point been installed by the phone company. Your modem would actually place a telephone call to your internet service provider (ISP), a company (for example, America Online) that served as a gateway to the World Wide Web.

Compared to today's seamless, integrated, always-on versions, these early internet connections were clunky and awkward, but they did have the useful side effect of making it clear who "touched" our data when we went online: the telephone company that received the call and the ISP whose portal we used were front and center in our internet experience.

Though the wires, special phone numbers, and distinctive dialup sounds have since disappeared, connecting to the internet still involves the same basic steps as it did decades ago. But today the companies that facilitate those connections have largely converged—and with them, the data about your online life. Where once your telephone company knew you had called your ISP but only the ISP knew what websites you had visited, today it's more likely that your home telecom and ISP services are provided by a single company that may also provide your mobile phone service, too. If so, where several companies once had an imperfect and incomplete view of your digital communications activities, today it is possible for one company to own an incredibly detailed portrait of both your physical movements and online activities. This means that any attempt to obfuscate who you are contacting or what you are researching must take this comprehensive view of your digital communications into account.

GETTING ONLINE WITHOUT WIRES

When wired connections to the web were the norm, the ability for people nearby to snoop on our internet activities was largely limited to "shoulder surfing"—someone literally looking over your shoulder to view your screen. In a world of wireless connections, however, there are much more surreptitious ways for those around us to eavesdrop on our digital communications.

For example, when you connect to a wireless router or hotspot, parts of your device's unique machine address code (MAC) are used to label your requests for web pages and other data, so that the router can make sure that each of the devices connected to it received the correct content. The way the router learns that MAC in the first place is from your device: whenever your Wi-Fi is on, your device is regularly broadcasting its MAC out to the world and waiting for something that looks like a router to respond. Interspersed among these announcements of its MAC, your device will also go through its list of remembered networks, shouting out their names to see if they're in range; your mobile phone does something similar when looking for a cellular signal. Under the hood of our "automatic" wireless connections is a noisy, ad hoc process in which devices are constantly announcing not just their presence but their identifying details and history, and then waiting for routers or cellular towers to respond. The problem is that when a router or cell tower *does* respond, your devices have no built-in way to know if they're legitimate.

THE IMITATION GAME

The rapid evolution of digital communications technologies has been made possible by an emphasis on *interoperability*—the ability of devices to interact or interface with one another. While this has been fostered through both open standards and trust-based models, it's the trust-based model that governs in the case of Wi-Fi connections. What this means is that *any* type of machine or device can declare itself a router, and your devices will believe it. Because there is no technical way for your devices to confirm that a given wireless network is trustworthy, it's up to *you* to make that judgment call before you let your devices connect.

Whom Can You Trust?

Trust plays a huge role in the proper functioning of digital communication technologies; large portions of the technical systems we rely on assume that the parties running those technologies are behaving honestly. There are moments when our systems call on us, as users, to decide what sites, apps, or networks should be trusted—and it's up to us to ensure that they should be. When we are connecting to a new Wi-Fi network, visiting a website that our browser has deemed unsafe or insecure, or installing apps or software on our devices, we'll usually see messages like "Connect?," "Proceed anyway," or "I accept." What these messages are really asking is: "Are you sure you trust the people running this hotspot/website/app?" For most of us, most of the time, the answer is usually, "I don't know. Maybe?"

Most of us use dozens of Wi-Fi connections, websites, and apps on a daily basis, but almost all of are them made, hosted, and administered by people we'll never meet and whose skills we cannot quantify. So there is something mildly absurd in the idea that we can make meaningful choices about whom and what to trust. Yet these systems do—and will continue to—require us to make these decisions. Fortunately, even without knowing the actual people—or sometimes even the companies—behind these systems, there are some simple heuristics that can help you evaluate how risky saying "yes" may be:

- *Wi-Fi hotspots*: Always independently confirm the network name (also known as the Service Set IDentifer, or SSID) before making the connection. Look for a physical sign in the area, or ask an employee to confirm the correct network. Spend the extra fifteen seconds to confirm that the name you see in your connection window exactly matches the one posted. *Bonus:* Only choose networks that require a password (it's OK if it's the same for everybody; more on this later), and don't tell your device to remember the network unless it's really necessary.

- *Websites*: Embedded in every web browser is a list of the certificate authorities (CAs) that the designers of your browser have decided to trust. While we'll address this in more detail shortly, a website's certificate is basically like a driver's license, ostensibly proving who owns and operates the site; CAs are the companies that issue those certificates. When you see a warning that says "connection unsafe" or something similar, it means either that there is something wrong with the site's certificate (it's expired, for example) or that your browser doesn't trust the issuing CA. This is why you sometimes get a warning for a given website in one browser and not another. CAs offer different levels of verification depending on how extensively they have confirmed the identity of a website owner—something like the difference between a library card and a passport. The most robust proof of identity is called "extended

CONTINUED

validation" (EV), and sites that have been authenticated in this way will have their company name appear in the URL bar to the left of the https or www. Since a large number of high-profile websites don't use EV, however, you will need to examine the domain (everything before the .com or .net, for example) letter for letter before trusting the site. No matter what, you should never enter username/password credentials into a site that isn't on HTTPS.

• *Apps*: The truth is, it's almost impossible to be fully confident about whether to trust an app or program. While major companies like Apple and Google do some vetting of programs in their app stores, the reality is that installing software on your device is like inviting someone into your home: you cannot watch their every move, so you need to feel comfortable that they won't rifle through your belongings or steal your valuables on the way to the bathroom. With that in mind, don't install apps you wouldn't let through your front door.

• *Software updates*: Once you've installed an app or operating system, you should *always* run updates as soon as possible. Since your operating system can verify that an update is legitimate, its origin will have been confirmed and vetted before you're ever asked to install it.

While the process that mobile phones use to look for nearby cellular towers is similar to that used for Wi-Fi, modern cellular signals (such as 3G, 4G, 5G, and LTE) do actually have a mutual authentication process that confirms the ownership of a tower before your device connects. The problem, however, is that if the strongest available signal is for an older, less-secure standard, then mutual authentication isn't required, and your phone will just trust that it's a real cell tower.

Unfortunately, this can open the door for cell-tower impersonators— also known as "IMSI-catchers" or sometimes by the commercial name "Stingray." For years, these devices have been used by law enforcement to track criminals and, allegedly, activist groups.[6] These days, however, such devices can be readily constructed out of off-the-shelf materials, often for less than US$100.

The reason it matters what routers or cellular networks you're connecting to is that *every data request your device makes is visible to the router or network operator*. This means that a dishonest router or a cell-tower impersonator can easily surveil your online activities, often without you being aware of it.

Even beyond confirming the network name, the privacy and security of your Wi-Fi connection also depend on whether the network is *secured* or *unsecured*. As users, the primary difference between the two is that the first requires a password and the second does not, but there are important differences between the two in terms of how your data is handled.

A Wi-Fi network that requires a password (these usually appear with a little padlock icon or are labeled "secured" in your wireless settings) will *encrypt* the data that your device exchanges with it, protecting your information from being snooped on by other devices in the area. Because an unsecured network doesn't encrypt your data, nearby devices can easily "overhear" your every exchange. Even worse, the data you're waiting for can actually be intercepted and modified on its way to you, opening the possibility of you seeing manipulated information.

Because they are so easy to monitor and manipulate, you should generally avoid using unsecured or "open" Wi-Fi networks. In a pinch, you can always "hotspot" your phone and use that to connect your computer to the web if needed; your cellular data connection is encrypted by default.

Connecting to known, secured wireless networks helps protect your data as it travels to and from the internet, but the broader security of your data also depends on the type of website to which you're connecting. Just like a Wi-Fi connection can be secured or unsecured, your connection to a website or service can be either secured or unsecured as well. In both cases, a "secured" connection means your data is encrypted; in an "unsecured" connection, it is not. And while an unsecured wireless network connection makes your data vulnerable to nearby devices, a connection to an unsecured website (that is, one that starts with http rather than https) makes your data vulnerable to *any device* between you and the website.

This means that as your data passes through any number of internet nodes—nodes that are necessarily operated by thousands of different people and organizations, as well as hundreds of governments and corporations—the data you exchange with an unsecured website will be visible to them all. So despite the fact that there is only a one-letter differ-ence between websites that start with http and those that start with https, the difference in how your data is handled and protected is truly worlds apart. This is true whether you're connecting to a wireless network, to a website, or even to another user.

What Exactly Can Encryption Protect?

Encryption is a big part of privacy and security in the digital world because it's the primary way that digital data can be transformed (essen-tially, "scrambled") in a way that makes it unreadable to anyone who lacks the correct "key." With the right key available, the digital scram-bling process can be reversed and the original data reconstructed (decrypted) from the encrypted version.

If this seems a little abstract, imagine this: You buy a new Rubik's cube and write a message on each side. To get this message to a friend without anyone else being able to read it, you scramble up the cube. As you do so, however, you record every turn and rotation and give that list of steps to your friend in advance. Now it doesn't matter *who* sees the cube; the message will be inaccessible until your friend uses your instruc-tions to reverse the "scrambling" process, thereby revealing your original message.

While your scrambling scheme (encryption) has protected the con-tents of your message, however, it cannot hide that the message exists: anyone who sees—or is asked to pass along—your cube definitely knows that data is being exchanged, by whom it's being exchanged, and that it is encrypted. Likewise, when you make an encrypted (HTTPS) con-nection on the web, the router can still see what web domain you're vis-iting, and every node that passes along those requests can still see both the origin address of the request and the destination address of the web-site or service being used. Every device—router, modem, and internet node—will also be able to tell that the data is encrypted, along with other basic metadata.

Hopefully, this example has helped clarify the basic protections and limitations of encrypting data. Nevertheless, the metaphor invites addi-tional questions. For example, what if someone messes with the Rubik's cube while it is in transit, that is, after you sent it but *before* your friend receives it? Why couldn't someone else solve the cube on their own? How do you get the solving instructions to your friend without someone finding or copying them? And if you can safely get the instructions to your friend, why would you need encryption for the actual message at all?

If you were asking yourself any of this already: Well done! A key part of information security is looking for potential "holes" in a system, and these questions represent some pretty big logistical and security hurdles. While the specifics are covered in detail in the bonus section at the end of this chapter, here's an quick overview:

• *What if someone tries to manipulate your encrypted data?* At least you'll know they've done it. Encrypted data can be changed, but generally it can't be forged. The interference will be obvious because what you (or your friend, or the website) receives will be nonsense. If data sent over an unencrypted connection is changed, meanwhile, you might not realize it.

• *What if someone solves the encryption on their own?* The best short answer here is that they can't; it would take too long. As the number of "steps" used to scramble your message increases, the time it would take another person (computer, really) to try out all the possible steps required increases exponentially. Without the instructions, the solving time can be many, many years. As computers get faster, however, it means that data encrypted with older, shorter instruction sets is no longer as safe.

• *How do you safely exchange the required "instructions" with your friend? If this is already possible, why bother with the encryption process at all?* The answer to the first question is: also encryption, but a different kind. The encryption/decryption protecting your transmitted data is known as "symmetric" encryption, where decryption consists of doing the encryption steps in reverse. "Asymmetric" encryption, which is addressed in the bonus section at the end of this chapter, uses some clever math to ensure that your friend can safely figure out how to decrypt your message even if you cannot communicate the instructions to her privately beforehand.

SEEKING AUTHENTICITY

As with wireless networks, it's up to you as the user to decide which websites are trustworthy. Not too long ago, the fact that a website offered an encrypted (HTTPS) connection was considered a key indicator of how trustworthy it was, because creating such a connection was expensive and time consuming. Today, however, encrypted connections can be created for free, which is a great thing for the overall privacy and security of the web. On the other hand, it means that you need to be even more meticulous when deciding which websites to trust.

This is where so-called certificate authorities (CAs) come in. CAs are organizations that essentially vouch for the identity of a web domain or website owner. In this process, the CA takes the place of the posted sign or cafe employee; it the CA that confirms to your device that the website you are visiting is operated by a particular organization. However, just as you might not expect a server to be able to guarantee that whoever set up the restaurant's router did so correctly and securely, CAs don't necessarily extensively verify the identity of every organization to which they issue a certificate. In many cases, they only confirm that the person requesting the certificate can actually update the contents of the website ("domain validation") or that their organization is legally registered somewhere ("organizational validation"). "Extended validation," meanwhile, also looks for a physical address, a publicly listed and functional telephone number, and a business history of at least a few years. You can tell if you're on a website that's been through the extended validation (EV) process because their business name will appear in green to the left of the https in your browser's URL bar; for the other two, you'll just see a padlock icon in that space.

Ultimately, however, your best protection against lookalike sites in particular is to check—letter for letter—that the domain in your browser's URL bar is the one you intend to visit.[7] Once you've confirmed that you're on the right site, do yourself a favor and create a bookmark or "favorite" in your web browser—and use that to be sure you're navigating to the correct URL in the future.

Where's the Dotted Line?

Web browsers come preinstalled with the names and signatures of trusted certificate authorities (CAs) chosen by whoever built the software; this is what your browser compares to the cryptographic signatures on a given website's certificate. If the CA signature that your browser receives from the website matches the one it has on file, it will add the little lock icon to your URL bar; if the signature doesn't match or is expired, however, you'll see some other icon and a message to the effect of "not secure" instead.

It's not just website certificates, however, that can be signed in this way; cryptographic signatures can be applied to any type of digital data, whether or not the data itself is even encrypted. Checking such signatures offers a way to confirm that the data hasn't been changed by a third party, because the signature is unique to a particular piece of content and to the date, time, and entity by whom it was signed.

This is how software makers ensure that their installation and security update packages haven't been tampered with before they get to your computer, and why you can trust (and should always install) them: your computer will already have the original program's basic signature on file and can use it to confirm that the content of the update really was made by the same organization.

WHEN ERRORS ARISE

What does it mean when you see a certificate error—which will usually manifest as a message warning that a site is "untrusted," "not private," or "not safe"—when you try to visit a website? Usually this indicates one of two situations:

1. *Your web browser doesn't trust the CA that signed the website's certificate*: Because of this decision by your browser maker, your computer has no comparison signature with which to authenticate the signature that the website has sent; this is also why the same site can generate an error in one browser and not in another. Which CAs to trust is another issue, and one that requires your judgment; you can either rely on your browser maker entirely or accept the risk of adding an unknown CA to your browser's existing list.

2. *The signature on the certificate is malformed or expired*: Like a driver's license or passport, website certificates are only valid for a certain period of time. Because an expired or malformed signature on the website's certificate may mean that the domain has since changed hands, you should be careful to independently confirm who runs the website before trusting any information it contains.

Because obtaining and maintaining a website certificate is up to the operators of a given website, in most cases your only real choice when you encounter certificate problems is between avoiding the website altogether and ignoring the warning and visiting it anyway. While obviously less than ideal, you should at least make the choice with your eyes open: If HTTPS isn't available, know that basically anyone can both observe and manipulate what you're seeing; the same is true for certificate problems, unless you decide to trust a new CA. Of course, even if all is well with the connection, you'll still need to decide—whether based on the level of validation or by doing a letter-for-letter check of the domain in the URL bar—whether the website you're on is really the one you're looking for.

BRINGING THE CLOUD DOWN TO EARTH

At this point, we've actually covered the major technical systems involved in both getting online and exchanging digital information with websites and services via the internet; we've also addressed the interplay between technical security mechanisms—like encryption—and inherently trust-based ones, like selecting wireless networks and certificate authorities.

Of course, our lives online are about more than just browsing the web; we also use "the cloud" to store, retrieve, share, and publish information. While there are legal dimensions to security in the cloud that we'll discuss in the next chapter, understanding the infrastructure of the cloud is another important aspect of information security.

THE CLOUD IS JUST SOMEONE ELSE'S COMPUTER

At base, the cloud is just a catch-all term for computers and programs that we access through the internet but that are owned, operated, and maintained by someone else. There is nothing ethereal about cloud computing; a document in the cloud differs from one saved on your computer only because it's actually saved on *someone else's* computer and you access it via the internet. Computers that are specifically configured and used for this purpose are typically referred to as "servers."

Almost every time we exchange data via the internet, the thing we are sending information to and receiving it from is a server. Servers store the content that we experience as websites, social media platforms, online data portals, and document storage and editing. While the connections and technologies of the web discussed thus far govern how we get to that content, servers are where it lives. We call these millions of machines "the cloud" because we don't generally concern ourselves much with where the physical server is located (also, "the cloud" is much more marketable than "some server farm in New Jersey").

The web servers in the cloud really only differ from your personal computer in that they are configured to correctly send, receive, and interpret the data and metadata that travel over the internet. For example, when you load a news organization's homepage, along with the main homepage content request, your device sends information about what type of browser you are using, how big your screen is, and what your display language is. This is how the server knows to send back data in a form that is theoretically optimized for your device and location, among other things.

Do You See What I See?

The metadata that gets sent from your devices to web routers, internet nodes, and cloud services is not something that most of us want visually cluttering our experience of the web. While that makes aesthetic sense, the relatively hidden nature of this data can make it difficult to appreciate just how much can be revealed by the undisplayed information that accompanies our content as it is uploaded, downloaded, transported, and transformed between our devices and a given web server.

In general, whatever you can see *on* a web server can also generally be seen *by* that server. If you can read the contents of some document on a website, in most cases, *so can the owner of that server.* This means that email you're able to read online can also be read by the service that hosts that email, and the same goes for photographs, audio recordings, and video files. So while an encrypted connection protects your data from observation and manipulation as it travels between your device and the web server, once it arrives at either of those endpoints, *it's no longer encrypted.* When we send an email to someone, for example, the reality is that we send an email to a server, which then passes a copy of that message on to our recipient's server. When she logs in, she can read the message—but so can both her server and ours.

The exception to this rule is when a system provides so-called end-to-end (E2E) encryption, which is now offered by a wide range of messaging apps and some specialized email services. Despite the distinct name, E2E messaging apps use precisely the same encryption process

CONTINUED

that HTTPS websites do, except that authenticating the identity of your conversation partner is handled by a certificate authority; that is something that you do implicitly by, say, looking someone up via their phone number. Once again, the system is relying on you, the user, to confirm (or "authenticate") who owns that phone number and know that it's the person you want to chat with. In order to offer a seamless experience, however, E2E-encrypted services require everyone to be on the same platform, sacrificing some interoperability, in this case, for privacy and security.

THE "META-" THREAT

The metadata that is exposed to online service providers when you visit their websites is often essential to ensuring that those sites and services work as intended. Even much-maligned "cookies"—another catchy name for what is actually just a text file saved on your computer—are essential to the functioning of something as basic as online shopping carts; without them, online retailers would have no good way to keep track of what items you have looked at or added to your cart without forcing you to log in first.

Between required billing information and the metadata that accompanies your every online request, however, suddenly the tiny, necessary bits of metadata required simply to visit a website add up to an enormous pool of information that is often aptly described as a "fingerprint": with our unique combinations of cookies and browser characteristics, it is increasingly trivial to distinguish (or reidentify) each of us via our online activities. This means that unless we take steps to obfuscate our work online, telecommunications companies can easily determine things like whom we are talking to and what we are researching. This is especially true because the majority of web cookies are created and controlled by a very small number of very large companies.

I highlight this not to make you throw up your hands in resignation (or despair) but largely because there are both technical and legal ways to avoid this information being used so effectively for surveillance, if individuals and legislators decide to put in the effort. In the meantime, understanding these technical requirements and assumptions of exchanging digital information online is essential for developing better information security, especially when journalism is so dependent on the incredible, resilient, robust, and surveillance-optimized ecosystem that is the internet.

BONUS SECTION: UNDERSTANDING ENCRYPTION

Cryptography is an essential component of contemporary information security. Though difficult to design and build properly, modern encryption tools are simply a way of obscuring messages using ciphers—a technique that has been in use for thousands of years.

The Romans, for example, used a strategy known as the "shift cipher" to protect the contents of confidential correspondence: each letter in the text was replaced by the one that appeared a specific number of places ahead of it in the alphabet (say, six).[8] Deciphering the message successfully is simply a matter of knowing the alphabet in use and reversing the "rule" used in the original cipher.

This type of "symmetric" cipher has been used in everything from statecraft to spy novels ever since. From the World War II–era Enigma machine to the book ciphers of *Sherlock*, a symmetric cipher (or symmetric *encryption*) mechanism remains a fast, strong, and efficient way to protect the contents of a message from prying eyes. Without access to the correct rule and reference (or "key"), a well-designed symmetric cipher is nearly impossible to break.

Yet symmetric encryption has its limitations. First, it depends on a *shared secret*—that is, both the sender and the receiver must know the key with which the cipher was built. At the same time, they must exchange or agree on this information without anyone else finding out, or that third party will be able to decrypt their messages as well. This presents a kind of first-contact problem that is familiar in journalism: How do you share a secret with someone you've never met?

The second limitation of symmetric encryption follows from the first: Because someone with access to the right key can decode *any* message it has been used to encrypt, protecting exchanges with two different correspondents requires a unique key for each of them. As your list of contacts grows, the task of managing the distinct keys needed to communicate with each of them grows unwieldy, if not impossible—much as it does with remembering all of our various passwords and logins.

In the 1970s, however, a group of cryptographers introduced a practical mechanism for using computers to perform what is known as "asymmetric" encryption,[9] which helps overcome these limitations. In asymmetric encryption, each individual has a unique pair of keys—one public, one private—that can be used to exchange encrypted messages with them: the public key is like a phone number or email address; it's what someone needs to send an encrypted message to you, and you can share it freely. The private key is required to decrypt messages, so it needs to be kept secret. Although the two alphanumeric keys are related, the private key, thanks to some sophisticated math, cannot be derived from the public key.

As with phone numbers and email addresses, of course, if you want to be able to send and receive encrypted messages, you need to have a set of encryption keys. This is done for you automatically by end-to-end-encrypted messaging systems like Signal and WhatsApp, or it can be done explicitly *by* you, as in platform-agnostic end-to-end-encrypted systems like PGP/GPG.[10]

Public/private key pairs are typically used one of two ways. Platform-agnostic key pairs can be used directly to encrypt data, either to you or to others. For example, Ed can encrypt a message directly to Laura's public key, and she can decrypt it using her private key. This is convenient because now any number of people can send Laura encrypted messages, and she only needs to keep track of her one key pair.

At the same time, if Laura loses control of her private key, anyone who gains access to it can now access anything that was ever encrypted to her public key. If that happens, Laura also loses "deniability," because the fact that her private key decrypts her messages proves that the corresponding public key belongs to her.

Deniability is essential if you need to protect your communications with encryption without *also* proving with whom you have been communicating; as we'll see in the next chapter, this is especially important for source protection. Fortunately, around the same time that asymmetric cryptography was invented, a way to use public/private key pairs to generate a "shared secret" between two entities who hadn't previously communicated was also developed. That shared secret can then be used to symmetrically encrypt future messages between Ed and Laura.

The advantage of this latter system is that it offers "forward secrecy," a crucial ingredient in deniability. Because they can generate a new shared secret at any time, Laura and Ed can exchange a few messages and then literally throw away the key. Once that symmetric key is gone, it's impossible to reconstruct the messages *and* to prove who exchanged them—thereby providing both encryption and deniability.

Most encryption systems "in the wild"—including encrypted Wi-Fi connections, HTTPS connections, end-to-end-encrypted chat applications, and even PGP/GPG systems—make use of both symmetric and asymmetric encryption. In each case, the public keys (website certificates are actually just public keys) are used to derive a numerical shared secret, which is then used to symmetrically encrypt the messages being exchanged, for as long as the "session" lasts. This combination offers the strengths of symmetric encryption while solving the problem of unmanageable key lists and first contact.

Beyond allowing Laura and Ed to derive a shared secret, however, asymmetric encryption also lets them cryptographically sign their messages using a combination of the message content, the date/time, and their private key; if Laura signs a message to Ed, he can use her public key to validate that it came from her. A valid cryptographic signature guarantees the *integrity* of the message, proving that it has not been tampered with since it was encrypted. The signature also proves the *authenticity* of the message, to the extent that it proves which public key belongs to the signer. This is precisely the opposite of the deniability discussed earlier: a cryptographic signature creates the property of *nonrepudiation*: if the signature is valid, the sender *must* have signed the message in question and thus cannot credibly deny it later. While nonrepudiation may be bad for source protection, however, it is great for things like security updates and website certificates, two types of situations in which you want to be sure that content came from a particular entity and that it hasn't been tampered with.

Of course, no encryption technology is perfect. Most flaws to encryption systems are introduced—intentionally or unintentionally[11]—through the standards and code used to implement them. Using encryption systems also comes with overhead of its own: using PGP/GPG, for example, requires using the software correctly and having exclusive control over some physical device—usually a computer—which may be a barrier for many journalistic sources. Even easy-to-use, encrypted mobile messaging apps require that all parties agree to use the same one, which can be a challenge in and of itself. Also, most encryption systems protect the *content* of our communications, not the metadata about it, which can also have significant consequences for sources because metadata is so identifiable.

Finally, although a cryptographic signature can authenticate the source of a message to the extent that it confirms control of a particular public key, this still does not prove *who* the person behind the key really is. In

2014, for example, Jesselyn Radack sent an email encrypted via PGP/GPG to "Glenn Greenwald"—the only trouble being that the public key she used didn't actually belong to him.[12] As always in journalism, verification is essential—especially when it comes to key ownership.

Despite its limitations, however, encryption remains an important component of modern information security. Understanding how and why encryption works will expand your toolkit for protecting your data, stories, sources, and colleagues. Especially given the many ways that digital communications can make all of those things vulnerable, being savvy about encryption is an invaluable journalistic skill.

CHAPTER 2

Digital Data in a Legal Frame

The right of the people to be secure in their persons, houses, papers, and effects, against unreasonable searches and seizures, shall not be violated, and no warrants shall issue, but upon probable cause, supported by oath or affirmation, and particularly describing the place to be searched, and the persons or things to be seized.

—U.S. Constitution, Amendment IV

Though colloquially known as protecting the "right to privacy," the Fourth Amendment to the U.S. Constitution includes neither "private" nor "privacy" among its fifty-four words. Though the familiar concept of a "reasonable expectation of privacy" can be traced to a 1967 Supreme Court opinion that dealt specifically with telecommunications, however, more than half a century later the United States still lacks any cohesive legislative approach to digital and communications privacy. This reality stands in stark contrast to the Founders' commitment, both constitutionally and legislatively, to guaranteeing and securing under federal law the privacy, security, and accessibility of postal mail, the most important communications technology of the time.[1]

This disconnect between digital and analog privacy rights means that understanding the landscape of legal protections (and loopholes) that governs digital information and communications in the United States can be challenging. At the same time, an awareness of how legal tools can be used to expose and exploit our newsgathering activities and materials is an essential aspect of modern journalistic information security. The following sections are designed to offer some insight into how the contemporary sense of a constitutional "right to privacy" developed and, perhaps more importantly, why it doesn't protect us against the collection, sharing, or outright sale of digital data (and metadata), even when it is "particularly describing" our interactions with our "persons, houses, papers, and effects," as mentioned in the Constitution.

"CONTENT," "METADATA," AND THE "THIRD-PARTY DOCTRINE"

In 1968, the Omnibus Crime Control and Safe Streets Act—commonly known as the Wiretap Act—rationalized and expanded upon a series of Supreme Court rulings establishing that the interception of communications in a physical space where an individual had a "reasonable expectation of privacy" required a warrant.[2]

In particular, the Supreme Court's decision in the 1967 case *Katz v. United States* asserted that the Fourth Amendment protected "people, not places."[3] As such, the Court ruled that when police used a recording device to capture the plaintiff's side of a telephone conversation in a public telephone booth, it had violated his "reasonable expectation of privacy." Because the act of recording constituted a "search" of Katz's conversation under the Fourth Amendment, the Court found that law enforcement should have obtained a warrant. In his concurring opinion, moreover, Justice Harlan noted specifically that "electronic, as well as physical, intrusion into a place . . . may constitute a violation of the Fourth Amendment."

Less than a decade later, however, the Supreme Court established in *United States v. Miller* that the defendant did not have a similarly "reasonable expectation of privacy" around records of financial transactions held by his bank, because in depositing money, cashing checks, etc., Miller had "voluntarily conveyed and . . . exposed" information that he knew would be shared with the bank and its affiliates "in the ordinary course of business."[4] In *Smith v. Maryland* just three years later, the court cited *Miller* when affirming that a warrant was not required to obtain the numbers dialed from a home telephone, under the rationale that "telephone users . . . typically know that the numbers they dial are transmitted to the phone company and recorded."[5]

The rulings in *Miller* and *Smith* help form the basis of what is now broadly known as "third-party doctrine," a line of legal reasoning that asserts that an individual has no "reasonable expectation of privacy" around information shared with a third party. Because police recorded Katz's own words in a public telephone booth, he was considered a "first party" to the contents of that exchange. Miller and Smith, by contrast, had "voluntarily" shared information about their financial transactions and calling patterns with a "third party" and therefore could expect no privacy protections to apply.

In the decades since the decisions in *Miller* and *Katz*, of course, the volume and variety of metadata that individuals "voluntarily" share with third parties has increased exponentially. Every time you open an app, click on a link, send an email, or receive a text message, you generate dozens of kinds of metadata that, legally, belong to the app developers, internet service providers, email hosts, and telecommunications companies that make those products and services. While recent Supreme Court rulings have carved out specific protections for metadata that provides a detailed record of an individual's "physical movements,"[6] whether those interpretations will be extended to other types of metadata is still unclear.[7] In the meantime, the vast majority of work we do with our digital devices and connections is, in the United States and many other jurisdictions, legally accessible to law enforcement and others without requiring the judicial oversight of a warrant.

CONTENT IS KING?

Unfortunately, the Stored Communications Act portion of the 1986 Electronic Communications and Privacy Act (ECPA)—still the only U.S. federal legislation to comprehensively address digital communications and data storage—only formalizes and extends the degree to which digital communications metadata is accessible to law enforcement.[8] In fact, its "Required Disclosure of Customer Communications or Records" provision enumerates the many forms of metadata that service providers *must* turn over to law enforcement when provided with a subpoena or court order, including:

- name (of account holder);
- address (of account holder);
- local and long distance records, or records of session times and durations, including type of service used;
- length of service, including start date;
- telephone, instrument number, or other subscriber number or identity, including any temporary network address; and
- means and source of payment, including credit card or bank account number if applicable.

Meanwhile, even the parts of the ECPA designed to protect the contents of digital accounts and files are incredibly limited by modern standards: a warrant is required only if the content is less than 180 days old. Otherwise, digital data stored with a third-party provider can generally be accessed through a court order or administrative subpoena, neither of which requires evidence of wrongdoing or significant judicial oversight to procure. Though technically obtaining information this way requires that the subscriber be notified, there are several exemptions that allow this notice to be delayed nearly indefinitely.

DIGITAL COMMUNICATIONS AND THE DEATH OF JOURNALISTIC PRIVILEGE

While open hostility toward the press became the norm in the United States following the 2016 presidential election, the aggressive prosecution of individuals who leak government information to journalists began under the Obama administration, which pursued ten leak prosecutions in eight years—more than all previous presidential administrations combined.[9] This trend accelerated under Trump, adding more than half a dozen leak prosecutions to the list.[10] Though politics may be encouraging the government's increasingly combative rhetoric around the press, the increase in prosecutions of government sources is essentially technological, as the degree of metadata connecting sources to reporters in recent years has proved more than sufficient for successful legal actions.

For example, even as the *New York Times* reporter James Risen waged a seven-year legal battle to avoid being compelled to name a source for material that appeared in his book *State of War*, prosecutors for the government relied principally—and, in the end, successfully—on metadata about Risen's communications with the former CIA operative Jeffrey Sterling to secure the latter's conviction under the Espionage Act for leaking classified information.[11] While Risen never testified at Sterling's trial, Fourth Circuit Judge Leonie M. Brinkema, who presided over Sterling's case, highlighted that the phone and email records connecting Sterling and Risen constituted "very powerful circumstantial evidence" that Sterling was indeed the source of the leak.[12]

In other words, even though for decades U.S. journalists successfully relied on state- and district-level shield laws—which exist throughout the country apart from Wyoming—as a means to protect the identity of their sources,[13] Risen's case and several others illustrate how thoroughly these privileges have been undermined by the technical realities and legal conditions of digital communications metadata. As one Department of Justice official noted during Obama's second term: "Prosecutions of those who leaked classified information to reporters have been rare, due, in part, to the inherent challenges involved in identifying the person responsible for the illegal disclosure and in compiling the evidence necessary to prove it beyond a reasonable doubt."[14]

Even legislation that explicitly acknowledges the need for government restraint in accessing journalists' metadata has often proved less than effective. The controversial "business records" section of the PATRIOT Act (which may be preserved in the coming years through the USA FREE-DOM Reauthorization Act),[15] for example, which gives law enforcement broad powers to "require production of any tangible things" as part of any "foreign intelligence" investigation, stipulates that such requests are lawful only "provided that such an investigation is not conducted solely upon activities protected by the First Amendment." Yet the mechanism for determining whether an investigation violates that standard is described only by the guidelines of the attorney general, which do not carry the force of law. So when the Department of Justice obtained the call records of several Associated Press journalists without notice in early 2013,[16] the company's only recourse was public complaint.[17] Despite the fact that the attorney general's own guidelines called for such subpoenas to be "narrowly drawn," some of the records subpoenaed were for the AP offices' general numbers. Hearst's general counsel Eve Burton pointed out that despite the apparent violation of policy, "the AP cannot march into court and sue the DOJ."[18]

Likewise, although the Privacy Protection Act (PPA) of 1980 helps guard news organizations against the use of search warrants to obtain materials that have been gathered "in anticipation of communicating such materials to the public," violations of the PPA can only be pursued via civil damage suits.[19] Recent cases of law enforcement trying to access news organizations' materials this way have only been stopped by last-minute court orders.[20]

WHERE LAW AND TECHNOLOGY COLLIDE

Metadata and direct testimony, of course, are not the only means by which the authorities can obtain information about a journalist's sources. Searches of digital devices and platforms, such as computers, hard drives, mobile phones, and social media accounts, have the capacity to reveal large quantities of sensitive reporting information, none of which is exempt from seizure if it is discovered in the course of executing a lawful—if unrelated—search.[21]

At the moment, the only meaningful exception to this rule is in the context of arrest. In 2014, the Supreme Court ruled in *Riley v. California* that while a warrantless search of someone's physical person upon arrest is reasonable "in order to remove any weapons" they might be carrying, since "data stored on a cell phone cannot itself be used as a weapon," it cannot legally be searched incident to arrest without a warrant.[22] Though recent district court decisions have also suggested that suspicionless forensic searches of digital devices cannot be conducted at border crossings, the broader reach of those decisions is not yet clear. The legality of "manual" searches (including of accessible files and accounts) at the border, meanwhile, has repeatedly been upheld.[23]

Within the United States, however, searches of encrypted devices and account contents can sometimes be resisted on legal grounds, depending on the decryption mechanism required. In 2013, for example, a Seventh Circuit ruling held that forcing a defendant to decrypt the contents of a drive to which he had not admitted having access was likely a violation of his Fifth Amendment rights. Specifically, the court asserted that while the act of decryption can be likened to handing over the key to a lockbox, even this simple "production" of materials—which does not typically enjoy Fifth Amendment protections—can in some cases have "communicative aspects" akin to testimony.[24] In general, however, decryption mechanisms that require only a fingerprint or facial recognition may not afford the same level of legal protection as passcode- or password-based decryption mechanisms, because the former do not "relate a factual assertion or disclose information" in the Fifth Amendment sense.[25]

THE GLOBAL PERSPECTIVE

Both U.S. legal scholars and the public at large believe that more should be done to protect Americans' privacy,[26] yet the creation of comprehensive privacy legislation in the United States in the near term seems unlikely. Though states like California and New York have begun to take action to protect individuals' data,[27] at the federal level even basic protections for digital communications like email have, for years, failed to make meaningful progress toward law.[28]

Globally, however, the European Union's General Data Protection Regulation (GDPR) constitutes a sweeping privacy regulation requiring, among other provisions, that consent be obtained before collecting *any* information about "users." It also provides options for legal redress on the basis of privacy violations or other harms. While Americans have enjoyed some incidental benefits from these changes, the impact of the GDPR in the United States has thus far been largely as a case study for how more comprehensive privacy protections may interact with a metadata-driven economy.

Stronger legal protections for Americans' digital information could go a long way toward restoring the legal potency of shield laws, whose effectiveness has been undercut by decades of technological change. At the same time, there is no set of legal precedents and legislative solutions that can eliminate digital communications' information security risks entirely. Instead, cultivating an understanding of both the laws and the technologies that govern today's digital communications systems serves as a starting point for understanding how to assess, prioritize, and, most importantly, mitigate the information security risks facing journalists and journalistic organizations. Because like journalism itself, robust information security is a *process*, not a product.

CHAPTER 3

Assessing Risks and Threats

At some point in our lives, most of us have had the experience of being taught how to cross a street. What we learned usually included some combination of "look both ways," "wait for the light," and "cross at the crosswalk"; if we were very young, they might also have included "hold a grown-up's hand." Crossing the street is something that most of us do several, maybe dozens of times a day—and few of us give it more than a few moments of thought each time. Yet while most of us can recall the instructions we were given as children, few of us strictly adhere to them as adults. We have places to go and not enough time to get there, or the streets we cross don't have stoplights or crosswalks. The times when we are most likely to follow the rules we were taught as children are when we are once again in their company.

That we can so often disregard the rules of crossing the street—yet still manage to do so safely—illustrates another lesson most of us learn from experience: safety is not really about following a fixed set of rules; it's about being able to perceive and respond to our *actual* risks in the moment. So on a sunny day we might sprint across traffic, but on a snowy one we might wait for the light. Over time, our confidence and accuracy in judging our actual risks and personal abilities improve, and judging what is safe becomes almost second nature whenever we step to the curb.

No matter how much of our lives we have spent online, however, few of us feel a similar level of confidence when it comes to moving around in cyberspace. There are many reasons why this is the case: online risks are more numerous and various, and, to the unpracticed eye, they are much harder to identify than an oncoming vehicle. Like health risks, moreover, the consequences of information security threats are both less immediate—and less immediately severe—than those posed by vehicular traffic. Counterintuitively, perhaps, understanding digital safety has nothing to do with being a "digital native."[1] And unlike the experience of learning to cross the street, few of us have ever been taken by the hand and shown what is necessary to keep ourselves safe when interacting with digital systems in the first place.

As we begin to appreciate the risks that digital communication systems pose to ourselves and our work, the first instinct for many of us is to look for simple rules that we can follow in order to navigate digital space safely. But while information security tipsheets, safety guides, and how-tos abound, these just-in-time resources are not designed to offer the nuance and scope required to develop adaptable, generalizable information security skills. So while the advice in such materials is often expertly sourced and thoughtfully curated, it can also be brittle: like "looking both ways" and "crossing at the crosswalk," it can be useful in addressing the particular set of risks its creators envisioned but may do little to clarify how to behave safely in even slightly different circumstances.

In a profession as fast moving, unpredictable, and inherently risky as journalism, trying to secure your work by following a set of prescriptive rules is simply not realistic: just as good interviewing means knowing when to stick to your prepared questions and when to ask an unplanned follow-up, good information security requires cultivating enough knowledge and experience to adapt to changing circumstances. As *Vice*'s security expert Destiny Montague describes it: "It's so much better [for journalists] to know how to think for themselves and how to be mindful of the threats they might face. . . . If I say, 'Well, use Signal,' that's not helpful—because you don't know why you're using Signal. Maybe you've heard that it's encrypted, but . . . does that actually help you, in your specific case?"

The type of skills we need to cultivate around digital communications and information security, then, are precisely the kind we've developed through a lifetime of crossing streets: the ability to *threat model*—that is, to efficiently identify and assess the risks we face in a given moment so that we can determine how to move ahead as safely as possible.

Threat modeling for journalism is in many ways essentially the same process as the risk assessments we reflexively perform on the street corner each day. What is different is that the foundational knowledge required—the online equivalent of being able to visually judge the speed of an oncoming car or the evaluate the likelihood that a braking vehicle will manage to stop before the crosswalk—is something that even those who have grown up immersed in digital culture may not necessarily have. That is why the technical operations of and legal rules around digital information systems were the focus of the previous two chapters: these are the literacies required for creating the independent, adaptable risk assessments and threat models required for effective twenty-first-century journalism.

CRAFTING A RISK ASSESSMENT

For most of us, the risks we face when crossing a street are easy both to identify and prioritize: *avoid getting hit by a vehicle.*

As soon as we interact with digital systems, however, we face a sometimes overwhelming variety of risks and threats, each carrying its own potential likelihood and severity. For example, there are risks that involve others' efforts to gain access to private information—from passwords, to photographs, to social security numbers—that may be used to take control of our accounts and manipulate our lives both online and off. There are also risks that involve our devices—whether it's the passive collection of our conversations by a smarthome device, the targeted installation of malware designed to harvest data about our contacts and activities, or "ransomware" that will hold our digital data hostage. There are also threats in which we are affected directly but targeted incidentally, whether because we have a connection—professionally or personally—to someone who is the real target of an attack or simply because we fall into a data collection dragnet designed to opportunistically collect as much information as possible.

Though technological systems are involved, creating an information security risk assessment is not a fundamentally *technical* task. As when we cross the street, the process of assessing, prioritizing, and even mitigating information security risk is one of estimation: just as we cannot know an oncoming vehicle's precise weight, speed, and stopping distance, we can never know exactly what resources an adversary has at their disposal—whether in terms of money, expertise, or attention. Yet the fact that most of us are not physicists does not make our practical judgments about oncoming traffic less effective. Similarly, the fact that we do not know the precise resources of a telecommunications provider, government agency, or trolling community doesn't prevent us from constructing a useful risk assessment and threat model or from taking steps to improve our information security against the possible threats they represent.

Where Do I Begin?

The time to conduct your risk assessment, build your threat model, and choose your mitigation strategies is, quite naturally, *before* you begin a reporting project or story—not halfway through or a few hours before someone will hit "publish." That said, if you're wondering whether you can do anything to improve the security of a project you already have underway, the answer will always be *yes*.

Is it ideal to do your risk assessment later in the reporting process? Of course not—but that doesn't make it useless, either. Conducting your risk assessment halfway through your project will change what your risks are, since now they will include whatever you have (or haven't) done thus far in the course of your reporting. In fact, even if a project is already *over* there's something to learn from it: an information security "postmortem" can yield valuable insights for similar projects down the road.

The temptation to avoid engaging with information security issues because it's "too late" is a symptom of what experts describe as security *fatalism*—the idea that if you haven't done everything "perfectly" then there's no point in doing anything at all.

This perspective is, to put it bluntly, bullshit. As *BuzzFeed*'s Eliot Stempf points out, "There are so many things you can be doing to better secure yourself."

Given the number and variety of tasks and challenges faced by journalists and newsrooms today, the temptation to write off information security as either irrelevant or impossible is relatable: many of us are loath to take on what seems like yet another set of responsibilities if we can possibly avoid it.

On the other hand, strong information security practices will not only make you and everyone you come into contact with safer; it will also make you a more organized, prepared, and informed reporter. And since journalism is, after all, mostly about discovering and synthesizing new information and ideas, developing information security skills is a no-brainer for professional development.

SETTING THE CONTEXT

Before you begin building any risk assessment or threat model, the first step is to choose the reporting project or process you're defining it *for*; these processes don't exist without context. True, there are a handful of security practices that are relevant to almost any threat model (as we'll discuss further in chapter 4), but there is no universal risk assessment that can protect you from "everything"—if that were the case, then information security really *would* amount to following a set of rules, and none of us would need to worry about data breaches, phishing emails, malware, account takeovers, or metadata trails.

If, like many journalists, you don't think you have a current project that *requires* a risk assessment, just pick any of those that you're working on already and forge ahead. It's a great way to get started practicing the skills you'll need when a higher-risk project starts up, and you're almost certain to identify some valuable resources and practices that will help increase your default level of information security regardless.

Am I Really at Risk?

For many people, the biggest hurdle to developing a good risk assessment is recognizing that you (or your sources, or your stories) are really at risk. In nearly a decade of researching journalists' information security issues, one of the things I've heard over and over again from journalists is that they don't really believe their work is really at risk. Often this is because they assume that their work isn't sufficiently provocative or controversial to inspire anyone to "bother" hacking them.

While it's true that a journalist covering national security will face different risks than a local beat reporter covering crime, that shouldn't be confused for a difference between "risk" and "no risk." In fact, while the national security reporter's adversaries might be better resourced and more technically sophisticated, the variety of possible attacks against a local journalist may be greater, and the resources required to execute those attacks may be lower. As Ela Stapley, an information security trainer for the Committee to Protect Journalists and the Rory Peck Trust, puts it: "Why is someone going to bother to tap your phone when they can just have someone wait outside your apartment and beat you up for your password?" Maybe you haven't experienced the risk of direct physical harm as a result of your work, but the fact remains that even if you are working "only" with public documents or "just" covering quality-of-life issues, there will always be entities interested in influencing, accessing, or restricting your coverage. That's why an essential part of any journalist's job is to understand how best to stop that from happening.

CENTERING THE JOURNALIST

Most traditional risk assessment approaches for journalism have been adapted from military-style hostile environment trainings, which have long been part of securing conflict and high-risk reporting assignments. These risk assessments often begin by evaluating the reporting environment: What types of violent attacks have taken place in the region over the past twelve months? Where are the nearby hospitals and consulates? While this information can be useful, says Eliot Stempf, *BuzzFeed*'s head of high risk, the traditional risk assessment's bias toward time-bounded risks and physical threats makes it less effective for thinking about information security risks: "The risk assessment is still built around the notion of the reporter going abroad to do an assignment and then returning to [a] safe home country . . . [and] that is obviously not the reality around the world and increasingly for journalists in the U.S." Instead, says Stempf, "We need to have sort of the processes that somehow capture the kind of workflow which doesn't have a discrete beginning and end."

For the past several years, Stempf, along with colleagues like the *New York Times*' Jason Reich, has been developing a process designed to center the needs—and the strengths—of the journalists working on a story. "It helps us move more quickly, so we're not just doing this thing where we're listing every single risk and every single mitigation—which will typically be a copy-paste job from a previous risk assessment—and then adding a section saying 'Oh the person's identity modifies the risk in X, Y, and Z way,'" says Stempf. "I am trying to sort of push away from that, as different reporters are going to face different risks and different threats and have different means to mitigate those risks." Indeed, even in the digital space—where the term "threat model" is more common—building out a risk assessment typically consists of asking (and answering, to the best of your ability) questions like the following about a given reporting project or process:

1. Who might be interested in the materials or information you have or are collecting?
2. Who might not want you to have or publish that information?
3. What resources might those people or organizations be able to leverage to access your information or (effectively) prevent publication?
4. What are the consequences to you, your sources, your colleagues, and your organization if someone who shouldn't gain access to your information does?

Unfortunately, the proliferating variety of risks facing journalists means that answering even the first of these questions can generate a rapidly expanding list of potential adversaries and "attackers," some of whose resources might seem either infinite or incomprehensible. While this type of threat modeling can seem appealingly straightforward, "it's very easy to go way down a rabbit hole and go extreme," says the Marshall Project's Tom Meagher. "It's fun for a few minutes, but then it's like 'We're overthinking this. Let's take a break and discuss. What's our real concern?'"

In most cases, Stempf says, identifying those "real concerns" means coming back to the reporter's own history and identity. "We foreground identity right off the bat, because for many folks there's going to be specific concerns around who they are. Maybe it's the background of the journalist. Maybe it's issues at the intersection of gender and safety. Maybe it's their nationality."

At the same time, Stempf points out, a reporter's identity is also often a key strength: "The way they're going to get the story is often connected to who they are," Stempf says. "There are many stories out there where people with particular backgrounds are just better suited to gain access to sources." The goal of centering the reporter in the threat modeling process, then, is to "bring identity right out in front, and let people say, 'Hey, these are the strengths I'm bringing to the story—how do we double down on those strengths?' And then, 'Here are some concerns,' because we're doing inherently risky work." In Stempf's view, "This hopefully provides a more holistic representation of the activities of the journalist and moves us away from the idea of 'Oh, so-and-so should not do this story because, for example, they are a woman,' which is an outrageous idea." In contrast, Stempf worries that "a risk assessment that doesn't start with a journalist's identity as a central point implicitly has the white male hetero journalist as the status quo."

IMAGINING AN ATTACK

Just because the journalist is the focus of the risk assessment, however, doesn't mean that the task of threat modeling is something they should be doing alone. Having journalists participate directly in the threat-modeling process is essential, says Stempf, because in addition to their unique understanding of their own risk factors and advantages, "many times a journalist in a specific area will have far greater access to actionable, on-the-ground information than I [as a security professional] will."

Whether or not you or any of your colleagues consider yourselves "experts," risk assessment and threat modeling is best done as a group. The key is to have your team put itself "in the shoes" of an adversary, taking all of the ingenuity, creativity, and focus that you usually apply to the work of sourcing and reporting and using it to imagine what you would do if you were working for "the other side." In imagining what an attacker might be willing or able to do, however, you will need to think outside the bounds of what journalistic ethics would allow: as has been demonstrated time and time again, lies, manipulation, and attacks on friends, family, and colleagues are fair game to most attackers. The more efficient you and your colleagues become at imagining how an adversary might compromise your reporting, however, the more effective your "defenses" will ultimately be.

The Art of "Red-Teaming"

The process of putting yourself in an adversary's shoes is a key part of a more general cybersecurity practice sometimes referred to as "red-teaming." Just as student journalists and novice reporters learn about the process of journalism through guided reporting assignments, future cybersecurity professionals often participate in "capture the flag" (CTF) competitions, where groups compete to attack—or defend—a set of digital resources. In CTF exercises, the task of the "red team" is to successfully compromise the resources being defended by the corresponding "blue team." As in the real world, nothing is off-limits to the "red team"—their job is to gain access to the blue team's resources by

CONTINUED

whatever means they can muster. While you and your colleagues might end up spending a long time discussing convoluted ways that an adversary might try to access your reporting notes (such as bribing your child's best friend to surreptitiously take photographs of your notes with their phone), you are also cultivating the important proficiency of "thinking like a group," which can not only improve your information security but can support your reporting, by helping you generate multiple story angles more quickly through the process of putting yourself in another's shoes.

THE MYTH OF ONLY TARGETED RISKS

A few years ago, I had a conversation with a high-level Google executive who described attending the annual gala of a nonprofit with which he was involved. The event took place in Washington, DC, and as a small bit of swag at the dinner, every attendee was given an organization-branded USB drive.

Just for kicks, he dropped off this USB with the security team at the Google office and asked them to analyze it. What they found was that the USB drive contained exfiltration malware: preinstalled software whose only purpose was to send data from the connected machines to servers somewhere on the internet (presumably—though not necessarily—controlled by whoever had manufactured the USB key). There was not, however, any evidence that this malware had been "personalized" to either the NGO that had hosted the event or the individuals who had attended. The security team's conclusion was that all USB keys from this company probably shipped with this malware, just in case some of the information sent back might eventually prove useful.

In other words, when it comes to digital information systems, all of us are at risk, no matter who we are. As members of a profession that specifically gathers unique, original, and otherwise unknown information, journalists are inevitably going to be more at risk than others. Because even if you were somehow to inhabit an impossible corner of journalism where no one at all is ever annoyed about or could profit from manipulating your coverage, does it then follow that you face no information security risks? No.

Whether you believe you face risks on your own behalf, there is no question that you face risks because of—and can equally pose a risk *to*—all of the people and organizations to whom you are connected. In other words, as much as we all rightly worry about who can access our text messages and stored documents, modern intelligence gathering is principally based on identifying and leveraging networks of connections. So even in the unlikely event that nothing in your email archive contains anything sensitive or compromising about *you*, it almost certainly contains key pieces of information about your sources or your colleagues. Moreover, because of the way that most organizations share digital resources, an adversary interested in accessing the story notes of your colleagues on the national security desk doesn't really need to target them directly; an attacker simply needs to trick someone *connected* to them—whether another reporter or someone in accounts payable—into creating an opening through which they can spy, usually through simple attacks that get them to install malware or give away their login information. This gives attackers a way to access the sensitive information they're after in the cheapest and lowest-profile way possible. In other words, "just" sharing an email domain, document access, or even contact information with a person who is a likely target means that, in effect, you are targeted, too. So the risk assessment for your bake-off story should be informed by the heightened risk your organization faces because of the real estate kickback piece your colleague wrote last week.

BUILDING "TREES" TO BREAK DOWN THREATS

Centering the reporter in the threat modeling process organically surfaces the ways that their individual identity and their organizational and community relationships are likely both to benefit their reporting and potentially put them at risk. Even so, it's simply not possible to address every imaginable threat. Instead, what you need is a systematic way to prioritize them, so that you can choose where to focus your mitigation efforts. A key tool for managing this process, which comes from the world of computer security, is known as the "attack tree" or "resource map."

While it may sound complex, an attack tree/resource map is really just a tree diagram or flowchart that helps you to first map out the actions and resources required to carry out a particular attack and, second, identify how you would respond to them. Imagine, for example, that a credible attack on your work might involve someone bribing your organization's cleaning staff to find and photograph your notes. Building out the corresponding resource map or attack tree would involve describing each step the adversary would need to take to execute that attack and arranging them in order (figure 3.1).

On its surface, the attack shown in figure 3.1 is quite simple: it requires only a few steps to complete. But how difficult or expensive is each step? If you rent space in a shared building, finding out who the cleaning company is might be possible by asking at the front desk, but then your adversary would also have to learn which individuals usually cleaned your offices in particular. Then again, if the building is small, your adversary might be able just to watch the parking lot until the cleaners arrive and note what company is doing the work. Step two is arguably trickier, because it means persuading at least one of the cleaners with access to find and photograph the relevant notes. And of course, the adversary would have to do all of this without raising enough suspicion that someone along the way alerts either you or the authorities.

Are all of the steps outlined here possible? Of course. But undertaking them would also require some amount of time and money. This is where

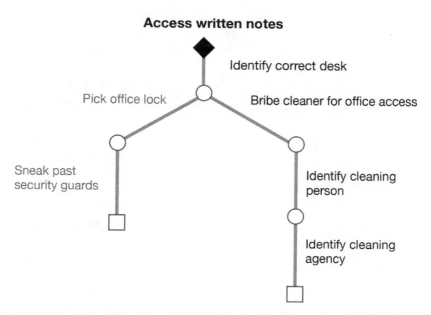

Figure 3.1   A simple resource map or attack tree.

annotating the various branches of your tree becomes essential: some paths to accessing your notes will be much more "expensive" than others, whether in time, money, influence, or a combination of all three. While weighting various branches according to their monetary cost is often the default approach, the valuation method you apply to your tree should also reflect your context; in some instances, for example, positive (or negative) publicity may be more influential than money. So while evaluating the cost of a private detective in financial terms makes sense, you'll probably want to evaluate a trolling campaign in terms of, say, community size or attention span. You might also classify the steps of an attack in terms of "special skills or access" versus "no special skills or access." Whatever combination of measures you use, the key is to ensure that you are clearly labeling your tree with both a particular goal and type of attacker in mind, so that each tree represents an internally consistent narrative of a particular adversary and attack (figure 3.2). All of these "valuations" will be estimates, of course, and that's fine. Just like assessing the movement of cars on the street, you and your team will get better at making these estimates as time goes on.

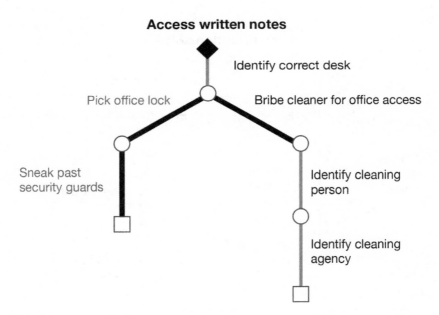

Figure 3.2   An annotated attack tree, with line weight indicating the "cost" of each step.

Once your tree is annotated, take a step back and evaluate this particular threat in context. How should this risk be prioritized? Would it cost $10K to bribe someone to photograph your notes, but the attacker only makes $60K per year? In that situation, the relative cost of the attack is high enough that its likelihood declines; you would do better to worry about deterring "cheaper"—and therefore more likely—attacks. On the other hand, if the attacker makes $60K per year but their brother runs the cleaning company, the cost of the attack drops almost to zero, since intimidation rather than bribery might become the most efficient way to get your notes photographed. Since the attack is cheap and relatively easy to execute, if this latter situation applies, you might want to take the attack—and ways to mitigate it—fairly seriously.

Just like centering the reporter's identity, the process of creating and annotating an attack tree or resource map allows you to narrow the list of possible threats into more *probable* threats by allowing you to visualize a well-defined set of dependent steps and associated costs. Once you have annotated your attack tree/resource map, you can then prune it to eliminate the attacks that are too complicated, difficult, or expensive for the attacker to execute reasonably. You can then prioritize and further annotate each of the remaining branches with specific mitigation and/or response strategies.

A Word About Vocabulary

For some readers, the term "risk assessment" may already be familiar as a phrase used when evaluating the "physical" security risks associated with a reporting project; in the digital space, most experts will use the term "threat model" as a comprehensive term that includes the risks, threats, adversary resources, and consequences of protection gaps.

In this chapter, I intentionally use both terms and add "attack trees/ resource maps" to help distinguish the process of *identifying* possible risks and threats from the processes of *atomizing* and *prioritizing* them. *Mitigation plans*, of course, are the steps one plans to take in order to, well, mitigate whatever risks you can.

Fortunately, as you gain more experience with these processes, you will see patterns emerge in terms of both possible attacks and effective mitigation strategies. As the next chapter will illustrate, there are a number of baseline security practices that will reduce the effectiveness of many attacks; as you adopt these, your attack trees will become sparser and more spindly as your overall vulnerability declines. In addition to making your work safer in general, this will also make preparing for high-risk assignments faster and easier—leaving you more mental and emotional bandwidth to focus on your primary objective: reporting.

MITIGATION TECHNIQUES: STRATEGY, NOT TECHNOLOGY

At both the organizational and individual level, there is value to documenting your threat model and risk mitigation strategies: it can provide a useful reference point for both future reporting projects and for evaluating the effectiveness of specific approaches. At the same time, simply generating paperwork is not the point. As *BuzzFeed*'s Stempf points out: "My goal is not to have a perfect [risk assessment] process. My goal is to help reporters and editors talk in a meaningful way about the stories they're doing and ideally find a way to think about risk that expedites things in a responsible way." Part of that responsibility, to Stempf, involves having the organization be the partner that acknowledges the role of identity in the risk assessment process. "It's saying, 'We as the organization are taking this seriously and we want to have this conversation with you,'" says Stempf. "Not, 'The onus is on you to raise these concerns that you feel uncomfortable raising because you're afraid won't get to do the story.'"

Just like the threat modeling process, designing mitigation strategies also has to be done in close conjunction with the reporter, as what will be effective for them is inevitably tied to their personal, organizational, and community contexts. A view-from-nowhere approach to security can lead to "mitigation" strategies that are unrealistic—which means they have virtually no security value at all. As the Freedom of the Press Foundation's newsroom security director Harlo Holmes puts it: "It's always a bad scene when what you're saying [from a security perspective] is not realistic within the context where people are."

Fortunately, mitigating risk is rarely about adopting a particular tool or technology; if anything, the purpose of laying out resource maps is literally to help illustrate the many points at which a given attack can be thwarted, often by relatively simple means. For example, as you read the last few sections, you may have thought to yourself: "Why wouldn't I just lock my notebook in a drawer?" Or, "Why leave my notes at the office in the first place?" If something along these lines occurred to you, you've already identified two strategic mitigation techniques: the first adds extra depth to an attack branch by putting a lock between your notes (the target of the attack and the "root" of the tree) and the adversary, and the second effectively eliminates the attack tree entirely, because no level of access to your office will turn up notes that simply aren't there. Of course, this latter strategy eliminates one tree but creates another, by shifting the location of the attack to your home or wherever you store your notes instead. As always, *eliminating* risk isn't possible, but you can make strategic choices that minimize it for your particular context. By learning to develop threat models and resource maps, you can create a methodical, modular way of characterizing information security threats and identifying mitigation options—whether those require a new technology or none at all.

WHAT ABOUT THE "UNKNOWN UNKNOWNS"?

Even the most dedicated effort to build a threat model and/or its corresponding resource map can be stymied by the sense that you simply don't have enough information about what is possible. After all, we often don't know definitively who might be looking to compromise our work, and things can get even murkier when it comes to assessing their potential skills and resources.

Fortunately, even when you can't precisely estimate the resources of your attackers, threat models and attack trees serve the crucial function of forcing you to get *organized*: to think about the information you have, where it is, and how others can (or might) access it. As we'll discuss in more detail in chapter 4, simply knowing where things are and thinking consciously about how you handle them constitutes the bulk of practical information security. Thus even highly imperfect threat models and resource maps are a valuable way to help kickstart that thought process and improve your information security, one project at a time.

Building attack trees can help you derive some heuristics for your work in a given context, as patterns across types of threats and mitigation strategies begin to emerge. Over time, these become your own information security equivalents of street-crossing strategies: a personalized understanding of how to interpret and respond to threats in real-time, based on your personal risks and resources.

As a result, organizing your thinking about risks and threats in this way will also enhance and streamline your work by offering a well-considered basis for making decisions like: Should I delete this? Where should I store it? For how long? As you integrate information security into your reporting practice more thoroughly, it can actually make day-to-day decisions about how you store, communicate, and access information easier—freeing up both time and mental energy to focus on the processes of reporting and publishing the news.

CHAPTER 4

Everyday Essentials

In September 1994, the National Science Foundation awarded $4.5 million to Hector Garcia-Molina for the Stanford Integrated Digital Library Project (SIDLP), which aimed "to develop the enabling technologies for a single, integrated and 'universal' library . . . [which] will provide the 'glue' that will make this worldwide collection usable as a unified entity, in a scalable and economically viable fashion."[1] A few years later, Larry Page, as an SIDLP graduate student, would create a program called "BackRub" in an attempt to "to store the connection graph for the web."[2] In 1998, Page and his collaborator Sergey Brin published a paper based on that work entitled "The Anatomy of a Large-Scale Hypertextual Web Search Engine," in which they introduced their new design, now named "Google."[3]

Over the past two decades, Google has expanded its services well beyond a single search engine, but its "search-first" approach to accessing digital information has become the dominant paradigm, far from the type of structured taxonomies used in the library work from which Google emerged. While using search to locate digital data and documents is efficient precisely because it *doesn't* require us to make decisions about the hundreds of messages, documents, files, and other materials that we interact with every day, this momentary efficiency, however, often comes at a cost: the ability to properly account for—and secure—the professional materials we use to do the work of journalism.

To put it simply: you can't protect something if you don't know where it is. Unfortunately, search-based methods of interacting with digital content encourage us to think only about how to *find* what we are looking for, not think critically about where it *is*. As a result, our ability to access almost anything means always having access to *everything*, turning our digital devices into all-access passes to our personal and professional digital lives. While having access to every document, data file, or email message no matter our context may superficially reassure us that we are never without the resources we need, it also means that, to a large extent, those resources are always at risk. For example, if the laptop you carry with you every day contains everything from your reporting notes to your last tax return, the consequences of it being searched, stolen, lost, or damaged can be astronomical. And for many of us, this boundary blurring doesn't stop with our devices—it extends to our digital accounts, where we may be mixing contact lists, reusing passwords, or forwarding emails from one domain to another—all of which places us one account compromise away from personal and professional chaos.

Will Security Slow Me Down?

In a research interview I conducted a few years ago, a security-savvy journalist aptly described the additional steps needed to secure his work as the "encryption tax": that marginal bit of additional effort required to use secure tools and processes instead of relying on more mainstream methods. Fortunately, the default security on everything from messaging apps to mobile operating systems has gone a long way toward reducing the severity of that tax, even in the space of a few short years. For example, most mobile devices are now encrypted by default if you use a numeric PIN, and the decryption happens automatically whenever you unlock your device.

Still, there are times when improved information security does require an extra step or additional effort. For example, the initial step of encrypting the contents of a laptop can take several hours, even though the "unlocking" after that is nearly instantaneous. Before writing these processes off as too tedious or time consuming, however, it's important to put their tradeoffs in perspective: most of us couldn't imagine not wearing a seatbelt in a car or a helmet when riding a bicycle—yet not too long ago those precautions were considered optional, despite their enormous safety benefits. Although digital safety mechanisms like full-disk encryption or multifactor authentication may require some adjustments

CONTINUED

in how we interact with our digital devices and data, it's no exaggeration to say that the protective benefits they offer rival those of seatbelts and bike helmets. Especially given the way that digital systems figure in our lives when it comes to health care, finances, and family—to say nothing of their role in our professional journalistic work—adding thirty seconds to the process of accessing our accounts or unlocking our devices is clearly a worthy investment.

DEVELOP YOUR "DIGITAL HYGIENE"

Moving away from the "all-access" approach to information management that so many of us use is perhaps the most fundamental component of good information security practice: by developing a systematic approach to identifying, storing, sharing, and accessing your data, you can effectively minimize risks to your data while still retrieving and using it efficiently.

Conceptually, "digital hygiene" is a way to think about the process of maintaining your information resources (especially those stored and accessed digitally) in a way that helps secure them, principally through a combination of *compartmentalization* and *data minimization*. By limiting cross-contamination—between personal and professional data, for example, or between login credentials for one account and another—compartmentalization helps contain the negative consequences of accidents or attacks while also making it easier to choose among services and accounts when you have a file to store or a document to share. Data minimization, meanwhile, means paring down the data resources you have accessible at any given time, as well as the data about you that is accessible to others—which helps reduce the likelihood of that data being exposed.

As the term suggests, digital hygiene is also about developing sustainable daily practices that support—rather than constrain—your journalistic work. As such, the most important aspect of adopting any of the following approaches is to do so in a way you can maintain in the long term: Whether you binge-scrub your digital footprint over the course of a week or slowly add accounts to your password manager as you log in to each service over the course of a month, the goal is to cultivate these as your new "defaults" for managing digital resources going forward.

If taking on new digital hygiene practices for ongoing stories is too disruptive, start small: build a risk assessment for an upcoming project and use it to test out one set of changes, such as giving sources only VOIP contact information instead of your actual mobile phone number. This approach lets you ease into these new habits while still reaping genuine security benefits; when you find a technique that works well for you, you can apply it elsewhere. If no new projects are on the horizon, complete the one-day "device diary" exercise described in the sidebar, and use that to think through ways to reduce your default information exposure—whether that means turning off your smartphone's Wi-Fi signal when you leave the house in the morning or moving old project files off your laptop and onto a backup drive. In the end, it doesn't matter precisely *how* you start, as long as you manage to get started somehow.

Writing Your Device Diary

The degree to which our digital devices and accounts are enmeshed in both our professional and personal lives makes the idea of trying to inventory our digital information a little like trying to organize your whole life during a weeklong vacation.[4] This is why starting at the project level can be helpful: you can start thinking about how you organize, access, and store information without trying to overhaul your entire digital life at once.

If you don't have a suitable project, however, creating a device diary can serve a similar purpose: recording and reflecting on your typical device usage over the course of a single day is a great way to become more aware of how you're handling your digital information—which is the first step to being able to handle it more securely.

The process is exactly what you might imagine: take note of what devices you have with you and how you use them over the course of a single day. I strongly recommend doing the actual note taking on paper, so you can easily annotate and modify it in real time. The objective of the exercise, however, is not to catalog every minute spent on your devices but to outline *how* you are using them. Some items to think about include:

- What Wi-Fi networks did your devices connect to, and when? Do you leave Wi-Fi on by default?

CONTINUED

- Do you have location enabled by default? If not, when did you enable/disable it? If so, how did you actually make use of it?
- What accounts have you accessed, and how? Did you need to reset passwords, or are you reusing them? If so, where and how? In what cases are you using an installed app, and in what cases a website?
- What devices do you carry with you, and which did you use for a given task? Why? For example, if you carry a laptop but answered emails on your phone, what was the reason?

While the overarching goal of this exercise is to find ways to improve your information security, the objective of creating your device diary is not to identify individual behaviors that you should stop but instead to identify your current habits—and what about them is or isn't working for you. In this vein, your device diary is also a great place to record all the things that annoy you about interacting with your devices—whether it's the way that webpages reload every time you return to a tab, say, or the frequent need to delete files to create more space on your device. In the end, the aim is to help you develop ways to organize and control your information that work for *you*—so understanding your existing habits and "pain points" is essential.

Once you have created your device diary, look over your "irritations" list: do you hate being interrupted with system notifications when you're trying to write or edit? Are you continually resetting passwords or typing the same information into online forms? Each of these things can actually serve as a place to start thinking about your information organization—and security. Scheduling a time each week to apply software updates might stem the tide of annoying "upgrade" reminders, and getting a password manager can make your login processes more efficient while also improving your overall information security. By thinking systematically about how you manage your information, you can both streamline and better secure essential tasks, leaving you more mental bandwidth for actually working. For example, setting up separate "work" and "personal" user accounts on your mobile device can be a simple way to manage notifications: switching to your "personal" user means you won't see work email notifications after hours, except when you decide to check them. Alternatively, you can set account-specific rules to ensure that you get

WRITING YOUR DEVICE DIARY, CONTINUED

notifications for urgent personal and professional calls but otherwise remain undisturbed.

While at first keeping a device diary might seem about as glamorous as organizing a junk drawer, taking the time to reflect on how you use your devices is the first step toward making them work better for you—not just from an information security standpoint but for all the tasks you use them for, every day.

UNDERSTAND WHAT'S OUT THERE

Whether your starting point was a risk assessment or a device diary, minimizing the data you expose in the process of collecting, storing, and synthesizing information for reporting is only half the information security story; the other half is dealing with the organizations and individuals out there collecting, storing, and synthesizing information about *you*. While some of this will be data—like old websites and social media accounts—that you have more or less voluntarily put into the world, much of it is collated and published by everyone from data brokers to doxxers. While it's often impossible to permanently "scrub" all of the online records you might like to, however, taking steps to minimize your digital footprint now can spare you some painful moments down the line. Even more, the skills you learn by uncovering information about yourself on the internet often make excellent reporting tactics, too.

DO YOUR OWN WHITE HOT DOXX

At *Vice*, the security expert Destiny Montague often gets journalists thinking about their digital footprint through an exercise that she calls a "white hot doxx": "It's basically me sitting there and acting as somebody would who's trying to doxx this person and seeing what information I can find. . . . Whatever I dig up I'll give to them in a report and say, 'Here's what I was able to find quickly—somebody who is motivated would also able to find this information.'"

Once she's completed the exercise, Montague will provide the journalist with a list of tips for removing their information and securing their accounts, but the first step, she says, is awareness. "A lot of times people just don't even realize that stuff is out there."

While doxxing is an old tactic in the online-harassment handbook, in recent years it has increasingly been used to target journalists. In 2019, for example, a far-right group doxxed dozens of journalists, prompting security specialists at the *New York Times* to publish a set of tutorials on how journalists could both proactively "doxx" themselves and remove the information they found.[5]

Removing *all* of your online data, of course, is neither possible nor desirable—from either a journalistic or a security standpoint. Potential sources often want to "vet" journalists based on their online profile, while leaving a little bit of information for would-be doxxers to find may actually deter them from digging more deeply. As Montague puts it: "If you lock everything down and make everything private, it's almost like inviting more attention in a way, because then it becomes a challenge."

Don't Have Time to Doxx?

If you don't have the time or energy to doxx yourself, there are services that can do some of the work for you—for a price. Services like DeleteMe and TallPoppy can help take over some of the burden of the opt-out process, which often has to be repeated at least annually. While this will mean handing over some private information to service providers so they can complete the opt-out on your behalf, this can be an efficient way for individuals and organizations to reduce online exposure relatively quickly and effectively.

COMPARTMENTALIZATION IS A *GOOD* THING

For most of us, the thorniest—and most essential—task we will undertake when it comes to organizing and securing our information will be untangling our personal and professional accounts, for everything from email to online storage. As always, the key to doing this successfully is to be systematic. Start with one service at a time and methodically work your way through them until you have separate professional and personal accounts (or addresses) for every major service you use. Here are a few ways to get started:

1. *Separate your email accounts:* Turn off forwarding, and choose a method for accessing each account on mobile and desktop. For example, you can

create separate personal and professional user accounts on each of your devices, or you can simply add multiple email accounts to your main profile.

2. Make a list of the digital services and platforms—such as social media and file storage—that you use personally, professionally, or both. For those you only use in one capacity, just update your login information with the appropriate email address.

3. For services you use in both spheres, open a second account if needed and "sort" your existing content into the correct account.

Should You Separate Your Social Media Accounts?

In a word: yes. Harassment and doxxing are some of the most common and serious threats that journalists face. Whether or not digital messages contain "credible" threats of violence, there is no doubt that the psychological and productivity toll of online threats is only increasing for journalists in every part of the world.

At the same time, however, most journalists are still expected to be both accountable and accessible to their audiences and, therefore, to maintain a presence on a variety of social media platforms. In my own research, I've found that even journalists who encounter significant threats and regular harassment online still see social media as both a critical tool for reporting and a valuable avenue for getting feedback on their work. And of course, many journalists wish to use social media to stay in touch with friends and family.

Since leaving social media altogether isn't often an option, "compartmentalizing" your social media accounts is an effective way to remain engaged with your online contacts—both personally and professionally—while also helping minimize the risk you face from bad actors. The main question is deciding whether to "move" your professional or your personal followers to a new account.

On the one hand, starting a new professional social media page or account means you are guaranteed to lose some number of followers along the way, but in making your existing account private, you'll largely avoid having to scrub old posts and photos. On the other hand, it may be easier to persuade your friends and family to follow you on a new, private account, just carefully reviewing the material your current public account contains.

CONTINUED

Either way, the question of what should persist or appear on a public account basically comes down to the degree that a post or photo contains information that can be used to infer details about your workplace, residence, family, or daily routines. Since nothing you share will be viewed in isolation, keep in mind that if you've posted multiple photos from outside your favorite coffee shop or showing the view from your office, it will be easier for someone to piece together its precise location.

In other words, treat your social media posts the way you would a piece of source content, and imagine how you personally would "verify" it. If you can determine where a photo was taken, for example, an adversary can, too.

ENCRYPT ALL THE THINGS

As discussed in chapter 1, encryption is *the* method for protecting digital information, whether it's in transit (moving across the internet) or at rest (saved to your local hard drive or on a cloud server somewhere). The good news is that encrypting your devices is one of the simplest ways to secure the data stored on them, and it's both simple to do and to "set and forget"—once you've turned on device encryption, you'll hardly ever have to think about it again (except to be glad you've set it up). As long as your device is "locked," its contents will be unreadable to anyone without your passcode or passphrase, no matter how long they have your device.

How Should I Lock and Unlock My Device?

Just as there are many types of physical locks in the world—key based, card based, and combination, for example—there are often multiple ways to lock and unlock our digital devices and accounts, from fingerprint and face logins to alphanumeric and pattern-based passcodes.

So which one is the best? Generally speaking, the strongest level of protection is offered by a passcode of at least 6 digits on mobile devices and a passphrase of at least 16 characters on laptops and desktops, as long as the passcode or passphrase is unique. Why? Though biometrics like your face, fingerprint, and voice are both ostensibly unique and convenient, they are easier to hack than good passcodes or passphrases. In 2013 and 2014, for example, Apple's Touch ID sensor was fooled by a fake fingerprint less than twenty-four hours after it launched.[6]

Biometric locks can also make it trivial for authorities to unlock your devices. In the United States, for example, revealing one's passphrase has previously been interpreted as a form of "testimony" that is subject to Fifth Amendment protections—this means you can legally decline to unlock a device with a passphrase or passcode. By contrast, law enforcement can easily use your image or finger to unlock your phone if they have you in custody.[7] Finally, there is the simple fact that biometrics are unchangeable, and this can have far-reaching privacy implications.

These days, many devices use a combination of unlock mechanisms in order to better maximize both security and convenience. Apple's iPhones, for example, can be configured to unlock via facial recognition as long as the passcode has been entered within a certain number of hours, so you can quickly unlock your phone without entering your longer passcode every time. But the real key is choosing the best balance between security and usability for your own particular level of risk.

OUTSOURCE YOUR PASSWORD PROBLEMS

If dealing with passwords irritates you, you're in good company: they annoy most users and frustrate security experts, too—efforts to do away with them have been ongoing for decades.[8] In fact, it's possible that the only people who truly "like" password systems are the hackers who are so effective at exploiting them. Nonetheless, passwords are here to stay—and because they remain the first line of defense for digital accounts and devices, finding a way to use strong, unique passwords is an essential part of securing your information resources.[9]

From a technical perspective, the strength of any password is directly proportional to its *complexity*—a measure of the computational resources (usually in terms of processors and/or time) required for a computer to correctly "guess" or "crack" it. In practice, there are only two characteristics of a password that influence its complexity: its length (number of characters) and its randomness (lack of predictability). This is what underpins all of the various recommendations and requirements for creating good passwords: requiring a mix of capital letters, special characters, and numerals is an attempt to discourage predictability, and minimum length requirements are there to encourage, well, greater length.

Though humans are excellent at remembering long things, we are terrible at creating and remembering random things. As a result, even when we manage to make long passwords (or passphrases), we often do so in a predictable way: by using facts about ourselves, for example, or by reusing passwords we've already committed to memory. This often makes it easy for hackers to "guess" our passwords by using dictionaries that combine common words *and* already leaked passwords to find the right one. So even though it could take years for a computer to "brute force" a relatively random eight-character password by guessing every possible character combination, an eight-character "common word" password can take less than a minute to identify. If you've reused the password, of course, then the match is instantaneous: the hacker can use previously leaked data to "crack" your password on the first try.

The simplest way for most of us to solve the password problem is simply to use a password manager, which stores all of your passwords safely inside an encrypted file. The "key" to this encrypted "master" file is still a password, of course, but creating and memorizing that one long, strong, unique password lets you take advantage of everything that modern password managers have to offer: password generation, storage, autofill, and selective sharing; you can even receive an alert if one of your accounts has been affected by a data breach. Password managers also offer great functionality for teams, as we'll discuss more in chapter 8. Even better, many password managers are either free or free to journalists.

If you're really opposed to a software solution, of course, there are other options. Using pass*phrases* (rather than pass*words*) that consist of multiple words (or even entire sentences—capitalization, punctuation, and all), lets you can create passphrases *so* long that the predictability of the individual words within the phrase doesn't matter—just make sure it's not something that would be easy to find (or infer from) any data you have online. Private jokes, wedding vows, lines from favorite recipes, or lyrics from childhood songs can all work well.

It's actually also just fine to write down your usernames and passphrases in a notebook—as long as you are thoughtful about where you keep it: a paper directory, stored at home, will be virtually immune to most digital attacks. You could also simply give up on trying to remember *all* your passphrases and instead focus on memorizing strong, unique passwords for a handful of essential systems, like your primary email, health, and financial accounts. Beyond that, you can simply rely on password reset functions to access your accounts: If you build in the process of requesting a new password to your login workflow, then you can protect those accounts with unique, strong passwords—that you'll never have to remember.

TURN ON ALL THE MULTIFACTOR

Enabling multifactor authentication (MFA) for your digital accounts is like adding airbags to your online life: when almost everything else goes wrong, MFA can really save your ass.

When MFA is enabled on an account, the service will require that the person trying to log in has not just the correct username and password but can demonstrate control of at least one physical device that you have previously connected to the account—such as a specific computer, mobile phone, or USB-style hardware key. Without MFA enabled, your account's username and password combination function basically like the key to a traditional lock: anyone who has a copy can access your account. Since the service providers who have copies of your username and password "keys" have an unfortunate tendency to get hacked, adding MFA is the best way to make sure your accounts aren't collateral damage when platforms make a security mistake.

If you're at all hesitant about adding MFA to your accounts, keep in mind that in most instances you won't need to use your additional factor for every single login. In many cases, you can choose to have a service "remember" your phone or laptop, for example, so you'll only get asked to input a passcode for MFA on the rare occasion that you're logging in from some unusual device. And if you encounter a service that doesn't offer multifactor authentication, you may want to look for an alternative: any service that can't be bothered to offer MFA probably isn't taking *any* security too seriously.

Which Additional Factors Should I Use?

Like many of the information security technologies in use today, second- or multifactor authentication mechanisms have been around for decades; some readers may remember the employer-provided LCD-display "fobs" that were required for certain company systems; for data-driven businesses, the added expense of buying and maintaining hundreds or thousands of these devices was more than worth it.

As journalists, of course, we are *all* in the information business, so protecting our accounts—both professional and personal—with additional factors wherever possible is just good sense. At the same time, many services still let you choose from several forms of additional authentication. Which one(s) should you use?

First, set up more than one additional factor for a given account if possible; many services support this, and it gives you flexibility: if you don't have access to some particular device when you log in (because your phone is dead) you can simply use another (like a hardware key). At one point, for example, Google accounts offered at least four distinct types of multifactor authentication (MFA), all of which could be enabled simultaneously.

At the same time, not all types of MFA are created equal. "Security questions," for example, are an early form of MFA that assumed there was certain information only the genuine account owner would know. In today's social media/surveillance capitalism climate, of course, even moderately obscure information like "the name of your first pet" or "the city where you were married" might easily be available online—whether as part of an affectionate post by a childhood friend or a profile built by a data broker. As such, security questions are often poor additional factors for twenty-first-century information systems.

SMS-based MFA—which texts a numerical code to your phone—also suffers from significant usability and security vulnerabilities. Because it is phone-number dependent, SMS-based MFA works poorly for anyone who frequently changes their SIM card, doesn't have active cell service for some reason, or doesn't have exclusive control over their mobile device. More crucially, SMS messages can be effectively intercepted through "SIM-hijacking," a form of identity theft in which an attacker convinces your mobile service provider to attach your phone number to another SIM card. While it may sound complicated, it can be surprisingly easy to do: in 2016, it even happened to the security expert Lorrie Cranor, who was the FTC's chief technologist at the time.[10] This is why the U.S. National Institute of Standards and Technology (NIST) has been explicitly discouraging the use of SMS-based MFA since 2016.

Fortunately, most services also offer "authenticator" apps that display regularly changing numerical codes similar to those delivered by SMS but without the risk of interception and spoofing. Essentially the modern descendant of those employer-provided fobs, these apps can be used for several online services simultaneously and work even without mobile service or Wi-Fi. Of course, they won't work at all if your phone has been lost, broken, confiscated—or is simply out of power.

That's why USB-style hardware "security keys" are in many ways the most robust option for MFA. Unlike SMS methods, security keys can't be phished, hijacked, or spoofed, and they don't require any wireless signal or battery to function. They also don't require you to transcribe numerical codes; you simply plug them in and touch the key when prompted. As device port formats like USB-C become more standard, moreover, a single key can be used with both phones and laptops. Hardware keys also work well for people who don't have exclusive control of a mobile device, and, like authenticator apps, a single key can be used simultaneously for dozens of online services. And while security keys—like mobile phones—can be lost, their primary drawback is probably that they come with an additional financial cost: a single key can run from roughly US$20 to US$70.

Whichever forms of MFA you choose, however, make sure to update your passwords and then configure at least one additional factor for every major account you control—you'll almost never need to think about your account login security again.

DON'T LET THE PHISH CATCH YOU

Most of us have been there at some point: it's an evening or a weekend, or you're simply out of the office on an assignment or errand. You receive an urgent email from your boss, who's away from her desk and needs you to make a quick fix to a story. You drop what you're doing, log in to the CMS, and make the update, glad that you were able to take care of it quickly.

That's precisely what a senior executive at *Forbes* believed she was doing in 2014, when she received an early-morning email from someone at *Vice* asking for her to comment on a recent *Reuters* story. Assuming it was related to the company's pending sale, she tried to click on the story link—but her webmail page reloaded, forcing her to log in again. When she did finally manage to follow the link to the *Reuters* story, it turned out to be broken. Though the executive left for work without thinking much of it at the time, chaos was unfolding inside *Forbes*'s digital systems during the course of her commute. The executive—and, shortly thereafter, an editor with high-level access to the *Forbes* publishing system—had, in fact, been *phished*.[11]

Simply put, "phishing" is *tricking*—usually with the objective of getting the targeted person to give away their login credentials. A typical phishing attack works like this: You receive a seemingly urgent message from someone in danger or authority, requesting that you take an immediate action—one that requires downloading an attachment, visiting a website, or logging into an online service; to help ensure you act quickly, the sender includes the links or files needed so you can easily complete the request. While generic phishing attacks tend to play on general anxieties (about terrorist attacks, for example, or weather emergencies), so-called spearphishing attacks will often contain details that seem like they should only be accessible to the (apparent) sender of the message or someone close to them. The attack has succeeded as long as you follow their directions: the attacker's malware can now take control of your computer, or they can use your credentials to access your accounts. Depending on their goals, the attackers may begin to noisily make their presence known or just quietly gather information for later use. Either way, identifying and recovering from the attack can take weeks or even months—and it can be difficult to ever be sure if an attackers' access has been eliminated entirely.

In the case of the *Forbes* attack, for example, the email from *Vice* was in some sense genuine—it had been sent from the account of a real *Vice* employee whose own email account had been recently compromised. Once the *Forbes* executive had entered her username and password on the attackers' lookalike website, her own account was used to send a phishing email to *Forbes* staffers. This was enough to convince her colleague to follow the link in *that* email, thereby giving away his login details to the attackers as well. For several days afterward, *Forbes* struggled to regain control of its systems: publishing was interrupted, and staffers were locked out of their email accounts while IT administrators worked with the FBI to lock out the hackers and restore normal access to services. In the meantime, the

Forbes website was briefly defaced, and data about millions of visitors was stolen.

Phishing attacks are designed specifically to play on our personal and professional impulses to get the scoop and be ahead of the curve. A phishing attack's effectiveness turns, in part, on how well it plays to either our ego or our anxieties, and the most successful attackers will mine our public identities to learn how they can most efficiently exploit one or both. This type of manipulation is also sometimes described as "social engineering"—a pseudotechnical term for what most of us would describe, quite simply, as *deception*.

The standard advice for avoiding phishing attacks, while straightforward and effective, is basically useless for journalists: Just don't click links in emails, the wisdom goes, or open attachments sent by people you don't know. But journalists are in the business of following leads and connecting with new people, so ignoring unsolicited emails or documents is hardly a strong career move. At the same time, journalists have more at risk than most people if they fall for a phishing attack: compromised accounts can lead to fake stories or social media posts appearing under your name, and malware can send sensitive information into the wrong hands—putting your stories, sources, and colleagues at risk.

Fortunately, the skills required to stave off even sophisticated phishing attacks are ones that as a journalist you already have: a strong sense of skepticism, a commitment to verification, and an eye for detail. So while no two phishing attacks will ever be exactly the same, a combination of awareness, practice, and discipline can help you avoid being tricked by them.

First, any urgent-seeming message that encourages you to follow a link should be treated warily and—first and foremost—verified. Compose a separate message (*not* a reply) to the alleged sender, ideally using a different "channel." So if the suspicious message arrived via email, consider a telephone call or a text message. If your contact confirms they sent the original, go ahead and do as they ask. If they haven't—congratulations! You've just foiled a phishing attack.

What if you *do* reach out for confirmation but don't hear back for a while? No one wants to delay in a breaking-news situation. In that case, it's OK to log in to the service specified, as long as you *don't* use the link in the message. Type the URL directly into your browser or use an app or saved bookmark, and then look for the material being referenced. If you can't locate it, there's a reasonable chance the message was a phishing attack, and you should report it if possible.

Avoiding the malware that can be part of digital documents is a somewhat thornier problem: In many cases, the person sharing a malware-infected file may not even know that there's a problem with the file they're sending. As such, your first step is to estimate the potential sensitivity of the shared materials. Is it likely to be high or low? If the sensitivity level/secrecy required is low, all you need to do to avoid most malware is to preview the documents in Chrome or any other frequently patched browser that implements "sandboxing;" this prevents the previewed files from actually running code on your computer. Since you have to allow this type of code execution to print, start by opening any files you need to print in Google Drive first. This will subject them to a scan that will purge a large proportion of malware automatically.

If the sensitivity of the documents is potentially high, start by saving them directly to an external drive, and then open them on a computer that doesn't connect to the internet. In practice, this can be the oldest, crummiest computer that can still open the files you need to view, because then it doesn't matter if the files contain malware: Without an internet connection, even the baddest malware is basically a bug in a jar: it can't get into your network or send data back to the attacker. While having this type of "air-gapped" computer may feel a little bit 1995, just think of it as the Bloomberg terminal for the modern newsroom: the machine that everyone on the floor uses for one particular task. And if you're worried about revealing your work to your colleagues, you can always buy or repurpose an old machine of your own.

A Few More Words About Malware

If you've ever opened an adolescent's computer, you already know that nefarious email attachments aren't the only way to get malware. It's all over the internet, and there are plenty of ways you can end up with a malware-affected machine.

For many years, online ads were a significant source of malware because of security vulnerabilities in Adobe Flash. Flash was officially phased out in 2020, so make sure to disable it in your browser(s) if you haven't already; while this may "break" your experience of some older or more niche websites, most of them are probably pretty broken already.

Another common source of malware is pirated software, which has, by definition, already been hacked. When you install a program that you already know has been compromised, you're basically blowing a giant hole in any security measures you've already taken.

Unfortunately, there is no easy solution, especially for occasional users and those on very tight budgets. Basically, you can either pay for legitimate software, or you can switch tools: rather than going for the name-brand software package, learn to work with an open-source alternative. These programs offer many of the same features as their better-branded counterparts but—like all sophisticated software—can have a fairly steep learning curve. While there's no way to avoid this time-or-money tradeoff, kicking the pirated software habit may be the most important thing you can do for your overall information security.

DON'T SKIP THE SOFTWARE UPDATES

"Oops, your files have been encrypted!" Along with a demand for roughly $300 in Bitcoin, this was the message that greeted physicians and hospital personnel across the United Kingdom on May 12, 2017, when they tried to connect to the National Health System's (NHS) appointment services. Yet this was only a small part of the global WannaCry ransomware attack that hit 150 countries and caused billions of dollars in damage. Barely a month later, the NotPetya ransomware attack similarly crippled shipping companies, corporations, and governments throughout Europe, costing billions more and requiring months of recovery. What made these organizations vulnerable to these attacks? Failure to install a Microsoft Windows software update that had been released months earlier.[12]

It's a scenario that we're all familiar with: you arrive at work in the morning, ready to respond to emails or get started on an article. You log in to your computer to find that the dreaded pop-up notification has appeared: Your operating system needs updating. Restart now? it asks. If not now, then when? In an hour? Tonight? Tomorrow? You reluctantly select "Install" and sit tapping your fingers, waiting to get back to work. The original estimate of three minutes turns into fifteen. By the time you can actually use your computer again, your intended schedule for the morning has already collapsed.

Software updates are among the most reviled of all security measures, with less than half of regular users opting to install them automatically. This is part of why they hackers continue to target known security vulnerabilities long after their patches have been released: most people will avoid updating their software "as long as possible," despite the potentially devastating consequences.[13]

As with pirated software, there isn't a clever way to make software updates go away: you just need to install them as promptly as possible. The only thing you can do is try to make this process more painless: designate a time to let it happen (actually put it in your calendar if that's your style), and let your operating system go to work. If you must put it off for a few days, fine, but make sure you set aside time to install updates at least once a week. Alternatively, you can just configure your devices to update automatically—and use the interruption as an excuse to go get a cup of coffee or read a few extra headlines.

How Do I Know It's Legit?

Keeping software up to date is particularly challenging if you're not sure whether a "software update" reminder is a scam or a hoax.[14] This can be even more difficult if you have antivirus software installed, since these programs often raise many alerts per day.

The good news is that notifications that come directly from the operating system or program are almost always legitimate; through the "magic" of public-key cryptography (as discussed in the bonus section of chapter 1), your computer can mathematically verify that a software update is actually coming from your operating system's maker.

Fraudulent software update messages, by contrast, will generally appear when your web browser is open (as opposed to when you start your computer or open an already-installed program), and they are much more likely to contain urgent, phishing-style language ("Your computer is at risk!"). If you're unsure (and especially if it seems like you can't "click out of" whatever message has appeared), hard-restart your device by holding down the power button. If the message reappears when you turn the device back on, it's probably legitimate. If not, you may have just dodged a nasty malware bug.

SHOULD I USE ANTIVIRUS SOFTWARE?

Antivirus software operates much like an annual flu vaccine: it can only protect you against a subset of already-known viruses. While this can be useful, these programs sometimes raise so many alerts we end up ignoring all of their security warnings. If you find that using an antivirus program has you "clicking through" security messages without reading them, then it's probably time to uninstall.

In other words, if you want to run antivirus software, go ahead—just recognize that you will still need to be vigilant about identifying and running software updates and other essential security patches as well.

BEYOND THE BASICS

If applied consistently, the practices outlined in this chapter will help protect you and the people in your networks from some of the most common and severe information security risks that face journalists—and the world—today. Though not exhaustive, many of the approaches detailed here act as sort of security "multipliers": each technique helps reinforce the value of the others. Multifactor authentication, for example, helps neutralize phishing attacks; using a password manager can help you manage compartmentalized accounts more easily.

A journalist's job is to seek out things and be in places and talk to people that others aren't, and there is inherent risk in that. Whether you are reporting from down the street or across the globe, you will need to collect and carry sensitive information, so considering security should be an integral part of your practice. As we'll see in the following chapters, however, minimizing risk in reporting work is much more about thoughtful planning and preparation than it is about technology.

CHAPTER 5

Fundamentals for Field Reporting

On Thursday, August 13, 2014, the reporter Wesley Lowery was charging his phone at a McDonald's in Ferguson, Missouri, when a group of heavily armed police officers entered the restaurant. Lowery, then a staff reporter for the *Washington Post*, had been on assignment in Ferguson for about a week, covering the protests following the shooting death of Michael Brown by police officer Darren Wilson. After providing officers with identification, Lowery began recording police activities within the restaurant, after which he and Ryan Reilly, a *Huffington Post* reporter, were instructed to leave the premises. While attempting to follow conflicting instructions from police about which exit to use, officers physically restrained Lowery, forcing him to drop his reporting equipment—including his mobile phone, backpack, and notebook. Though Lowery and Reilly (who was also arrested) were released shortly after being brought to a local police station, their reporting equipment remained in the hands of police the entire time they were detained.[1]

On paper, the United States remains a world leader in legal protections for the press. In practice, however, the risks to reporters' information—both online and in the field—have escalated to the point that in 2017, dozens of media organizations came together to launch the U.S. Press Freedom Tracker. The site has since recorded hundreds of incidents like those in Ferguson, where journalists have been arrested, detained, or had their equipment damaged or confiscated as a result of their reporting activities.[2]

Still, even the most robust legal protections cannot, in the moment, protect your work from a compromised hotel Wi-Fi connection or an overzealous police officer. As such, preparing for effective, secure field reporting requires some threat modeling and security preparation of its own.

WHAT IS THE FIELD, ANYWAY?

Today, the devices, accounts, and activities used to produce journalism are largely the same whether you are in the field or in the office: an increased reliance on third-party services and reporters' own devices means that there are limited differences in the technology being used inside the newsroom and on the road. In one sense, this can streamline our work by minimizing the need to switch devices or workflows based on our physical location. At the same time, however, the fact that we can maintain the same workflow irrespective of our physical environment may also make the very real security differences between being at home or in the office—versus out in the field—less obvious to us. Whether the protest, rally, or press conference you're covering is outside your local city hall or several states away, any time you have to rely on physical and/or digital infrastructure that is unfamiliar or out of your control, you need to make sure that you're threat modeling for "the field."

ON THE STREET: COVERING REAL-TIME EVENTS

At a political rally, protest, or even large-scale concert, your physical context at live public events can shift from orderly to chaotic almost instantly, putting your reporting equipment and safety at risk. The nearby physical and digital infrastructure, moreover, is often overwhelmed and may break down entirely: ATMs run out of cash, cellular networks jam and fail, transportation services halt, and even physical movement is often curtailed. Even if you're fully credentialed and have worked in the area or on the beat before, ensuring that both your physical person and all of your materials— from notes to photographs to video recordings—are as well protected as possible requires some advance preparation. To help guide your efforts, the following sections highlight some particular information security concerns you'll want to consider as you begin your risk assessment process for working outside your home or office.

GETTING THERE AND BACK AGAIN

Despite having traveled extensively in the Time Before Cell Phones, sometimes I still often catch myself wondering how I'll find my way around a new place without being able to search online maps. The answer, of course, is "offline"—specifically, paper—maps. Whether purchased, printed, or drawn, paper maps are an essential resource to have on hand when doing any reporting on a live event. This no-batteries-required view of the area should be labeled with key resources and amenities: bathrooms, banks or ATMs, potential device-charging locations and Wi-Fi hotspots, and safe places to escape the crowd. Map in hand, you should clearly outline both how you plan to get to the site (car? bike? public transit?) and identify multiple ways to leave—taking into account that ridesharing services and nearby public transit may be overwhelmed or inaccessible. As much as possible, arrive well before the crowds and orient yourself by taking note of prominent visual landmarks.

ONLY BRING WHAT YOU NEED

Mapping your physical surroundings and movement strategies is a crucial aspect of information security when reporting from the field: it means you won't be wasting precious time, attention, and battery life figuring out where you are or how to get where you need to go. It also helps ensure that you won't have your phone out except when you're actually reporting—reducing the chances that your device gets dropped or knocked, jeopardizing whatever material you've gathered already.

That risk-minimizing approach should also inform the process of choosing what devices to bring with you in the first place. Reporting from a live event is not the time to be carrying your primary laptop or possibly even your primary phone. Unless you'll actually be editing photos or video directly from the event, a blank loaner or "travel" laptop or a Chromebook is more than sufficient for checking emails and submitting photographs. And because such devices will have little to nothing stored on the hard drive, there's much less at stake if it gets stolen, damaged, or confiscated.

Likewise, if you don't *absolutely* need to have your primary phone with you, consider carrying a secondary travel phone. Inexpensive, pay-as-you-go (and even pay-by-the-day) options are plentiful, especially in the United States, and using a separate device makes it easy to ensure that you don't inadvertently lose (or expose) all of your regular contacts, photos, and accounts. It also means that if something happens to the device, the replacement cost will be lower. Since a travel device is likely to be a different model than your usual phone, try to borrow or buy it at least several days in advance so you can get a feel for its battery life and how to use it efficiently. This will also give you a chance to preload it with essential contact information for your editor, reporting partners, emergency contacts, etc.

You'll also want to make sure everyone who needs to knows your travel phone's number, so that an urgent call from you doesn't go unanswered.

Of course, if an alternative device isn't an option, consider creating a travel profile on your existing device (for longer assignments, you may want to back up your device to the cloud and reset it entirely). This lets you leverage both the hardware quality and familiarity of your usual phone while still streamlining your app and contact information. This can help you work more efficiently and reduce the visibility of the material that's on your default profile.

BE STRATEGIC ABOUT WHERE YOUR DATA IS GOING

If you haven't done so already, now is the moment to check your device settings to confirm where your data goes once it's captured on your phone: is it stored locally on your device, or is it uploaded to the cloud? Though many devices and accounts can be configured to do both simultaneously, making an intentional decision is crucial. Here are a few things to consider as you design your reporting plan.

THE PROS AND CONS OF SAVING LOCAL

The primary advantages of storing your data locally (that is, directly to your device's hard drive, an SSD card, or an external hard drive) is that the process is fast and reliable: saving your materials happens quickly, so you're not left waiting for overloaded cell and Wi-Fi signals to finish syncing or uploading your data in order to move on to the next task. SD cards and flash drives, in particular, can be easily swapped out as needed; this offers both flexible storage capacity and built-in compartmentalization, since even if your device gets trashed, you can pop out the SD card and access your media using a different device later on.

The drawback of local storage, of course, is that if those physical storage devices—such as SD cards, external drives, mobile phones, or audio recorders—get lost, damaged, stolen, or confiscated, then your materials are most likely gone for good. Moreover, while the flash memory found in most phones, SD cards, USB drives, and even some laptops is pretty damage resistant (as long as it's not crushed or short-circuited), for the most part you have to secure your local storage devices physically in order to protect them. That means having a secure (and preferably discreet) place to keep SD cards and thumb drives in particular: since most cameras don't yet support encryption, most kinds of removable storage media are unencrypted by default, meaning anyone who gets their hands on them will be able to access their contents.[3]

THE PROS AND CONS OF THE CLOUD

Saving data remotely, of course, offers exactly the protections that physical storage media cannot: even if your devices get pulverized, there's no real risk to information that has already been uploaded to the cloud.

At the same time, cloud storage isn't the information security panacea it might initially seem to be, especially when it comes to field reporting. Successfully uploading your materials requires substantial bandwidth, which is always in short supply in large crowds. A more insidious drawback to cloud storage is what happens afterward: once data is in the cloud, most of us tend to leave it there. Sure, hitting your current storage limit might prompt you to purge some older files or folders. But the truth is that most of us tend to let data accumulate in the cloud, which can be a risky proposition in the long run.

For one thing, it is easy for data stored in the cloud to suffer from "permissions creep": although you start out by carefully controlling precisely who has access to which files, over time more and more people get added to folders and archives, and soon there are names in the list that you don't even recognize—or that you wouldn't, if at some point you bothered to check. So the edit permissions that you've given to a reporting partner are extended to a weekend editor who's filling in on the story; that person then shares the files with their personal account, so they can more easily access it from home. Suddenly, a compromise of someone's old Yahoo email account could be putting your carefully collected reporting materials at risk.

Cloud storage, then, introduces another layer of complexity for information security: you need to know what you have, where it is stored, and, crucially, *who has access*. If you're already disciplined at keeping track of the first two, then your best approach may simply be to move data out of the cloud on a regular basis to limit its potential exposure; it's also a good idea to review project folders regularly and pare down who has access.

THE "HYBRID" APPROACH

Choosing where to save your work need not be an either/or proposition, of course; many systems (especially on mobile devices) can opportunistically do both. This type of redundancy can be a good thing, as long as it doesn't make you lazy about managing your information altogether. Information security is about minimizing both upfront risk and the negative consequences if something does go wrong; you can't do either without a clear understanding of where your information is. In this sense, the specific choice you make is less important than the fact that you make a choice proactively. That way, if the unexpected happens you will have confidence that you know how to respond.

COMPARTMENTALIZING: HARDWARE EDITION

Today's mobile phones can do pretty much everything: let us post social media, take high-quality photos, record interviews, and manage calendar events and task reminders. They let us send and receive phone calls, text messages, emails, and instant messages; review documents; and browse the web. With the ability to switch reporting mediums with the tap of an app, the idea of traveling light and using a single device for all of your reporting and communication needs may seem like a no-brainer.

But that convenience can also be a liability, as your all-in-one reporting device can also become a single point of failure. Dropped, lost, confiscated, dead battery—if you're depending on your phone for all your reporting needs, its failure can take your reporting along with it. Inexpensive digital cameras and audio recorders can be both less distracting and more discreet than smartphones, and using them also helps you avoid relying on mobile apps for capturing audio, photos, and/or video that may "share" your data with third parties. This last point is crucial, given that even experts struggle to determine what information mobile apps are actually collecting and transmitting.[4] Using dedicated devices—especially those without internet connectivity—is one more way you can better control who has access to your reporting materials and so better secure your reporting more generally.

ON THE ROAD: REPORTING AWAY FROM HOME

Covering protests, campaign rallies, concerts, and conferences always presents a range of logistical and reporting challenges. When those events happen locally, however, we at least usually get the physical and psychological respite of returning to a familiar space at the end of the day. Whether at your home or office, having a relatively comfortable, secure place to process your reporting materials and mentally decompress is a valuable resource. How, then, can you help create a similar level of security for yourself and your work when you're on the road?

Sometimes, being away from home can itself be something of a break—an opportunity to focus on your work away from the pressures of daily life in your home context. On the other hand, addressing even simple, daily necessities can quickly become exhausting when you're on the road. Whether you're staying in a traditional hotel or a short-term rental, everything from managing your laundry and finding breakfast to securing your equipment and connecting to the internet takes on an extra layer of complexity when your home base is not a physical space that you really control. Unsurprisingly, these are also the moments when most of us begin to truly appreciate the overlap between digital and physical information security, since we have to think about not just what is happening to the information that we capture and store on our digital devices but also consider where and how those devices are being kept, connected, and protected whenever they are out of our hands.

GETTING ONLINE

One of the simplest—and most significant—information security hurdles facing journalists away from home is the task of adequately securing your internet connections when you have to rely on hotel or rental Wi-Fi.

Larger hotel chains will often provide a username and password for their Wi-Fi network, but the actual signal may still be unsecured. The login allows them to throttle or even terminate your internet access if your activities are putting them at risk.

In order to protect your work in those contexts, what you'll need is a virtual private network (VPN). These services essentially use whatever internet access you have to build an encrypted "tunnel" through which all of your subsequent web browsing and other internet activities are sent. As a result, the only thing your host connection (including whoever runs the Wi-Fi router and the broader network it connects to) can see is a single connection to your VPN provider; the details of your web traffic are visible only to the VPN provider itself.

Of course, a VPN-protected connection is not going to behave identically to the internet connections you're used to at your home or office. By their very design, VPN connections protect your internet traffic from snooping by first sending *every single one* of your requests to a physical location controlled by the VPN provider, meaning that your data might have to travel hundreds or even thousands of miles round trip just for you to load a basic webpage. As a result, VPNs tend to be slower and experience more lag time than you might be used to. Using a VPN also requires trusting that service provider almost implicitly—because while the hotel or conference center won't be able to see your browsing activity, your VPN provider will see every connection you make. Just like other online services, a good VPN is something you'll have to pay for if you want a substantive level of security and privacy. Fortunately, there are high-quality VPNs available for as little as US$40 per year if you sign a multi-year contract.

WHEN YOU'RE AWAY FROM YOUR DEVICES

As we'll discuss in more detail in chapter 6, methodically backing up your reporting materials is an essential aspect of any information security plan when you're on the road, whether in another city or on the other side of the world. In many cases, backing your materials up to the cloud can be a valuable option if it's feasible: once they've been uploaded, sensitive reporting materials can then be "wiped" from your physical drives and storage devices, limiting what data remains accessible if they are searched or stolen.

At the same time, moving your data off of hard drives and memory cards isn't always possible: limited time, bandwidth, and storage capacity can all curtail your ability to make comprehensive online backups. Likewise, while encryption can make the data you store on these devices unreadable to others, the time required to encrypt large quantities of data may also be prohibitive.

If you need to leave devices containing sensitive data in a rental or hotel room, then, protecting them really comes down to traditional physical and operational security: place them in the room's safe if one is available, or find unlikely places to conceal them. Wherever you put them, consider leaving "breadcrumbs" nearby that will help you confirm that they have not been discovered or tampered with in your absence. In a safe, for example, you might position certain items on top of the drive in a particular orientation. If you return and those items have been disturbed, it may signal that the safe has been accessed by others.

While some of these scenarios may seem more the stuff of spy movies than regular reporting, remember that information security is more about planning ahead than it is about adding any elaborate new routines to your actual reporting process. Just as importantly, engaging in these practices when the stakes are low will make them familiar and comfortable, so that when you're in the higher-risk situations where you really need them, making smart, secure decisions will already be a habit.

CHAPTER 6

Reporting Abroad

Seth Harp, a reporter for *Rolling Stone*, learned the limit of his rights the hard way when he was stopped by Customs and Border Patrol (CBP) at Austin-Bergstrom International Airport in June 2019. Harp, a U.S. Iraq war veteran who has also covered armed conflict and the military for the *New York Times* and the *New Yorker*, was returning from a week-long reporting trip in Mexico when CBP agents pulled him aside for secondary screening. Though Harp traveled to Mexico frequently, this was the first time he had been detained at the border. Because he was not under arrest, Harp's request to speak with a lawyer was denied; instead, CBP agents lied to Harp, telling him he wouldn't be allowed into the United States unless he cooperated.[1] Over the next several hours, CBP agents searched Harp's electronic devices in detail, perusing chats with sources, emails with editors, and personal photographs. Though agents more than once took his devices out of his sight, Harp did observe them taking down his laptop's serial number and the IMEI of his mobile phone. Eventually, the CPB agents returned his belongings and told him he was free to go.[2]

Harp's experience is not unique. In 2018, the Committee to Protect Journalists spoke with dozens of journalists who had been subject to invasive searches at the U.S. border. While a 2019 ruling by the influential Ninth Circuit held that forensic device searches at the border required "reasonable" suspicion that a device contains contraband, manual searches like those Harp observed are still considered "routine."[3] This is especially problematic because CPB is authorized to share information with other federal agencies but does not disclose what information is shared or how.[4] Even for American journalists, this makes the U.S. border one of the riskiest geographies they will encounter when reporting abroad. Because of this, a coherent information security strategy is essential preparation for any international travel, regardless of your assignment or destination.

Given the degree of preparation that international travel already involves—from arranging accommodation and currency to choosing local fixers and mobile phone operators—addressing information security concerns actually requires minimal additional effort. In fact, once you've developed a risk assessment that addresses a handful of information management concerns, you'll probably find that it makes the remainder of your planning easier. Especially if you've already been practicing the compartmentalization and data minimization habits discussed in previous chapters, preparing to travel abroad will probably take less time than it used to, as long as you have answered four key questions:

1. What information will I bring?
2. How will I communicate with contacts, both in-country and back home?
3. How will I document my reporting?
4. How will I transmit or transport that information?

WHAT SHOULD YOU BRING?

In the United States, the context where individuals enjoy the greatest privacy and security protections are within their homes and rental properties. With few exceptions, even law enforcement cannot enter your property without your express permission or a search warrant; even some "noninvasive" surveillance technologies, such as infrared cameras, cannot legally be used to observe these spaces without a warrant.[5] When you travel, however, many countries demand access to the devices and materials that you bring with you and may detain you or deny you entry on the basis of their contents, including social media accounts. As a result, the best way to protect almost *any* type of information while you're traveling is simply to leave it at home.

Not carrying information with you over a border doesn't necessarily mean not using it at all during your reporting, however. If you expect to have good internet connectivity at your destination, organize an online storage space with the materials you'll need ahead of time, and download them once you arrive. If downloading once you're in-country is dangerous or unreliable but there is material that you absolutely *must* bring with you, opt for small drives or storage cards that can be transported discreetly. After all, authorities can't search a device they haven't found.

DEVICES: WHAT TO CONSIDER

MOBILE PHONE

If you (or your organization) can afford it, a travel phone can be invaluable when reporting both domestically and internationally. Because you can optimize its hardware, service plan, and features to make connecting, backing up, and wiping the phone as straightforward as possible, a dedicated travel phone can make travel preparation simpler and more secure.

For example, a GSM phone with an easily accessible SIM slot (or two) is extremely versatile: you can choose, purchase, and use a local SIM (be prepared to present your passport, as identification is required to purchase a SIM in most countries), or you can equip the travel phone with a U.S.-based SIM that includes some international service (some U.S. carriers offer low-speed international data and SMS on certain plans).

Before you leave, perform a factory reset of the device in order to ensure it is a clean slate in terms of contact information, apps, and accounts; if the device has a separate SD card, make sure you empty and/or erase that separately. Since the objective of using a travel phone is to leave your primary phone at home, you will want to add (only) essential contact information and accounts before you depart.

If you depend on flight alerts and digital boarding passes, make sure these are routed to email and/or SMS accounts accessible on your travel phone; you may even wish to direct these to a throwaway travel email account that you use only for a single trip. If you'll need to add work and social media accounts to the device once you arrive, make sure you know your passwords, and double-check that you can access at least one multi-factor method that doesn't depend on your primary mobile phone. Hardware security keys and/or preassigned backup codes are supported by most major services and can be configured for the relevant accounts before you travel.

If a travel phone is not in your budget, you can always double-check your MFA options and back up your primary phone to the cloud, then perform a factory reset and SD card wipe. You then have the option to restore your phone at your destination or (preferably) after you return home. While this approach can simplify things like accessing accounts after arrival, it also means that the consequences of your phone being lost, damaged, or confiscated are more severe, since it's probably a relatively expensive device and, once restored, still contains all your typical accounts and data. Ultimately, of course, you need to select the options that work best for your particular needs and budget.

What About "Burners"?

While a popular topic of discussion around hacker conferences, "burner" phones are more an object of lore than an actual information security measure.[6] Often portrayed as cheap phones that you use for a limited time to thwart surveillance, the reality is that any security such a device offers lies entirely in the fact that it isn't traceable to you and isn't carrying any of your data. If you're already being diligent about resetting your primary or travel phone before going abroad or into the field, then a burner device has nothing to offer you except crummier hardware and fewer features. Of course, if that's what it takes to keep you from loading up your Twitter account in a context where you know you shouldn't be, go right ahead. Otherwise, don't worry about what you call your device and focus instead on how you'll use it: that's how real security is achieved.

LAPTOP

Having your primary laptop with you can sometimes feel like a security blanket: no matter what the outside circumstances, it can be comforting to know you have your digital world at your fingertips.

Unless something goes wrong. If your computer is lost, damaged, confiscated, or searched, that "security" becomes a massive liability, as journalists like Seth Harp have learned all too well. As such, it's best to travel with the cheapest, most basic laptop computer that you can. While technically this can be any computer with an up-to-date operating system and a straightforward factory-reset process, Chromebooks in particular are almost always a good option.

Why Chromebooks? Since they are basically Android phones in a laptop format, even the best Chromebooks are relatively inexpensive, and the operating system updates automatically; they also have a one-step "power-wash" function that performs a factory reset almost instantly. And since your apps, data, and profile information are all drawn from whatever Google account you use to log in, you don't even need to worry about doing separate, explicit backups first.

Chromebooks' limited storage space also naturally discourages accumu-lating lots of (potentially irreplaceable) files and data on the device—and the less you store on a travel laptop, the less you have to lose if something happens to it. At the same time, you won't be able to do advanced photo or video editing on a Chromebook (although if you happen to be a data nerd you can program pretty effectively with the Linux apps enabled). If those capabilities are essential for you, using a refurbished machine to travel can help minimize costs, though you'll need to set aside time to configure and install any necessary software before your trip. But if you simply need a travel laptop that will let you write, edit, and upload reporting materials, a Chromebook is often a great place to start.

HOW YOU'LL COMMUNICATE

An average of 90 percent of the world's population owns a mobile phone; in the United States, that rate was 96 percent as of 2019, and more than half of Americans had only wireless service at home.[7] Naturally, then, most of us reach for a mobile phone when we want to communicate with others.

Designing a communication plan for reporting abroad is about more than learning how to top up a local SIM or find a usable cell signal, how-ever. Once you've decided on a device, you'll need to learn about the legal and behavioral norms for digital communications (such as social media) in the region you'll be visiting, and choosing which mobile networks you connect to—and how—will need to be tailored to your threat model. Here are some elements you'll want to consider before you depart.

WHAT KIND OF MOBILE SERVICE WILL YOU USE?

Whatever device you choose, you need to decide whether you will rely on a U.S. service provider plan with international coverage or whether you'll buy a local SIM in the region where you'll be reporting. Beyond the cost differences—which can be significant—your selection will have implica-tions for both you and your contacts in-country. If you choose to retain your regular service, standard voice calls and SMS messages to sources will clearly be coming from an international number; this can have safety impli-cations for them if speaking to foreigners (or journalists) is at all taboo. Using a local SIM can help you communicate with locals somewhat more discreetly, but purchasing a SIM in most places requires registering with a significant form of identification—often a passport number—making calls and texts to and from your device easily traceable by local authorities.

Since there is really no way to use mobile services anonymously, your best option will depend on the threats that you and your sources are facing. Would calls from an international number raise suspicions in a source's family or community? Are you already under scrutiny from local authorities, making your locally registered SIM easier to identify? While in many cases we cannot know the identity—much less the circumstances—of every source before we begin our reporting, think carefully about the type of story you're pursuing and the risk that your sources and collaborators may face before you decide on the type of mobile service you'll use for your project.

WHAT APPS WILL YOU USE—AND HOW?

Nearly three-quarters of the world's population has access to a device that can support mobile apps.[8] This is a boon for information security, since many popular communication apps offer better security than traditional phone connections or SMS services. Because they can operate over Wi-Fi, moreover, communication apps are often more reliable, efficient, and accessible than standard phone and SMS services that depend on spotty and expensive cellular signals to operate.

Messaging apps like WhatsApp and Signal, for example, offer security features like the end-to-end (E2E) encryption discussed in chapter 1. While an E2E app is only as secure as the device it's running on,[9] of course, using an encrypted messaging app to communicate offers significant protections from both real-time surveillance and efforts to expose an exchange after the fact—even by the app maker. As such, these apps can be a strong choice for both local communication with sources and fixers and long-distance messaging with editors and loved ones.

At the same time, some E2E apps—especially proprietary ones—may still collect metadata about the way you use them. As discussed in chapter 2, this information may be more than sufficient to identify sources for legal purposes. As of this writing, for example, WhatsApp's privacy policy states: "You provide us the phone numbers in your mobile address book on a regular basis, including those of both the users of our Services and your other contacts. . . . We collect device-specific information when you install, access, or use our Services. This includes information such as hardware model, operating system information, browser information, IP address, mobile network information including phone number, and device identifiers."[10] This information would be more than enough for authorities to identify your sources, even if the contents of your messages could not be read.

In other words, you'll need to consider the logging and data retention policies of the apps you use—along with their more "technical" security features—in order to choose communication options that fit the threat model of both your project and your sources.

What's the Problem with Proprietary Software?

If you've done any reading about "secure" apps and software, you've almost certainly seen some of them touted as "open source" rather than "proprietary." For a lot of security folks, any application that isn't open source (or at least "source available") is a nonstarter from a security perspective, because there's no way to know for sure what the app *actually* does—and therefore if the security features it promises are for real.

Choosing open-source software is not a security guarantee, however. In principle, anyone can review the code behind open-source software for potential security risks, but that doesn't mean anyone really does. That's why some of the most catastrophic security bugs on the internet— like 2014's "Heartbleed"—have been rooted in open-source software: though there are good incentives to *use* it, there have historically been fewer incentives to audit and maintain it.[11]

In other words, proprietary software isn't *necessarily* less secure than open-source software. Since most of us are not in a position to effectively review the code and judge the security of open-source tools ourselves, in practical terms it comes down to trust: Do you trust the company or community behind this tool? If so, try to confirm its security properties with one or two experts—and then get on with your work.

Beyond an app's own data policies, it's important to understand the prevalence and/or profile of particular platforms in the region where you'll be working. Especially in times of unrest, just having the wrong app on your phone can be enough to trigger arrest.[12] Especially in places where encryption is only marginally legal, encouraging sources to use E2E-encrypted apps could put them at risk. Instead of focusing on technical security features in those instances, you and your sources may be better off carefully using a more common app, so your exchanges invite less scrutiny.

Finally, you'll want to evaluate whether the specifics of an international assignment warrant adjusting some of your typical use patterns for apps. For example, while you might avoid geolocation services domestically, these may help your security team monitor your safety outside of the country. Likewise, you may want to turn on automatic backups if the risk of device damage or destruction is high, even if you usually don't use that feature in the United States.

HOW YOU'LL DOCUMENT

The expectations for a journalist's default skill set today is what just a few years ago would have made them a "unicorn" in the industry: they need to be able to research, interview, and write, certainly, but also produce audio, take photographs, report on-camera, and do data analysis; designing graphics and having several thousand followers on social media is helpful, too. Even if you never anticipate publishing a podcast in your life, however, you'll almost certainly be collecting images, audio, video, and even data in the course of your reporting. Because these media can be so much more sensitive than written notes, moreover, your reporting plan for work abroad should include how you'll capture that content with both quality *and* security in mind.

NOW YOU SEE IT?

Whether you are crossing a border or entering an office building, the chance that your person and effects will be searched while reporting is high, especially outside of your home country. Because of this, "carry only what you must" should become a mantra when reporting abroad: if possible, back data up to cloud storage as much as possible and remove it from your local devices as best you can. Likewise, if there is a risk that your devices may be damaged or confiscated, having more than one way to conduct your reporting is essential: a small digital audio recorder or point-and-shoot camera can substitute for more specialized equipment in a pinch, and they may be more easily concealed if a search seems imminent.

In other words, a key strategy for protecting devices that you *must* carry with you is to minimize or deflect interest in them: avoid stickers or logos that might draw undue attention to laptops, and consider tucking smaller drives and devices in places that are less likely to be searched thoroughly. Many women, for example, find that male security personnel don't closely inspect menstrual products, making them a convenient place to stow flash drives or SD cards you'd rather not have scrutinized.

The success of this type of operational security depends on following the reporter-centric approach to risk assessments discussed in chapter 3. When you are relying on obfuscation as part of your security strategy, your best, most reliable security measures depend not only on *where* you are but on *who* you are or appear to be: using menstrual products to hide reporting materials might work well for journalists who present as stereotypically female but could draw heightened scrutiny for those who present as stereotypically male. This is why risk assessments and threat models should always begin with the reporter and then expand to include relevant social and political contexts: attributes that could seem like limitations in one sense often prove to be advantages in another—and the best journalistic and security outcomes depend on accurately assessing and leveraging those characteristics.

Plausible Deniability

Often a way to enhance your personal and information security in any reporting context is to operate in a way that is as low profile (or "low signature") as possible. When traveling abroad, this can be as simple as adapting your dress and habits to accommodate local norms. At the same time, there is no such thing as "no-signature" reporting; at some point, others will become aware that you are a journalist, and that fact will influence how you're treated.

How much you reveal about your activities can have security implications for both you and your sources. If you want to effectively deflect questions about exactly where you've been and whom you've been speaking to, you'll need to develop a persuasive alternative narrative. If you don't want to reveal that you were conducting interviews at a refugee camp, can you offer a credible explanation for why you were in the area? If authorities were to search your devices, would they find evidence of activities you've denied?

Sometimes, reporting safely means being able to offer "plausible deniability": a believable explanation for activities or materials whose true nature you cannot disclose. Plausible deniability is especially important when you have no feasible way to protect something other than to hide it; if it *is* discovered, you need to be prepared to explain

CONTINUED

its presence. Like all information security, plausible deniability only works to the extent that it accounts for both what you are doing and for who you are or appear to be.

HOW YOU'LL TRANSMIT

Whether you'll be filing at regular intervals or returning home before producing your piece, any international reporting project requires a robust plan for how you will get your notes, stories, and other materials out of the reporting area safely.

Just as you can either store data locally or remotely, you can transmit your reporting materials either virtually or physically. "Virtual" transmission will require an internet connection and some form of cloud storage or data sharing service. Physical transmission will mean just that: carrying your physical storage devices (flash drives, SD cards) on your person or in your luggage—or else using physical shipping, mail, or delivery services.

Whether transmitting data virtually is feasible will depend on both the size of your files and the speed, reliability, and bandwidth of your internet connections. When working abroad, transmitting your data virtually and then removing it from local devices is usually preferable, because your greatest information security risk is typically from regional groups and authorities.

If uploading your data is not possible, either because there's too much of it or because you have poor or untrustworthy internet access, backing data up to physically discrete memory cards or drives will likely be your next best option. If you have time and your devices support it, you may want to encrypt your files; at minimum, you should strive to remove them from devices that can natively open/play their contents, such as computers, cameras, or audio recorders. At this point, your main source of security is once again obfuscation—whether you are carrying the devices on your person or concealing them within a package, you are protecting your data principally by making it hard to find. In this case, you'll need to rely on your own experience and that of local experts to assess which options are likely to receive more or less scrutiny: Will a drive shipped inside a souvenir be more likely to make it safely across the border, or will an SD card tucked into a hidden pocket be sufficient? For those decisions, there's no replacement for a thorough risk assessment that takes into account the facts on the ground.

What About Encryption?

You may have noticed that while the security potential of E2E-encrypted apps has been discussed in some detail in this chapter, the idea of encrypting individual files and physical drives has not. Why?

Encrypting the data on your drives or devices is an effective protection against technical and legal threats but does little to reduce your security risks if you can be forced to reveal the password that protects them. In situations where your physical safety is uncertain or your legal rights are minimal, refusing to decrypt your materials can be downright dangerous. Add to this the fact that encryption is simply illegal in many places, and its utility as an information security tactic when reporting abroad diminishes even further.

This is not to say that having access to encryption tools when working abroad isn't useful: many E2E-encrypted messaging apps, for example, are so widespread that even countries where encryption is technically illegal do not attempt to block their use. And if you are uploading sensitive materials to an email account or a third-party data sharing service, encrypting them beforehand adds a meaningful layer of additional security, as they will be unreadable to both opportunistic hackers and law enforcement who might obtain copies of them. But given the many vulnerabilities we face when traveling abroad, minimizing and obfuscating the data you carry is almost always a better strategy than relying on encryption, since there are other ways the latter can put you at risk.

Optimizing your information security when reporting abroad is largely a matter of planning, taking into account both who you are and where you are going; this will help you create both a risk assessment and mitigation strategies that make the most of your specific skills and attributes, without wasting effort on generic—and potentially inapplicable—threats.

Fortunately, this additional bit of pre-trip planning will help you make practical security and reporting decisions. Just as importantly, it can contribute to your peace of mind: instead of worrying about what will happen if a device is damaged or your bags are searched, you'll have a plan for how to respond if something like that happens. As a result, you can be more present in—and responsive to—your actual reporting work, which is what doing high-quality journalism is really all about.

CHAPTER 7

Creating a Culture of Security

For reporters, the first job of journalism is to get the story; for editors, it is to make sure the story works. Whether collaborating principally with staffers or freelancers, an editor's job is to shape coverage so that it meets the needs of the news organization, both substantively and stylistically. Because editors are a key interface between reporters and the larger institution, their role is much more significant than simply editing copy or even approving pitches: editors exert enormous influence over the reporting culture of an organization, serving as front-line representatives of its needs, values, and requirements. As such, building strong information security practices depends significantly on the robustness of editors' engagement with these issues.

Research indicates that reporters would like to see more involvement from their organization on information security: a 2015 Pew Research Center survey, for example, found that while 64 percent of investigative journalists believed that the U.S. government had "probably collected data about their communications," half of them also felt that their organization was "not doing enough" to protect them and their sources from hacking and surveillance.[1] At least part of the difficulty in securing journalists' work stems from the degree of autonomy reporting demands: journalists (and journalistic organizations) need to be flexible and adaptable, and they need information security approaches that are, too. This is probably why, despite editors' interest in information security, many are reluctant to impose security measures on the journalists they manage, even if they have the authority to do so.[2]

Fortunately, good information security—like good editing—is less about imposing hard and fast rules than it is about creating an environment

where reporters can easily integrate key principles into their work and recognize when they need to ask for help. Because of the overwhelmingly
digital nature of newsgathering and production today, the benefits to editors of cultivating good information security within their teams go beyond
avoiding the embarrassing—and sometimes dangerous—fallout of a security failure. By educating themselves—either directly or by identifying
security "experts" with whom to confer—editors can equip themselves to
make the policy, technology, and time management decisions that will best
support the efficacy *and* security of the reporters they oversee, which is good
for everyone. As Miriam Elder, a former world editor at *BuzzFeed* put it:
"Somebody who takes security really seriously, their reporting tends to be
all the more thorough . . . the care that they put into their security is also
reflected in the care that they put into their stories, their ideas, their
reporting—everything."

BECOMING A SECURITY CHAMPION

As an editor, improving your team's security means building your own
understanding first. You'll need to identify what security measures your
team needs—bearing in mind not just the where, what, and how of the
reporting your group does but the characteristics, strengths, and preferences of the individual reporters you work with, as well as the resources of
your organization. In other words, you need to develop a risk assessment
or threat model. If you work at a smaller news organization, you may want
to revisit chapter 3 for a refresher on how to approach this process; if you
work at a medium or large news organization, now is the perfect opportunity to seek out your colleagues' expertise.

A newsroom of almost any size already employs people with some degree
of security expertise. Some of them may specialize in physical security; others may be focused on securing the organization's networks and digital
infrastructure. In some cases, the person with the best understanding may
be a fellow newsroom employee whose beat or reporting method has
exposed them to security issues. If you don't already know whom to reach
out to, now is the time to apply your reporting skills to the problem and
identify what security (re)sources your organization already has.

If you're at a larger news organization, you may well discover that there is
an existing team that can help you perform risk assessments; in most cases,
they will be grateful to hear from you and will gladly develop a customized
risk assessment with or for you, making short work of what can be an

otherwise daunting task. Even if your organization doesn't have a specialized team in place, however, finding a well-informed colleague to collaborate with will make sketching out your risk assessment both faster and more fun.

With a threat model in hand, you can now begin to prioritize your most relevant threats and identify appropriate mitigation strategies. If harassment is weakening morale or making certain types of coverage harder to generate, you may decide to focus on getting team members to compartmentalize their social media accounts and "scrub" their online profiles. If your organization has been targeted by hackers, your first emphasis may be to encourage team members to set up multifactor authentication. If you are frequently collaborating with groups outside your organization, you may decide that using a password manager to facilitate and audit access to resources and accounts is your first priority.

Once you have identified your security objectives—whether they are broader goals such as "team members seek security advice when needed" or more specific ones like "team members use non-SMS two-factor authentication on professional social media accounts"—it's time to determine how can you best engage and motivate your team members toward adopting those behaviors. While the ultimate goal of your efforts is to improve the security, reliability, and efficiency of your team, achieving those ends first requires developing a robust culture of security.

CREATING A CULTURE OF SECURITY

Even in academia, most journalism education relies on the apprenticeship model: newer or less experienced reporters learn through an iterative process of trying, being corrected, and trying again. The role of the editor is essential to this process: through their editors' feedback, reporters learn where they need to add more stakeholder perspectives or expert corroboration, how to structure or fill gaps in their stories—and whether their pitch is really a story at all.

Whatever the experience level of the reporters you work with, developing a culture of security will mean weaving information security considerations into the entire pitching and editing process: you'll need to ask about how sources have been contacted, where notes or recordings are stored, and whether the reporter has received online blowback after publishing stories on a similar topic before. While some reporters may initially bristle at being asked to explain so much of their process, your objective is to get a clearer view of how their reporting is being conducted, because security is not something that can be bolted on at the end of a reporting process. Without integrated security practices, you will not only have no idea if your security goals are being met, but you—and your reporters—risk losing out on big stories because you've failed to lay the appropriate groundwork. As Reuters's global managing editor Reg Chua puts it: "[The times when] you're working on anything that is moderately sensitive is when you don't recognize it until it's too late. So by the time [a reporter] calls up to say, 'Hey, my source has just given me this great set of documents,' you say, 'Well, how many times were you e-mailing with her before she did this? How much of a trail have you already left? And my God what are we going to do now?'"

Avoiding those "my god" moments so that your team can pursue more exciting stories requires diligence and preparation. Even if your team is willing, developing a robust culture of security requires more than good intentions and enthusiasm; it requires the right combination of knowledge, incentives, and support in order to translate those good intentions into genuine *behavior change*.

UNDERSTANDING BEHAVIOR CHANGE

In his 2013 *New Yorker* feature "Slow Ideas," the surgeon and essayist Atul Gawande examines the trajectory of two crucial medical discoveries of the nineteenth century: anesthesia and "Listerism"—the practice of disinfecting the hands and instruments for surgery. Once discovered, Gawande writes, anesthesia swept through the medical world in months and was standard practice in the United States and Britain within seven years. Joseph Lister's methods for sterilizing the surgical environment, however, took decades to become more than a perfunctory part of surgical practice.

Both discoveries were medically important, if technically complex. So what drove the difference in adoption rates? Why did surgeons' behaviors around sterilizing the medical environment not change more quickly? As Gawande writes:

First, [anesthesia] combatted a visible and immediate problem (pain); [Listerism] combatted an invisible problem (germs) whose effects wouldn't be manifest until well after the operation. Second, although both made life better for patients, only one made life better for doctors. Anesthesia changed surgery from a brutal, time-pressured assault on a shrieking patient to a quiet, considered procedure. Listerism, by contrast, required the operator to work in a shower of carbolic acid. Even low dilutions burned the surgeons' hands. You can imagine why Lister's crusade might have been a tough sell.[3]

For many organizations, information security may seem like the Listerism of the twenty-first century: information security threats are usually "invisible," affecting digital systems in ways that are hidden from us. As with the spread of illness, not every instance of bad security results in a breach, so it can be hard to connect the insecure activity to its (eventual) consequence. Like disease, however, individual behaviors can have far-reaching implications; poor information security can expose a journalist or news organization's entire network to risk. Likewise, the consequences of even a single information security breach can be severe: sources can be jailed, and news organizations can lose significant credibility when information security fails. As the security expert Matt Mitchell says, "You might have a hard time recruiting talent; you might have a hard time retaining talent; you might have a hard time even getting ads . . . [a security breach] has a really bad ripple effect."

Yet information security still often seems a hard sell, even to journalists working on sensitive beats with vulnerable sources. Here, too, Gawande's examinations of the medical profession offer intriguing parallels: health care workers have long suffered from an "illusion of invulnerability" regarding their own susceptibility to infection, as well as cognitive bias in their recollections of when, for example, failing to wash their hands may have led to an illness.[4] Similarly, journalists who have not experienced security incidents may insist that information security concerns are not applicable to their beat or may rationalize past security incidents as having been out of their control.

Fortunately, public health experts have spent decades researching how to foster behavior change around precisely the type of complex and time-delayed risks found in the health care environment, and many of those lessons can help support better information security practices. Unsurprisingly, there is no magic bullet for creating behavior change, but the following framework can help you systematically initiate and sustain better information security practices within your team.

At a high level, some of the key factors that influence behavior change can be summarized as follows:[5]

1. The messenger: Who is delivering the information?
2. Incentives: Our responses to incentives are shaped by predictable mental shortcuts, such as strongly avoiding losses

3. Norms: How strongly others influence us
4. Defaults: We follow preset options
5. Salience: What is relevant to us usually draws our attention
6. Priming: Our acts are often influenced by subconscious cues
7. Affect: Emotional associations can powerfully shape our actions
8. Commitments: We seek to be consistent with our public promises, and we reciprocate acts
9. Ego: We act in ways that make us feel better about ourselves

While not every new behavior or workflow adjustment will require a nine-point plan to be successful, having *a* plan is essential. It's the nature of news that there will always be another fire to put out; having a plan in place will help prevent security initiatives from falling by the wayside. With a little bit of tailoring, you can design, introduce, and adopt information security practices that work with your team's specific strengths, needs, and personalities.

CHOOSE YOUR MESSENGER

In organizations with a strong, well-established institutional culture, personally acting as "the messenger" for new security practices may well be the most effective approach. If you, as both a team leader and representative of the news organization, clearly understand and support a new practice, tool, or protocol, your team will likely trust that it is worthy of adoption. Likewise, even if you are part of a newer or more fluid organization, if you have a strong personal rapport with your team members, your endorsement of a new approach may be sufficient for your team members to take it seriously.

On the other hand, you may be leading a newer, less cohesive team or face influential team members who may challenge your expertise or authority. In that case, having your organization's technical personnel or even an external consultant recommend or endorse the new security practice may be a more effective way to introduce it to your team.

IDENTIFY THE INCENTIVES

There are few things more attractive to journalists than the promise of a bigger, better, or more exclusive story. For this reason, making information security considerations a requirement for greenlighting an exciting project may well be the best mechanism for getting reporters to buy in to new security processes. For this to work, however, the converse must also be true. At Reuters, says Chua, "There are protocols: what you're allowed to do and what you're not allowed to do. And obviously if we catch you doing those things [that you're not allowed to do], then we give you a good talking to, or we don't let you go back in again."

Depending on your team, even small incentives (and disincentives) might work in some cases. If your team has a friendly competition with another in the organization, the chance to "prove" themselves in a head-to-head competition could be motivating for your team members, as could a within-team leaderboard. Offering collective benefits—a sponsored coffee break, for example—for teamwide task completion might encourage more skilled members to help others get up to speed. In mission-driven fields, appealing to a sense of professional responsibility can also be powerful; health-sector research around hand-washing behavior in hospitals, for example, revealed that messages emphasizing *patients'* health was more effective at changing providers' behavior than messages emphasizing their own personal risks.[6] In journalism, messages that appeal to reporters' sense of loyalty to both colleagues and sources may be effective in motivating information security practices that protect the team as a whole, such as securing accounts, devices, and documents.

APPEAL TO NORMS

Extensive research shows that individuals tend to evaluate their behaviors with respect to existing social norms and that these can be used to influence behaviors within communities. If other teams in your organization—or on your beat at other organizations—have strong information security practices, this can be used to encourage your team's adoption of similar practices. If the behaviors you are encouraging are significantly more secure than those of other teams, however, then your efforts can have a "boomerang effect," in which community members resist even a positive behavior change because it, too, deviates from the norm.[7] In this case, you'll want to identify the positive perceptions and consequences of "deviating" toward more secure behaviors and communicate these clearly to your team. For example, you might want to highlight scoops and sources that arrived through more secure communication methods or try to secure recognition from company leadership for your team's outstanding security practices.

Norms, of course, govern far more than information security behaviors, so working *with* the norms of both your team and your organization will be crucial to reaching your information security goals. If your team or organization typically follows more participatory decision-making processes, using a collaborative or consensus approach to selecting a secure communications platform will be more successful than trying to impose your own choice on the team. While this may mean compromising your own preferences, failing to honor existing norms can cause friction or open conflict; even worse, it may lead team members to feign compliance while actively subverting or working around new practices, creating greater and more entrenched security problems. As *ProPublica*'s deputy managing editor Scott Klein observed of early concerns around mandating MFA on email accounts: "If [*ProPublica*] made it too hard to check your e-mail, people would just forward their [company] e-mail to their Gmail, and then we would have no idea how people secure their email, and then corporate e-mails would be everywhere . . . if you make the controls too tight, users—and especially sort of newsroom culture—will just get around it." As MFA has become the norm for everything from bank accounts to social media platforms, however, concerns about mandating this security behavior have declined. According to the Marshall Project's senior editor Tom Meagher: "Now it's to the point where anybody new coming in, it's like, 'Oh yeah, I do this with my bank—it's no big deal.'"

CREATE CLEAR AND SENSIBLE DEFAULTS

Though for many of us the concept of "defaults" is inextricably connected with technology, defaults are also an important way to reduce the mental energy your team members spend on the nonreporting aspects of their work, including security measures. By clearly defining, for example, what second-factor device team members should choose for their accounts, for example, you save them the effort of making a unique decision every time they join a new platform or service. As Reuters's Chua points out, this helps you enhance your team's information security without it "eating up cognitive space that [reporters] could spend doing something else."

KEEP IT RELEVANT

Relevance (or salience) will, like norms, be defined in large part by the existing structures, values, and priorities of your team and organization. If employee satisfaction at your organization is connected to its strong reputation, highlighting the ways that account compromise threatens that reputation may increase team members' appetite for account protection strategies such as using a password manager or enabling MFA. Likewise, if your organization has a strong investigative history, share stories about how security measures can support that. Conversely, talking about attacks that have targeted similar organizations to yours may help team members appreciate the security risk they face—and therefore the value of a new security solution.

DELIVER YOUR MESSAGE WITH PRIMING

Priming (also sometimes called "nudging") takes advantage of the fact that humans are invariably affected by cues within the environment that they do not process consciously. Nudges are found everywhere in marketing, for example, from online account registration forms with prechecked "Send me updates" fields to supermarket checkout lines bordered with candy, magazines, toys, and travel-sized toiletries.[8] The presence of these visual elements is an implicit "suggestion" toward the product or behavior—one that can influence your behavior unless you think about it actively.

The Ethics of Nudging

For some people, the psychology of nudging has ominous undertones, evoking images of *They Live*–style subliminal messaging. Like many complex ethical questions, however, it largely comes down to issues of benefit and agency: who benefits from the adoption of a particular behavior, and how much agency should individuals have when it comes to making that choice?

In marketing, many of the behaviors we are "nudged" toward by product and experience designers are not clearly (or even probably) to our personal benefit: a store looking to maximize sales is not necessarily concerned with whether we really need that energy bar or magazine. Part of the equation of designing a successful nudge, however, is ensuring that the cost of regret is not too high: if I spend 99 cents on a bottle of lotion that I use once and then lose under the seat of my car, I'm unlikely to feel enormous regret. At the same time, in cases where individual agency is paramount, societies often restrict opportunities to nudge. In the United States, for example, electioneering is banned within and near polling places on election days, and in France there is a forty-four-hour media blackout on election-related reporting before any legislative or presidential election.

In many industries, the security of a company and its products is an unequivocal priority, even if it demands heavily restricting employees' activities. By contrast, flexibility and speed are essential in news, and the work is inherently risky. As a result, promoting security without compromising newsgathering activities is essential.

It is precisely because of this that nudging can be an important tool for reinforcing secure behaviors in newsrooms: while the benefits of security accrue to both the individual and the organization, relying on suggestive—rather than prescriptive—security measures still provides journalists with sufficient agency in going about their work. Because almost any reporting task can be completed in a range of ways, nudging can help provide just-in-time guidance toward secure behaviors without placing undue restrictions on how journalists go about their work.

Priming and nudging are not necessarily surreptitious or nefarious, however. They can also be overt, such as signs on the office wall or reminders in an email signature—about how specific behaviors help improve security both individually and collectively. When researchers sought to improve hand hygiene in hospitals, for example, they added signs to existing soap and sanitizing-gel dispensers reminding users of the risks posed to patients by poor hand hygiene.[9] This nudge was both overt and direct; the key to its success was its salience (health care workers were motivated by patient concerns) and its just-in-time nature (the reminder happened at the exact place and time when users could act on it).

UNDERSTANDING AFFECT

Affect—essentially a person's mood or emotional state—has a huge influence on our ability to learn and acquire knowledge. Very broadly speaking, a positive affect supports openness, creativity, and better learning, while a negative affect tends to restrict perceived options and limit knowledge acquisition.

Given the significant risks associated with poor information security, it can be tempting to try to encourage secure practices using scare tactics. Yet research shows that these "fear appeals"—which frame a security behavior as the means to avoid negative consequences—are broadly ineffective when it comes to achieving adoption of better information security behaviors.[10] In general, successful behavior change depends on cultivating a positive sense of agency and self-efficacy with respect to the task at hand. Thus, while a fear appeal may briefly draw team members' attention to information security issues, demonstrating how a proposed security behavior or protocol enhances the team's reporting work is essential to ensuring that team members actually adopt the new tool or approach. Otherwise, they will eventually find ways to avoid or work around the secure behavior in favor of tasks that bring them positive rewards.

MAKE—AND HONOR—CONSTRUCTIVE COMMITMENTS

Before introducing any new information security process or protocol to your team, take it for a test drive: add MFA to all of your accounts, for example, or compartmentalize your social media accounts. Keep track of your experience, including things that went wrong or tricks for managing the new process efficiently. Not only will this put you in a more expert position when your team members ask questions about the new practice, but it will show that you personally are committed to it—an investment that your team members are likely to reciprocate.

Failure to do this, conversely, will undermine the entire process. As the organizational security expert Angela Sasse observes:

> The ultimate test for the leadership is that they are always very clearly acting in line with the rules and principles that are being put forward. There's nothing more corrosive [than] . . . being able to flaunt the rules as a badge of seniority. And if that happens, particularly in knowledge organizations where people are very smart, they immediately see, "Do as I say, not as I do." Then immediately that undermines the fact that [security] is an important value—and that's absolutely toxic.

Fortunately, by offering to be accountable for your own adoption of new behaviors—whether by holding regular check-ins, using buddy systems, or inviting other teams to learn about your process—you are likely to get a similar level of commitment from your team. As long as these commitments are made voluntarily, most people will follow through with them.

LEVERAGING EGOS, NOT JUST MANAGING THEM

At times, managing reporters' egos can feel like a full-time job—journalism is no stranger to highly demanding personalities. Of course, it takes a certain level of self-regard to take on big, complex stories—and the ego boost associated with a byline is an important mechanism for both transparency and accountability. By appealing to the part of a reporter's professional ego that views protecting their sources as honorable or altruistic, for example, that ego can be a powerful way to encourage more secure behaviors. Similarly, since being entrusted to handle the sensitive materials at the center of high-impact stories—like the Snowden revelations and the Panama Papers—increasingly requires strong information security skills, appealing to team members' desire to be part of high-profile reporting can further motivate them to embrace new information security skills.

MOST OF ALL, MAKE TIME

Even with an eager team and an impeccable plan, changing habits and routines takes time. As an editor, one of the most significant things you can do to help your team meet its information security goals is to proactively schedule time for team members to undertake the tasks involved—whether that's setting up a password manager, adding MFA to their accounts, or engaging in an antiphishing training. Without this, information security becomes an empty ambition. As Angela Sasse explains:

> If people have to do something or change the way they're working or they need to learn something new—that needs to be scheduled; it needs to be acknowledged that some productive time has to be given up to do this. And that is not a decision an individual will make without being given explicit permission. . . . This is one of those things where leaders really need to really organize, lead, and manage the time. [You] have to basically put a schedule in place.

By thoughtfully introducing and implementing a new information security practice, you can accomplish much more than even improving your team's security; the concern that you put into designing and managing the effort and the time required will not go unnoticed by the reporters you work with. Helping your team members achieve even a modest security goal will increase not just their safety and preparedness but their overall sense of self-efficacy, which will foster the confidence they need to take on new security and reporting challenges of all kinds.

Case Study: The Panama Papers

While the computer security literature is replete with examples of security shortcomings and failures, one of the most notable examples of a successful security culture at work in a modern organization actually comes from the world of journalism. The Pulitzer Prize–winning Panama Papers project, led by the International Consortium of Investigative Journalists (ICIJ), involved hundreds of journalists from around the globe conducting high-stakes investigations based on a huge trove of documents leaked from the Panamanian law firm Mossack Fonseca. Not only was the Panama Papers one of the most wide-ranging and complex investigations in journalistic history; it also demonstrated how much a strong culture of security can accomplish, even outside the trappings of a traditional organizational culture.

Throughout the course of their initial year-long collaboration, the Panama Papers journalists—hailing from dozens of different news organizations around the world—managed to preserve the security of their work, despite the fact that they were working across beats, languages, and time zones. The security challenge was significant: the massive document trove at the heart of the project's reporting had to be both remotely accessible and searchable; locked rooms and air-gapped computers were not an option. Yet even in the several years since the initial stories were published, neither the identity of the documents' source nor the documents themselves have been publicly revealed.

The adversaries who might have targeted ICIJ's work were powerful: global financial institutions and large corporations—and more than a dozen world leaders—were implicated in their work. The consortium of reporters actually working on the project, moreover, lacked many of the information security tools available to traditional organizations. They could not control access to the documents by placing them in a secure physical facility or by hosting them on a secured, dedicated network. For the most part, the Panama Papers journalists had to be able to access their source documents and share information using the same devices, technologies, and internet connections available to the rest of us.

Through interviews with journalists who worked on the project and with members of ICIJ's leadership and technology teams, my research partners and I learned that the key to getting more than three hundred journalists to maintain the project's strict security protocols was a clear sense of shared priorities and a pervasive culture of security. As an editorial leader at ICIJ told us: "In every editorial note I would write, I would remind [contributors] about some security measure; how it takes one of us to make a mistake for the whole thing to basically fall to hell, and you would lose an entire year of work, and we would be—a joke basically. Nobody would ever come to us again with any confidential information."

ICIJ leadership was a key messenger for security priorities from the start of the project, when only ICIJ members were involved. For that group, the incentives to not lose an entire year of work *and* to preserve the possibility of future leaks were highly motivating. Moreover, the invitation-only nature of ICIJ as an organization helped foster a strong set of institutional norms and commitments around information security.

As the project grew and ICIJ members onboarded others, those commitments extended to the new reporters on the project, whose access to the Panama Papers' documents was predicated on their adherence to the established security protocols. At this point, many teams relied on clear defaults to facilitate their work: "In this project we just routinely encrypted everything we wrote. . . . Because we were just used to doing it, and that helped us a lot as a team, that we understood that it's not such a big thing, it's not such a pain in the ass—but you're always on the safe side of it."

Of course, the Panama Papers project wouldn't have been possible without technology, and selecting the right technologies for the project— for everything from MFA to information sharing—was essential to its security success. As we will see in the next chapter, however, when a strong security culture and well-chosen technology solutions come together, journalists don't just adopt more secure practices—they actually embrace them.

CHAPTER 8

———

Security Strategies for Teams

When a handful of *Gawker* reporters were exchanging jokes on Camp-fire, the company's group-messaging platform, in October 2012, it's unlikely they ever imagined that their comments would become part of the legal record in a lawsuit filed against the company.[1] Yet that's exactly what happened when, in March 2016, reporters' chat transcripts were presented during testimony in an invasion-of-privacy case filed by Terry Bollea (a.k.a. Hulk Hogan) against Gawker Media. After a jury awarded Hogan $115 million in damages a few months later, Gawker Media filed for bankruptcy.

Introducing a new technology to a workflow will always have secondary effects; some of them end up being more perverse than others. In 1999, for example, researchers found that even as organizations adopted computers and internet technologies, they continued to consume as much or more paper than before; the introduction of email increased paper use by roughly 40 percent.[2] Shortly before Gawker Media filed for bankruptcy in 2016, the reporters and editors of another tech-focused media group—*Vice*'s Motherboard vertical—took a week-long sabbatical from Slack, their preferred group-messaging platform. The reason for their experiment wasn't security—though the team was highly conscious of the app's security limitations.[3] The problem, it turned out, was efficiency. Even though Motherboard folks thought of Slack as a way to make their team more efficient, their editor, Adrianne Jeffries, characterized the app as "just baseline distracting."[4] And while the app did support better communication with offsite colleagues, it also served as a managerial crutch, according to *Vice*'s editor-in-chief Derek Mead: "[Slack] makes limping along with a terrible hierarchy and structure possible, so you don't have to solve inherent problems to your staff model."[5]

This type of decreased efficiency was once among the common secondary effects of most "secure" technologies, as poor usability made the tools that offered security features like encryption both complicated and time consuming to use. As one news editor described it in a research interview:

> There's kind of like an encryption tax on the work of journalists these days. . . . We have to spend time doing things that we otherwise wouldn't do in order to communicate securely with sources and with each other and to responsibly use documents that we have. And it takes time. It means that we have less time to talk to people, to go and travel, etc. We still do all those things, but there's a chunk of our time that's spent on security, and not on other forms of reporting.[6]

Fortunately, major technology and service providers (including Slack) are now often integrating better security options into their products, so using a popular tool doesn't necessarily mean using an insecure one.[7]

Information security is about much more than choosing technologies with the right encryption options, however. It is about finding tools that serve your team on multiple levels: tools should offer the right security options, but they also need to be accessible and usable by team members and solve a problem *apart from* security. Perfectly secure systems are easy to come by, after all; they just don't help you do anything useful.

INVEST IN INTEGRATED SECURITY SOLUTIONS

As an editor, you want to do everything you can to ensure that the journalists on your team produce timely, accurate, interesting stories that hopefully connect with your audience and don't put your organization unduly at risk. By now, you know how to shape a headline for social media, fill gaps in stories, produce coverage and publishing schedules—and you also know when it's time to call the legal department. Some of these tasks have been part of the profession for fifty years, some for less than fifteen. At most news organizations, information security has been on the horizon for less than five. Yet as hostile attitudes toward and coordinated attacks on the press increase worldwide, understanding how to secure the work and safety of their journalists is quickly becoming an essential part of every editor's job.

Improving security doesn't always involve adopting new tools; sometimes it's about streamlining them. When Reuters's global managing editor Reg Chua made the choice to ban Telegram, for example, his reasoning was informed as much by compatibility as security. "It's not that Telegram is safe or it's not safe," says Chua. "It's that we can't have fifteen different communication systems around the organization. You need to have a few. So we've settled on a few."

Fortunately, there are a number of tools and services that can enhance the processes of newsgathering, editing, and publishing *as well as* your team's security. For example, setting up VOIP phone numbers for each of your team members can make it easier for them to manage communications whether they are at the office or in the field; at the same time, this protects their personal phone numbers, which can otherwise be used for harassment or identity theft.[8] Likewise, upgrading a file-sharing software license let them keep all of their reporting materials in one place, streamlining their access while also helping them better "compartmentalize" their accounts. In both cases, evaluating a new technology choice in terms of both workflow impact *and* security reveals that very often a well-chosen tool can improve both. Here I offer an overview of such dual-purpose technologies, followed by a discussion of how to select the specific product or vendor that will best meet your team's needs.

PASSWORD MANAGERS

As addressed at length in chapter 4, passwords remain a pervasive—and problematic—reality of digital technologies and services. Every single one of us has more passwords than we can possibly remember, much less associate with the correct account, device, or username. Password managers solve this problem by acting as a digital storage locker for all your other account credentials and safeguarding them with the two-part protection of a unique alphanumeric key and a master password.

If securely storing and autofilling login credentials were all that password managers did, it would be more than enough. But many password managers go well beyond this and, in the process, become an invaluable tool for managing teams. For example, many password managers allow you to collect sets of login credentials into distinct "vaults." When a new team member needs access to, for example, your shared social media accounts, you can simply invite them to that vault, and they can instantly use the logins and other information it contains. Even more importantly, if a team member leaves, removing their access is as simple as removing their access to the vault—or even from your password manager's account entirely. Password managers can also be used to store and share contact information, credit card details, and other information that you need to communicate securely—and selectively—to your team. Many password managers even have options to notify you if a service where you have an account has experienced a security breach. And because they can both generate and autofill strong, unique passwords across all your devices, they reduce the temptation toward password reuse that can make the security breaches that are beyond your control so damaging.

While the specific features they offer differ, the fundamental characteristic all password managers have in common is that they encrypt the vaults or databases containing your credentials; without this feature, you may as well be storing your credentials in a shared spreadsheet (it's been done!). Thanks to the two-part key system (alphanumeric code + master password), however, even password managers that store your data in the cloud are relatively safe from hackers, because the alphanumeric code acts as a kind of second factor—without it, even the company that makes the password manager can't access your accounts.

SELECTING A MULTIFACTOR SOLUTION

Although there's no great productivity argument for multifactor authentication (MFA), there is definitely value in selecting—and supporting—a preferred MFA approach for your team. Researching MFA options saves your team members from having to do this themselves and makes troubleshooting easier for everyone. And because MFA is such a powerful prophylactic against common security risks, knowing that your team is using strong MFA will offer you precious peace of mind the next time you hear about another service provider's security breach or a large-scale phishing campaign.

ENCRYPTED-COMMUNICATION SOLUTIONS

As the experiences of Gawker Media, Sony Pictures, and others have aptly demonstrated, what feels in the moment like harmless workplace banter—whether via chat, email, or text message—never reads quite the same way once it's part of news coverage or a courtroom deposition. And while many journalists prefer to conduct sensitive conversations face to face, digital services of one kind or another are often the only option for connecting with your team.[9]

Fortunately, an increasing number of mobile messaging apps support end-to-end (E2E) encryption for text, voice, and even video communications; some even have desktop counterparts. Your team will need to choose just one or two of these platforms, however, for the sake of both efficiency *and* security: you don't have the time to manage six different messaging apps, and end-to-end encryption—the security feature that helps protect your chats from ending up on someone else's front page—is only available when all users are on the same service or platform.

If you work at a larger organization, of course, you'll want to start your selection process by reviewing what may already be available, supported, and/or licensed by your company; some apps have enterprise-level security features that may not be available to you if you start your own account. Just as importantly, company-sanctioned software often comes with company-sponsored support, meaning that you and your team can rely on existing help desk solutions for troubleshooting if needed. As always, however, you need to consider your threat model when making your choice: the contents of an enterprise system may be better protected from outside attackers but still be accessible to your company's IT team. Making the best choice for your team on a technical level will depend on your particular risks and threats.

BROWSER-BASED VIDEO/VOICE CALLS AND CONFERENCING

While in-person interviews are usually preferable, sometimes a video call is the next-best way to speak with sources or team members face to face. Agreed-upon apps for voice and video connections are a great first step, but for team members or sources who need to use shared equipment, installing and configuring an app can be impractical—or even generate new security risks.

Fortunately, there are a number of voice and video solutions that offer robust security by using a standard web browser as the "shared app" for establishing an end-to-end encrypted connection. In addition to bypassing the need for administrative rights to the device being used, moreover, web-based video and voice solutions make it relatively easy to hide or destroy the traces of their use through the web browser's "incognito mode" and/or by logging out and deleting the web cookies and browsing history. This can be an especially important feature for sources from vulnerable and marginalized communities and for reporters who are operating in hostile environments. By avoiding the need to register an account altogether, both sources and reporters can connect securely, while minimizing the risk of their activities being exposed if someone inspects their device. For example, when *Vice*'s security expert Destiny Montague prepares reporters' equipment for a risky assignment, she ensures that nothing will "tie [the reporters] back to the company, down to account creation . . . [even] the software we license for them is on a separate licensing agreement where it's not licensed to *Vice*, maybe it's licensed to some random Gmail account."

What About PGP?

One of the best-known pieces of security software, the Pretty Good Privacy (PGP) protocol, was designed by Phil Zimmerman and made freely available online in 1991. PGP was the method by which Edward Snowden—with some help from Laura Poitras—eventually managed to share his famous document collection with Glenn Greenwald, and Snowden has gone on the record many times in defense of its security properties.[10]

PGP—and its popular open-source successor GPG (Gnu Privacy Guard)—was the first software to make strong, asymmetric encryption (see the bonus section in chapter 1) available to the general public. Though often characterized as "encrypted email," the core PGP/GPG software can be used to encrypt and decrypt *any* type of digital data, including text files, data files, audio, photos, videos, and more.

In other words, PGP/GPG remains a useful tool for protecting data that has to be transmitted using an otherwise insecure channel, such as email or a third-party file-sharing service. Since the "keys" needed for PGP/GPG are typically saved on a specific computer, it's best suited to situations where everyone who needs access has a machine that they have full control over. Though PGP/GPG software can be tricky at first (and famously so, in academic circles),[11] the strength, flexibility, and proven security of PGP/GPG make it a tool worth exploring.

If you do try out GPG, I highly recommend using this "manual" approach: install the relevant software for your operating system and then individually encrypt files as needed and share them with others as email attachments or via third-party file-sharing services. Since almost every high-profile security failure associated with PGP has actually been

CONTINUED

about the software written to integrate it into, say, email applications,[12] this lets you be confident that you're getting the best security—and also the simplest user experience.

USABILITY, UTILITY, AND TECHNOLOGY ADOPTION

Even after carefully determining how to get your team on board with new security measures and weighing the pros and cons of specific tools, closing the gap between your team trying a new system and actually integrating it into their workflow is a significant challenge. As the previous chapter's examples around hand hygiene demonstrate, even the combination of knowing what needs to be done, appreciating why it's important, and having the resources readily available to accomplish the task isn't always sufficient to ensure that a new tool or protocol becomes part of your team's regular routine. If learning a new technology is also part of the mix, the likelihood of real adoption diminishes even further.

Part of this stems from the fact that adding just one new tool or process is composed of many steps. For example, even adding MFA to a single social media account entails at least the following discrete actions:

1. Open social media app
2. Go to "settings"
3. Choose "Enable 2FA"
4. Select "App-based"
5. Install authentication app
6. Verify device
7. Login from primary computer; choose "remember device"
8. Login from guest computer to test logging in with additional factor
9. Repeat steps 7 and 8 as needed

While these steps are not complicated, they imply an entirely new approach to the login process that will have to be followed at least once for every primary device and, perhaps most importantly, negotiated after any logout/system refresh/forgotten password incident—in other words, during circumstances in which both time and patience are in shortest supply.

At some point, your team members must choose to continue using a new system despite the real, if temporary, inconvenience caused by the change in routine it requires. For your team to make it over this thresh-old, you will need to make sure that you have carefully balanced the combination demands and incentives of your new system such that it can satisfy this critical equation: usability + utility = technology adoption.

ASSESSING USABILITY

In recent decades, researchers across a number of technology-related fields have focused increasing attention on the *usability* of their systems, so that real people can complete their desired task using that system in an effi-cient and satisfying way.

Perhaps unsurprisingly, early security technologies failed miserably when it came to usability. In the last several years, however, a broader awareness of security issues—driven, in part, by journalistic coverage—has inspired more care and attention to be paid to whether technically secure systems are usable enough to actually improve security in the real world.

For example, one recent study compared the usability of five different methods of MFA in two specific scenarios: the setup phase and regular use. Though research participants rated authenticator-app-style MFA as the most usable on a day-to-day basis over a two-week period, those same users felt that authenticator apps were the most onerous MFA option to set up and configure.[13] This suggests that editors who want their teams to adopt app-based MFA will need to ensure there is a lot of support and positive reinforcement available during the setup phase, but then they can be con-fident that once reporters have the system up and running they will con-tinue to use it without much additional intervention.

Of course, in most cases you don't really need an academic study to assess how usable a tool will be for your team. With some experimenta-tion and a few thoughtful conversations with colleagues, you will proba-bly be able to identify which tools are likely to meet your needs best. At the same time, you'll want to explore how the system performs in at least a few different contexts in order to evaluate it for that other essential char-acteristic: *utility*.

EVALUATING UTILITY

Although good usability makes it easier to adopt a new system, there is no reason to bother doing so unless it makes reporting, editing, and/or pub-lishing more effective, efficient, or enjoyable. An attractive interface or more intuitive controls, on their own, offer little reason to depart from the status quo.

At the same time, utility can manifest in many different ways. For some reporters, utility may come in the form of increased access to sources, approvals for new assignments, a reduced risk of harassment—or even simply recognition from their peers. In other words, it doesn't matter if team members see security as contributing to the utility of a new tool or process: a study of password manager users, for example, found that increased convenience was their top reason for adoption, not security.[14] Likewise, it's not necessary that every team member feel a new tool is useful for the same reasons—it only matters that for each person, the sum of its utility and usability is sufficient that they will continue to use it.

This means that while *some* usability and *some* utility are required for a particular technology to see adoption, the balance between these vary considerably and doesn't need to be alike for any two people. An immediately and obviously useful tool with poor usability (think: every content management system you've ever used) will still see adoption because it's essential to the publishing process. On the other hand, a process that offers little or no immediate utility to an individual reporter (such as reporting suspected phishing attacks to the company's IT team) will need to be highly usable for team members to take it up.

In all of this, remember that as a team leader, you can positively influence the perceived usability *and* utility of the security measures you select by providing support and offering incentives where needed, which will help ensure your team's adoption of important new tools and strategies.

Case Study, Continued: The Panama Papers

The culture of security that ICIJ and its journalists built during the Panama Papers project consisted of much more than weekly exhortations to maintain secure practices. ICIJ provided trainings and on-demand assistance and even developed their own secure communications tools in order to support the intense level of secure, remote collaboration upon which the project depended. While this led ICIJ to develop some custom technologies, most of their security protocols relied on the kinds of tools that are available to all of us: multifactor authentication, PGP, and encrypted chat apps.

For example, in order to access Blacklight, the Panama Papers' document repository, ICIJ enforced a strict multifactor authentication login process that required journalists to provide their second factor code for *every single logon*. A similar process was required to access the "Global I-Hub," the secure forum for posting messages and sharing information among reporters on the project. During the course of the investigation, ICIJ even came to require that every single journalist create and use a PGP encryption key in order to receive weekly email updates and password reset information.

These security measures were met despite the poor usability of PGP, which has been critiqued by academics for decades.[15] Even more surprising, however, is that in a survey conducted at the end of the initial phase of the Panama Papers investigation, well over half (63 percent) of the journalists on the project rated complying with its security requirements on the "easy" side of a seven-point scale—even though nearly half of them had either never heard of or never used *either* multifactor authentication or PGP when they joined.

A large part of the credit for the success of ICIJ's security measures is due to the thoughtful way their protocols were both selected and introduced to the participating journalists. For example, after experimenting with both computer-based virtual machines and web browser extensions, ICIJ eventually chose the Google Authenticator app as their MFA solution. For participating journalists who lacked smartphones, ICIJ determined that buying them new devices was more efficient *and* more usable than any other option.

Similarly, at the start of the project, journalists were allowed to use either PGP or a Hushmail account for email communications. Once the project had launched, however, ICIJ grew uncomfortable with outsourcing the security of email communications and decided to mandate that each participating team member generate and be responsible for their own PGP encryption keys. Anticipating that PGP's poor usability would make the transition challenging, however, ICIJ provided several weeks' notice about the impending change and offered group trainings and on-demand help as needed in order to reduce the usability burden it presented. On the utility side, ICIJ also only introduced the PGP requirement after the project was mature enough to ensure that participating journalists knew how valuable access to ICIJ's platforms really was. So while the move to PGP necessarily presented usability challenges, the clear utility to project partners of both continued data access and weekly updates was sufficient to drive successful adoption. As one member of the ICIJ leadership put it: "We have people to teach them how to [set up their PGP key], we have a support team that can help them. . . . It went well because they were interested in keeping the access to the [platform]."

Despite its ambitious goals and challenging context, then, ICIJ's security work with the Panama Papers project was successful in part because they found the correct balance between the journalistic utility of their systems and the usability of the security mechanisms required to access them. As one member of the ICIJ technical team commented: "You have to keep a balance between functionality and security. Because if you start with all the good practices in security at once, journalists will react to that, and they will resist it, because it will be less functional."

In some cases, moreover, as reporting partners learned more about security, they also began to see security itself as a valid source of utility. In the words of one Panama Papers journalist: "I would like to receive more training at digital security tools. It was really useful. I learned for myself how to encrypt my computer and find out how vulnerable my information was, due to my lack of expertise using digital security tools."

With the correct combination of utility, usability, and a culture of security, adopting more secure processes and technologies is more than possible, and it can even grow an appreciation for security among team members who don't recognize it at first. As another Panama Papers journalist put it: "[Security is] always a pain and even slowed us down. But this work is important, and anything to keep it secure is fine."

CHAPTER 9

Working with Freelancers and Community Contributors

Freelancers and stringers are integral parts of the journalism ecosystem. While many large newsrooms may work with them only occasionally,[1] for many magazines and smaller organizations, freelancers are a crucial resource: they often have the skills, experience, and flexibility to do stories on topics or in locations that would otherwise be out of reach, and they can help bring a wider range of perspectives to your publication. Just because freelancers operate independently, however, doesn't mean that they should be left to handle their information security alone: commissioning editors need to participate in addressing freelancers' unique security challenges. In the case of community contributors, moreover, leadership from editors around information and personal security is even more crucial, as many community contributors are poorly prepared for the reality of what it means to have their content be published, especially in the digital space.

GENERAL CONSIDERATIONS AND "DUTY OF CARE"

Whether or not you regularly engage freelancers or work with user-generated content, understanding how freelancers are managed in your organization and developing protocols for working with them are valuable ways of preparing for dealing with a wide variety of security concerns. As much as possible, freelancers should be treated with the same duty of care as their on-staff counterparts, but since external reporters and contributors won't have access to many of your organization's technical systems and resources, you will need to consider how you can make collaborating outside those systems both efficient and secure. Some of this may simply involve clarifying the communication platforms your team prefers, but it may extend to additional behaviors you expect the freelancer to adopt on their own. As *Vice*'s Destiny Montague describes it: "In order to do this job—if you're going to even do freelance—you should take these basic measures: Have two-factor on your accounts. Understand passwords. Make sure that you're good with your privacy and security settings on your online accounts."

Developing these materials will not only streamline the process of onboarding your next set of freelancers or community contributors, it also will help protect both your organization's infrastructure and reputation. As Adrianne Jeffries points out, "The freelancer is also kind of a threat. . . . That person could introduce vulnerabilities into your newsroom." While this risk is serious, working with a freelancer or contributor who suffers an information security failure is perhaps an even greater one. If a freelancer is compromised, the security expert Matt Mitchell says, "Reputational damage will be caused, and it's long lasting. . . . Because people don't understand [security] that well, they want to believe you that it's not [the organization's] fault—but they can't."

While each freelance reporting assignment will require its own risk assessment, curating your own baseline information security expectations for freelancers—as well as strategies for securely handling the commissioning, editing, and compensation for external contributors—will still pay dividends, especially in those time-sensitive situations when an external contributor is your best or only option to get the story.

COMMISSIONING

Editorially speaking, spec work is in some ways the safest bet when it comes to freelance material. The already-written or -recorded piece—even if it demands substantial editing or re-reporting—is the best (in some ways, only) guarantee that the reporter can and will actually deliver what they have pitched. At the same time, spec work presents significant security (and, arguably, ethical) challenges: professional and financial pressures may encourage freelancers to do risky reporting in order to get an editor's attention. Whether it's reporting from a conflict area or delving into the online activities of an extremist group, you may find that potential contributors are taking on bigger risks with less preparation than your organization's safety and security standards would allow for staff. These considerations led Miriam Elder, during her time as world editor at *BuzzFeed*, to stop accepting spec work altogether. "You don't want to encourage people to go somewhere dangerous where nobody else wants to go," she says. "If you take their work, it just kind of encourages them to do ever more risky things."

News organizations can help reduce this temptation by being explicit in their public instructions to freelancers about any caveats—including security concerns—that can affect the likelihood of spec material being accepted for publication.

Ensuring that the pitch evaluation process incorporates security considerations is also crucial; freelancers are often not in a position to accurately weigh the risks associated with a given story themselves. As Matt Mitchell puts it: "An individual cannot properly do a risk assessment. They're too close to it . . . the 'Go/no go' is always on 'Go.' "

At organizations like Reuters and the *Wall Street Journal*, this problem is addressed by requiring editors to flag any pitches that involve a greater-than-usual security risk, whether they come from staffers or freelancers. The pitches are then run through a formal risk assessment process so that the relevant editorial and/or operational managers can make the call about whether to move ahead with the story. Even these formalized systems, however, require editors to make an initial judgment about the potential risks involved in a pitch and engage the review process appropriately. At smaller organizations, it will also fall to the editor to assess the risks and set the boundaries for the stories you commission.

EVALUATING RISK IN PROJECT PITCHES

If you are part of a large organization, you can probably expect to receive training on how to evaluate pitches for risk and escalate them for further review. If you are at a smaller organization, however, this process can be more challenging: you won't have the resources to conduct a full risk assessment for every pitch that crosses your threshold—which means you'll need to develop some heuristics based on your own knowledge of the beat. While many traditional security assessments emphasize geography, they may not account for risks like especially aggressive online communities. This is where drawing on your expertise as an editor is crucial: few people will know the risks for your reporters' beats—whether they are staffers or freelancers—better than you will. Leverage your prior threat modeling/ risk assessment work on similar stories to help hone your sense of what is worth worrying about when evaluating new pitches.

Once you have a sense of the risks a story involves, you'll need to be clear about what precautions you expect freelancers to take. If the material is reported from a physically dangerous area, ask prospective contributors to provide evidence of adequate insurance or for details about their digital and physical safety protocols. Similar requests can be made for those working in the digital sphere: if someone pitches a story about an online community that has a reputation for abuse, confirm that freelancers have taken steps to protect themselves against identity theft and doxxing. For example, have they locked down their credit and recently reviewed their online footprint for information about their location or personal relationships?

At the same time, it's important to take a collaborative approach with experienced freelancers (or staffers) in particular: good risk assessments are based on more than externalities. For example, *BuzzFeed*'s head of high risk Eliot Stempf begins every risk assessment with identity characteristics that may influence the reporter's risk profile. "If we don't do that," Stempf says, "I worry that the 'default' risk assessment is for a straight, white man." Though you have to rely on your best judgment, true security starts with making sure that reporters can be open about their vulnerabilities *and* their strengths.

ESTIMATING ADDITIONAL COSTS

Many times, assuring freelancers the same level of security as staffers means taking on some up-front costs. For example, you may need to provide training or resources to freelancers who do not already have sufficient security around their digital accounts, or you may need to lend or procure them equipment to use while traveling. If your organization cannot provide these resources, some amount of cost sharing should be included in the reporting agreement or stipulated as already completed and/or in hand. For particularly dangerous assignments, organizations should be prepared to advance payment for certain expenses, such as adequate insurance. According to the freelancer advocacy group ACOS (A Culture of Safety) Alliance, which counts Agence France-Presse (AFP), Bloomberg, CNN, NBC, WAN-IFRA, and dozens of others among its membership, "editors and news organizations should be aware of, and factor in, the additional costs of training, insurance and safety equipment . . . news organizations should endeavor to provide agreed upon expenses in advance, or as soon as possible on completion of work, and pay for work done in as timely a manner as possible."[2]

Though many of these principles are framed by ACOS in terms of "traditional" conflict reporting, Reg Chua of Reuters, an ACOS signatory, points out that the safety risks faced by reporters are not at all confined to physical conflict areas, as online threats and vicarious trauma constitute widespread risks to both staffers and freelancers. "Managers are now much more trained to look at things like harassment," says Chua. "They're much more sensitive now to the notion that, you know, it isn't bombs that gets you. It's looking at videos."

If assessing risks or providing resources to freelancers is beyond your organization's capacity, there are many groups that can help ensure your freelancers' safety. In addition to the ACOS Alliance, the Frontline Freelance Register, Rory Peck Trust, and others offer helpful risk assessment tools as well as formal and informal mechanisms for sharing information and evaluating risk. While much of this information may be related to physical safety issues, information security concerns are increasingly being integrated into their broader safety resources, and are a great way to stay up to date.

WORKING WITH LOCAL REPORTERS

One of the great benefits of digital communication systems is that news organizations can more easily connect with local talent when commissioning coverage. The very speed and simplicity of that information exchange, however, can also reduce our ability to appreciate the risks those local journalists may face. While local journalists' work is often "lower signature" than that of journalists who arrive on assignment—and their background knowledge and sourcing networks may be more robust—local reporters often face risks that persist long after the assignment is complete. Local journalists can face reprisals against themselves and/or their families, including legal sanctions or prosecutions, physical and financial penalties, and online attacks. Thus while local reporters may face fewer risks during the reporting process, you may need to think more carefully about how their work is handled when it's time to publish.

What's Your Sign?

In military contexts, the "signature" of a person or operation is roughly associated with its detectability; low-signature weapons or activities are harder to identify or distinguish from their surroundings. Taking a low-signature approach to reporting—whether by working with local journalists or fixers, adopting regional dress or customs, or traveling with more discreet equipment—can often be a valuable way to minimize risk. This is one of the reasons why accurately understanding how individual reporters' personal characteristics interact with a given environment is an essential aspect of any risk assessment: the better they are able to blend in, the lower their risks may be. Of course, sometimes high-signature reporting activities are unavoidable; there is no way to camouflage high-quality video broadcast equipment, for example, such that it will escape detection, and sometimes the best reporter for an assignment will very much *not* blend in with the crowd. As with all other aspects of security, the key is simply to ensure that your risk assessment and security protocols are designed to reflect and address the signature level of the work, whether that's high or low.

EDITING

Because freelancers typically won't have access to the same editing infrastructure as staffers, such as organizational accounts for email and other services, securing the editing process may require some adjustments from your usual routine. From agreeing on a communications strategy when freelancers are in the field to determining how they will share reporting materials and participate in the editing process, planning ahead will be crucial for both efficiency and security.

SHARING MATERIALS

The ubiquity and interoperability of email make it a convenient fallback for transmitting digital information, especially when working with reporters outside your organization. While hardly ideal from a security perspective, there are creative ways you can minimize email's security risks as long as you have a clear sense of what needs to be protected.

For example, imagine a local reporter is filing a text-heavy story about LGBTQ youth in sub-Saharan Africa—a region where homosexuality is often viewed as illegal. In this case, you and the reporter may agree that while digital drafts and email exchanges will contain only first names or pseudonyms, necessary identifying information will be captured on paper and shared only through an E2E-encrypted app with disappearing messages. This approach allows you and the freelancer to reap the convenience benefits of email while still helping protect the subjects of the story by keeping their real identities off of insecure digital channels.

What Does Anonymity Really Mean?

In computer security, the formal definition of an "anonymous" communication is one in which a message cannot be traced back to the person who created it. Technically, this is usually achieved through a combination of location and/or timing obfuscation, as well as minimizing or eliminating other metadata.

In the world of journalism, of course, an anonymous source is usually one that is anonymous in name only: their legal identity is often known by at least the reporter and editor, if not by others within the organization. At companies like the Associated Press, for example, using an anonymous source in a published article is not even an option unless your editor knows the source's identity.[3]

In a global digital publishing environment, however, anonymous sourcing is more complex than ever: given the abundance of information available online, effectively maintaining a source's anonymity requires much more than simply withholding their name from publication. In 2019, for example, the *New York Times* came under fire for publishing contextual details about the identity of the whistleblower whose complaint helped precipitate the Trump impeachment inquiry.[4] Many readers worried that the details about the individual's work history and expertise would uniquely identify them to the administration and subject them to retaliation.

This illustrates the additional care that must be taken when granting—or even considering granting—a source anonymity: even if your security measures are sufficient to protect their identity, can your story still include enough detail to be meaningful without effectively identifying them? If not, then you need reevaluate either your offer or your story.

Of course, there are many secure options for sharing text files; most text-only documents are small enough to be easily sent through secure mobile messaging apps. Sharing high-quality image, audio, and video files, however, presents a substantial challenge: not only are such files too large to send by email, but they are also inherently identifiable, and if they fall into the wrong hands they can quickly put their subjects at risk.

Unless your contributor plans to obscure her subjects' identities in all of the material she captures, handling such materials safely requires thoughtful preparation. If the materials will be shared digitally, using end-to-end encryption methods like PGP/GPG with third-party sharing services (as described in chapter 8) is ideal. If legal or technical limitations make encrypted solutions untenable, mailing physical storage media with a secured shipping service may actually be more efficient, as they allow you to obtain high-resolution files while also letting the journalist destroy the originals for safety if needed.

Finally, if securely receiving digital materials comes up enough, you may want to investigate whether your organization can build and host an HTTPS web form—or even a SecureDrop—that contributors can use to upload material directly to your servers; even a short-lived Google or Microsoft form (whose link you share securely via an E2E app) could work in a pinch, especially if your organization has an enterprise account.

Most importantly, be sure to document and agree upon your information-sharing approach with your contributor in advance. This will be invaluable if another editor needs to get involved in the project. Keeping a clear record of what has and hasn't worked—and why—is also useful when planning future projects *and* can help when pitching internally for additional security resources—such as software, licenses, or training support.

ASSESSING THE PUBLICATION CONTEXT

In the days of print-only journalism, publications—and their on-the-record sources—often enjoyed a sort of geographic indemnity: there was limited risk in publishing information about someone who was half a world away from your circulation area.

In the digital publishing environment, however, even content from relatively small, regional outlets may be picked up, recirculated, and amplified online in communities and contexts far different from those for whom it was intended. Activists whose work wins accolades abroad may be targeted for retaliation where they live, and even legally protected activities may still put subjects at risk. During the 2020 Black Lives Matter protests, for example, news editors grappled with the implications of publishing identifiable images of protesters, given the surveillance that targeted the movement.[5]

This is not to suggest that editors or publications should shy away from investigations in order to avoid ruffling feathers; in fact, organizations seeking to "be vigilant and courageous about holding those with power accountable," per the Society of Professional Journalists' code of ethics, should carefully "weigh the consequences of publishing or broadcasting personal information" about private individuals. Editors should also consider the reporters' safety along with that of sources. As the ACOS principles highlight, freelance journalists should always be "given fair recognition in bylines and credits for the work they do . . . unless the news organization and the freelancer agree that crediting the journalist can compromise the safety of the freelancer and/or the freelancer's family."[6]

As always, a thorough risk assessment at the start of a project will minimize the need for additional prepublication safety reviews; still, almost all content will benefit from an editing pass that takes safety considerations into account, whether those are likely to manifest online or offline. Far from compromising coverage, this process will ensure that all parties involved in the story—including reporters, editors, and sources—are well prepared, both logistically and psychologically, to handle potential responses to the finished piece.

MANAGING THE PAYMENT PROCESS

Even when the story is done and the piece has been published, freelancers often face one final security hurdle in working with news organizations: getting paid.

In the United States, for example, freelancers are usually required to provide personally identifiable information (PII—often a Social Security number) in order to get paid, and they should be provided with a secure means of transmitting this, even if that means calling it in to the office. As usual, this security measure protects the news organization as much as the individual: if a data breach were to expose freelancers' PII, your organization could face stiff financial penalties. Keeping this data off unencrypted systems is in everyone's best interest.

WORKING WITH COMMUNITY CONTRIBUTORS AND
USER-GENERATED CONTENT

More and more newsrooms today find themselves in the position of working, at least occasionally, with "user-generated content" (UGC) and/or community contributors, whether as part of breaking news coverage or as part of a more general integration of social media into the reporting process. While the actual content may be anything from photographs or videos to tips or story leads, working with UGC presents a set of security issues both distinct from and often more complex than working with journalistic freelancers.

As Fergus Bell highlights in the *Verification Handbook for Investigative Reporters*, many individuals who are accidental witnesses to newsworthy events may not realize the significance of their materials or a well-developed understanding of the implications of sharing it with news organizations.[7] This means it falls to editors to make a good-faith effort to help such contributors understand the potential consequences of republication (including the safety and security implications) before securing permission and running contributors' content.

Perhaps the most tragic example of this is the experience of Ramsey Orta, who released the video of Eric Garner's death to the *New York Daily News* a day after Garner was killed by police in 2014.[8] Orta subsequently experienced years of harassment by law enforcement and has expressed ambivalence about his choice to capture and share the video, telling *Time* in 2015 that if he had it to do over again, he would release the video anonymously.[9]

News organizations are naturally reluctant to publish "anonymous" materials, but the experiences of Orta and others are powerful illustrations of the risks that face community contributors. Editors should remind such sources of the consequences of being credited: using their legal name could expose them to pressure from law enforcement, as it did with Orta, while attributing content to a social media handle could make that account a conduit for a barrage of abuse.

While time is often short when considering UGC for breaking news events, duty of care should extend to anyone who supplies content to a news publication, whether they are a professional or "citizen" journalist. As a result, it is up to editors to prepare sources as much as possible for the risks they may face if they choose to be credited for their work, in addition to offering them as much protection as possible should they wish to share it anonymously.

As with more formal commissioning processes, editors should be clear about setting safety parameters for acceptable UGC in order to minimize the risks taken by community members at the scene of an event. Editors should also provide a method to share the content that preserves the contributor's privacy (and therefore security). Especially when it comes to dealing with controversial or emotional issues, the process for using their work should made be clear to contributors in advance. For example, if they will need to agree to be interviewed or confirm their identity, this should be made clear *before* sources submit content, so that they can manage their expectations accordingly.

Case Study: Scenes from *Charlie Hebdo*

Jordi Mir was writing emails in his apartment on January 7, 2015, when he heard gunshots outside his apartment. Moving to the window, he mistook the armed men running down the street for SWAT police, perhaps responding to a bank robbery. Reflexively, Mir captured the scene on his cell phone and later uploaded it to Facebook.

"I had to speak to someone," Mir told the Associated Press.[10]

Although Mir took down the video less than an hour after posting it, it had already gone viral—and been picked up by news organizations, many of which did not edit out the horrific, close-range killing of a police officer, Ahmed Merabet, at the end of the forty-two-second clip. Although Mir declined offers to buy the footage, many news outlets chose to run the unedited video regardless. While the footage may have galvanized the public, however, it devastated Merabet's family. Mir, meanwhile, described his regret for the "stupid reflex" that led him to post the video on social media.

While many newsrooms today would be unlikely to run content without going through a robust verification process—including obtaining permission from the original poster—the experience of Mir and other community contributors around the *Charlie Hebdo* attack illustrate the many questions that arise when working with UGC.

Claire Wardle, a UGC expert and founder of the verification-focused *First Draft News*, for example, says Mir's experience also raises the question of whether someone can withdraw consent for sharing content. "Can somebody change their mind?" asks Wardle. "Once they've made it public and then hidden it, what does that stand for? What does that mean?"

Wardle has also observed firsthand the concerns that many would-be contributors feel about having their content attributed to them at all. While news principles generally require crediting content to help ensure transparency and accountability, this can sometimes put contributors at risk. "If you speak to these people, you recognize how unprepared they were," says Wardle. "I used to be really militant about, 'We should be using people's names when we're crediting,' and then it became really clear that eyewitnesses were like, 'I don't want my name associated with this stuff,' either because they were getting abused . . . or because they're like 'I don't want my name to be associated with this terrible event that I was once caught up in.'" If your publication doesn't already have clear guidelines about how to handle the wishes and safety concerns of UGC contributors, now is a great time to start that conversation.

CHAPTER 10

Essentials for Small Newsrooms

In the early 2000s, the average American newspaper had a staff of almost fifty; by 2013, that number had dropped to under twenty-five. Unsurprisingly, as newsrooms have continued to shed employees, workloads have risen: in 2016, reporters said they were expected to produce more stories and digital features than just two years prior. In 2020, more than ten thousand newsroom jobs were lost in the first half of the year alone.[1]

In these circumstances, it's tempting to think that information security is a less pressing concern than, say, keeping your website online, especially for smaller news organizations. Yet this is a false dichotomy: strong information security is precisely what *can* keep your website online—whether in the face of an incursion by local law enforcement, for example, or after a ransomware attack. Whether your enterprise is a handful of local reporters or a single investigative partner a thousand miles away, strong information security will always be the most effective—and least expensive—way to protect your business and promote your journalism, by ensuring that it remains both credible and accessible.

Fortunately, securing the work of a small newsroom is not an expensive undertaking; in fact, it may even *reduce* some of your upfront and ongoing costs. What it requires more than anything is thoughtful planning and policy development, which can help you avoid the kind of information security events that might otherwise jeopardize your organization's ability to report, publish—or even survive.

YOUR ORGANIZATION NEEDS *YOU*

If you lead a small newsroom, you already know how much work it takes to keep a newsroom running. Whether it's managing reporters, reader feedback, or revenue adjustments, the noneditorial aspects of the business are just as crucial to producing quality journalism as is choosing coverage areas or assignments. Good business decisions are what make good journalism possible.

What may be less obvious is the extent to which good information security can protect the integrity of both your business and your journalism. A hard-hitting series on local environmental damage won't come to much if your website is down and your social media accounts have been hacked. Fortunately, developing strong information security practices and policies doesn't require you to go to hacker camp or learn to decipher lines of code. "You can start at a really untechnical point," says organizational security expert Angela Sasse, "which is the definition of security: 'Things that should happen, do. And things that shouldn't happen, don't.' [As an organizational leader] it's your responsibility, at a high level, to start writing, 'This is what we want to happen, this is what we don't want to happen.'"

Of course, journalism is an inherently risky business—which is exactly why having newsroom leaders be the ones to set information security policies is so essential: If your newsroom is going to take risks, they should be journalistically worthwhile; conversely, if you're going to invest in a project editorially, you should make sure you're taking the security steps necessary to protect your investment.

No matter the size of your newsroom, developing and implementing new information security practices is a multistage process. First, you need to take stock of the existing practices and preferences within your organization, with a particular focus on digital tools and communication platforms. Second, you need to identify your security needs and priorities and be willing to explore how technology can support meeting them. Finally, you need to develop and share a set of internal policies that clearly articulates how any new process or technical systems should operate and—most importantly—how the security they provide supports the editorial mission of the organization as a whole. While this may seem daunting at first, many of the most crucial security practices you adopt may require relatively little ongoing attention; those that do need to be revisited regularly will reward you with peace of mind and the confidence that in the unlikely event of a serious incident, your entire organization knows how to respond.

So, You're About to Start a Podcast

Most of this chapter assumes that you are part of an existing organization that's looking to revamp or improve its information security practices. While integrating information security into your work processes from the ground up is easier and more cost effective than doing so after the fact, you may not yet know what your organization's processes—or prospects—actually are. If you're just starting out, is it too early to think about information security?

Whether or not you have a five-year plan in place for your organization, you are almost certainly already using digital systems to do journalism. Begin by evaluating those under the "what should and shouldn't happen" rubric to identify any adjustments you need to make (is account access being shared insecurely?) and set aside time regularly to reevaluate your practices as they change and grow.

Perhaps most importantly, recognize that spending time on information security is an important way of investing in the journalistic work that you're doing and ensuring that its impact isn't subsumed by attacks from some army of trolls. Use this chapter as a jumping-off point for developing the habits and strategies that will keep your work safe for the long term, even if right now it's just you and a SoundCloud account. "Larger news organizations have learned these [information security] lessons time and time again," says Harlo Holmes, the Freedom of the Press Foundation's newsroom security director. "But nobody really says, from a security perspective, 'So you're about to start a podcast—here's what you do.'"

Well, if you're about to start a podcast, or a blog, or a newsletter, this chapter is for you.

INVENTORY YOUR ASSETS

When Runa Sandvik first began her security work at the *New York Times*, there was no internal directory of all the company's social media accounts. "I spent a year finding all of them," Sandvik said. She chose to focus on social media accounts because it was clear to her that the platforms were central to both disseminating and reporting the news, and she couldn't help secure accounts she didn't know about. While smaller newsrooms may be able to inventory their systems in a few days or weeks, the central lesson remains: you can't secure something if you don't know what and where it is. By methodically documenting all the accounts and systems your organization relies on, you can begin to develop a comprehensive view of what you have—and from there, how to secure it.

In most cases, getting a handle on your newsroom's information resources will involve looking at four categories of systems and applications, organized broadly by their function in the reporting/publishing process. While not mutually exclusive, these groupings are intended to help you develop a thorough overview of what you're using. Alternatively, you may prefer to start with a story- or project-based "device diary," like the one described for individual reporters in chapter 4. Either way, the primary goal of this phase is to enumerate the systems your organization relies upon for reporting, publishing, and distributing your journalism.

PHYSICAL INFRASTRUCTURE

The physical infrastructure of your digital systems comprises the devices that your organization uses to do its work: computers, smartphones and other mobile devices, Wi-Fi routers, cameras, audio recorders, and so on. While it may take some time, gathering this type of inventory data should be relatively straightforward; simply build a list of all the devices your reporters and other staff are using, making a note of the following:

- Device type
- Manufacturer and model
- Operating system
- Software and apps, including version
- Internet accessibility (can the device connect to the internet directly?)
- Ownership (business/personal)

If possible, you'll want to learn these details about *all* the equipment your staff relies on, including personal devices (such as home routers) that newsroom members use for work. While some employees may find this intrusive, remind them that having this information will help the organization better support and secure their work wherever they are, as well as anticipate and troubleshoot problems for them if something goes wrong.

DATA STORAGE

Where are reporting materials being stored? For each of the storage locations identified, determine the following:

- Storage type
- Internet accessibility (can the device connect to the internet directly?)
- Ownership (business/personal)

RESEARCH AND COMMUNICATIONS SERVICES

What company is running your organizational email services? What apps are reporters using to communicate with one another and with sources? What subscriptions does your organization maintain (or do your reporters use) to complete their work? For each service account, note:

- Account type (free/paid)
- Location of privacy policy/terms of service
- Ownership (business/personal)

PRODUCTION AND PUBLISHING

For this section, you want to examine the accounts and services that are integral to your organization's online presence and publishing, including production software, web hosting, and social media accounts. For each of these, you'll want to note the following:

SOFTWARE
- License type: local/standalone license vs. cloud-based subscription
- Version number/expiration date
- Purchase price/annual cost
- Ownership (business/personal)

SOCIAL MEDIA ACCOUNTS
- Platform
- Handles/usernames
- Ownership (business/personal)

WEB PUBLISHING
- Domain name
- Domain registrar

- Expiration/renewal date
- Administrator account details

As you compile this information—likely through your own investigation and via one or two brief homework assignments for your employees—you'll also want to note key security features:

1. Are digital devices encrypted?
2. Do user accounts have unique, strong passwords?
3. Do user accounts have non-SMS MFA configured?
4. Are shared account credentials managed through a password manager?
5. Are account users/administrators all current employees who should have access?

In order to distribute the effort required for this task, ask each member of your organization to fill out a structured worksheet like the example provided here; this can also help you more clearly visualize and organize the data you collect.

Is There a Risk in a Master List?

In precisely the same way that you don't want to be using a shared spreadsheet to keep track of usernames and passwords, you also don't want a list of every device and system in your organization sitting unencrypted on someone's computer or cloud storage account. Whether you choose a third-party service or basic PGP, make sure the information about your organization's systems are end-to-end encrypted and backed up in the cloud; while you will need to update your inventory periodically, you'll want to protect the effort you've put into it without simultaneously creating a new security risk.

BUILD OUT YOUR ROADMAP

Once you've completed the inventory of your information systems, you'll have what you need to take on the "basics," as outlined in chapter 4: Just by ensuring unique and strong passwords, MFA, device encryption, and appropriate administrator access, you'll have improved your organization's baseline security level significantly—most likely without paying for anything other than (maybe) a password manager license.

Table 10.1 Sample device/service audit template

	Device/ service type	Model	Operating system	Software type + version	Internet enabled?	Ownership	Username/ email	Paid/ free	Purchase/ annual cost	Expiration/ renewal date	Encrypted?	Strong password?	MFA enabled?	Password managed?	Access vetted?
Infrastructure	Laptop	Samsung Chromebook Plus	Chrome-OS	n/a	Yes	Personal	***	Free	$0	n/a	Yes	Yes	Yes	No	Yes, August
Data storage	external hard drive	Western Digital	n/a	n/a	No	Personal	n/a	n/a	$60	n/a	Yes	Yes	No	No	Yes
Communication services	1password	n/a	n/a	Android app, Chrome extension	Yes	Personal	***	Paid	$60	September	Yes	Yes	No	n/a	Yes, March
Production/ publishing	Adobe Creative Cloud	n/a	n/a	Android apps	Yes	Professional	***	Paid	$960	February	Yes	Yes	Yes	Yes	Yes, July
Production/ publishing	Twitter	n/a	n/a	Android app	Yes	Personal	***	Free	n/a	n/a	Yes (hosting device)	Yes	Yes	Yes	Yes
Distribution	CMS	n/a	Word-Press	5.5	Yes	Professional	***	Paid	$300	December	Yes (https)	Yes	Yes	Yes	Yes, January

Whether it's because a license expires or a computer breaks down, however, at some point you'll need to bring new technology on board; by making security one of the criteria, you can get the best of both productivity *and* security. By contrast, holding onto old systems—whether to avoid the cost of purchasing or the effort of learning to use new ones—will almost inevitably backfire on both fronts. As Angela Sasse explains:

> When you're making the decisions about the technology you're buying, or when to upgrade or move to another technology platform—that is the point at which you need to think about your security. . . . The more you can actually integrate the security into the tools that people use all the time, the less friction and the less productivity loss you get.
>
> If you're unwilling to invest, and you're trying to push out and save money by not investing in new tools—that very often means you've got older infrastructure, which means you need more patching, you need more security. . . . By investing in a new technology platform sooner, you could get rid of that whole problem.

At the same time, your strategy for choosing new technologies will need to balance functionality, security, and cost—both upfront and in the longer term. Ensuring that you get the best value for your organization means looking not just at the capabilities of a particular system but at what type of *human* capital is required to realize those capabilities and keep the system secure. As Ankur Ahluwalia, vice president of technology solutions at the Associated Press, points out, "We're not going to just bring in the tool or the technology without considering the entire life cycle." He continues: "I could bring [a new technology] in, but do I need six people to run this thing?"

The near-constant maintenance required by digital systems is one of the reasons why so many organizations have moved to third-party providers: the cost of maintaining and securing services as essential as email is simply too complicated and expensive to do correctly in-house.

PHYSICAL INFRASTRUCTURE STRATEGIES: DEVICES AND CONNECTIONS

Even if you rely almost universally on third-party services, your employees will still need physical computing devices and internet connections. In general, you have one of two choices: design and purchase the machines that staffers will use for work, including computers, mobile phones, recording equipment, etc. Or, you can take a bring-your-own-device (BYOD) approach, in which employees use their own equipment and may be reimbursed for some or all of the cost.

COMPUTERS

While it may be tempting to have employees work on their personal machines to avoid the upfront cost of providing or replacing them, both the efficiency and security cost of ensuring that everyone in your organization can access all the tools, software, and services needed to report, collaborate, and publish effectively can be extremely difficult if no two machines are quite the same.

Fortunately, there is a better option today than going to a retail store and purchasing a new computer: whether you decide on Macs or PCs, it's now possible to purchase machines that come preconfigured straight from the manufacturer, ensuring that everyone has access to the same tools from day one—without requiring that someone (or everyone) in your organization become an expert at installing and configuring software. And while it may be unorthodox, organizations that rely mostly on web-based and/or open-source tools for reporting, editing, and publishing should give Chromebooks serious consideration: top-of-the-line hardware options can access most Android mobile apps (which can provide basic image, video, and sound editing); offer stronger, more seamless security; *and* cost hundreds less than their "traditional" computer counterparts.

MOBILE PHONES

Despite the security risks presented by the commingling of personal and professional accounts, BYOD strategies for mobile phones at most organizations is "a genie that's out of the bottle," says the Freedom of the Press Foundation's Harlo Holmes. The expense of the mobile phone hardware combined with the inconvenience of carrying multiple devices means that only the very largest news organizations commonly purchase "work" phones for their employees.

Even if you aren't purchasing phones for employees, you'll want to make sure that they have a work number that is separate from their personal one: widely sharing a SIM-based mobile phone number can pose significant security risks, as they are increasingly used for identity theft, locating people physically, and hijacking online accounts.[2] Fortunately, there are plenty of voice-over-internet-protocol (VOIP) and other service providers that will forward calls to employees' existing devices, many of them for free.

Whatever hardware solutions you choose, keep in mind that you'll ideally keep one or two sets of "travel" devices on hand to lend to employees when the risks of an assignment could lead to the device being either damaged or removed from the reporter's control (for example, when covering a protest or crossing a border).

INTERNET CONNECTIONS

Many office spaces now come prewired for internet and Wi-Fi, limiting your control over these devices. Still, try to work with your landlord to understand how your Wi-Fi routers are configured and secured. Whether part of a commercially rented space or as part of employees' home office setups, however, all Wi-Fi networks used for work should have nonobvious network names and be secured by a strong password. Moreover, the credentials for connecting to the router itself (in order to set up or change the networks it offers) should be changed from any manufacturer defaults and kept confidential. Finally, creating a guest network for visitors can help protect your essential systems from malware and other intrusions.

As discussed in chapter 5, access to a high-quality virtual private network (VPN) can be an essential resource for staffers when the security of the available Wi-Fi network (whether at a hotel, airport, or conference) is in question. Even "at home," however, using a VPN makes it more difficult for your current internet service provider to observe your web-browsing behavior—an increasingly important protection option for news organizations since sales of that information became legal in 2017.[3] Fortunately, the cost for either a commercial or self-hosted VPN for a small newsroom is only about US$100 per year.[4]

DATA STORAGE STRATEGIES

Reporters' practices vary widely when it comes to storing data; some have elaborate digital file organization methods, and others have drawers of notebooks organized by year.[5]

At the organizational level, correctly balancing local and cloud storage solutions requires weighing both the legal and financial aspects of these systems: if protections against physical intrusion are strong where you operate (as they are in the United States), offline storage of data in physical backup drives offers significant protections. By contrast, if a cloud service provider is *unlikely* to respond to law enforcement requests for data but on-site raids *are* likely, well-secured cloud data storage options can offer significant security benefits over physical drives. From a financial perspective, you will also need to balance the convenience and accessibility of cloud services with the monetary cost of maintaining accounts with greater storage limits.

Whatever combination of cloud and offline storage you choose, keep in mind that no data should exist only on an internet-enabled device such as a computer or mobile phone: backups—whether on local hard drives or to cloud-based services—are your best protection against ransomware attacks, which have hit an increasing number of news organizations of all sizes.[6]

Backups vs. Archives: What's the Difference?

What does it mean to have a "backup" of your website versus "archives" of your materials? In general, a backup of any content is a copy that is structured, formatted, and stored in such a way that its contents can be easily recovered and redisplayed in its intended format. A website backup, then, will be a copy of all the files and databases that comprise the articles, media, and appearance details of your website—saved in exactly the same form in which they exist online. Having a backup means that if something should happen to the live version of your site, you can simply replace the corrupted site files with the backup copy, and your site can be up and running again, usually within minutes.

What constitutes a true digital archive, meanwhile, is something about which even experts disagree.[7] It is, however, much more than the backup files from your website or the text of a published story kept on a hard drive or cloud service. Ideally, archives are "future proof"—meaning that they are human-readable even in the absence of special technologies; this is one reason why paper is still a favored archiving material. What it means to be future proof, especially when it comes to interactive, data-driven, or other dynamic applications, is less clear. While there are efforts to develop sophisticated emulators that can preserve the original experience of these pieces,[8] most attempts to archive unique digital experiences will be an approximation; for interactives, for example, simple videos of the work can capture some of the experience before the piece succumbs to digital decay.

CONTINUED

Ensuring you have adequate data backup systems is an essential business continuity question, while archives are more about the historical record: if catastrophe should strike your organization tomorrow, where will the records of your digital-only content live? Consider reaching out to local public or university libraries as well as NGOs to explore your options, but bear in mind that giving them your website's backup files probably won't cut it.

RESEARCH AND COMMUNICATIONS SERVICE STRATEGIES

EMAIL

Following the Snowden revelations in 2013, many news organizations were wary of outsourcing their email and other communication systems to third-party service providers, given concerns about subpoenas and other government monitoring. Today, however, there is no question that the best email security *and* functionality are offered by third parties, especially as phishing, spam, and denial-of-service (DoS) attacks have become increasingly common.[9] Still, the era of third-party email doesn't mean that legal considerations are now irrelevant. For example, Harlo Holmes points out, smaller organizations in particular may want to look for email providers that have "a stated mission of protecting groups who could find themselves on the wrong side of a court bench for some reason."

COLLABORATION SERVICES

Cost and convenience often dictate that communication and document collaboration services are handled by the same provider, which can be incredibly useful in streamlining your reporting, editing, and publishing processes. As long as the accounts and devices used to access them are properly secured, most large-scale service providers offer similar levels of security, though some may have special savings available for nonprofit and/or journalistic institutions.

Beyond account configuration, however, the security of these systems depends largely on how they are *used*, rather than on their technical specifications. Adding encryption to your workflows—whether through a zero-knowledge cloud storage service or local PGP/GPG—can certainly help, but the best security will come from training your staff to use these services in a secure way.

ADDITIONAL RESEARCH AND COMMUNICATION SERVICES

Newsrooms rely on a wide range of additional services to do their work—whether to facilitate FOIA/L requests, access court records, or create visualizations. For the most part, specific services should be selected for their functionality and cost and secured via proper management of account access and credentials. In the rare instance where equivalent services exist, close attention should be paid to the privacy policy and terms of service to understand how the data you generate or upload is handled.

PRODUCTION AND PUBLISHING STRATEGIES

SOFTWARE

Few of us enjoy being forced to buy or learn new software, but upgrading old software to subscription-based services has both productivity *and* security advantages: it makes the software easier to access from anywhere and reduces the temptation to defer essential security updates in an effort to use an older version of a program just a *little* bit longer. Coupling subscription-based programs with a password manager can also give you much greater visibility into who has access to what and how it's being used. Beyond greater information security and access control, this approach also allows you to understand which applications are truly central to your operations and which ones can be retired or replaced.

SOCIAL MEDIA ACCOUNTS AND MAILING LISTS

For many newsrooms, there is little to love about social media platforms whose algorithms and policies can shift without notice, sometimes to devastating effect.[10] Like collaboration tools, however, security around social media and mailing lists is mostly about securing account access and ensuring that employees understand the risks of posting information that can be used to locate them physically or track their own movements or those of their colleagues or loved ones.

WEBSITE AND CONTENT MANAGEMENT SYSTEM (CMS)

Redesigning your website and adopting a new CMS are invariably expensive and complex undertakings. Though the look and feel of your new site is editorially important, so is protecting your investment against hackers and trolls seeking to damage your brand or take your site offline. This means not only understanding how your website is secured from the outset but also how security updates will be identified and applied in the long term.

In many cases, the most stable and secure solution will be to use an integrated platform that hosts a common publishing system like WordPress. These services allow you to create a new website relatively painlessly, and they often come with significant technical support and security features—such as login tracking, SSL, and automatic backup services—that can help protect your readers, content, and brand long after the novelty of the redesign has worn off.

Of course, working with an independent designer to build a custom website will give you more flexibility in terms of features and feel, but adequately protecting your investment will require pricing in the costs of updating and maintaining the site—both for functionality and security. Even customizing an existing content management system will need this type of evaluation: if your design will require custom plugins and features, for example, how long will your site designer commit to maintaining those elements, especially if security vulnerabilities emerge? If they cannot provide maintenance, make sure you understand how disabling an outdated plugin or other feature will affect your site's overall functionality. Now is also a good time to ensure that your new site will be HTTPS and to explore options for services that can protect your site from threats like DoS attacks.

Reviewing security plans may not be as exciting as choosing a new layout or color scheme, but it's at least as essential to the future of your organization. Without good security, an attack may cost you more than your reputation; your entire web presence could be at risk. As Harlo Holmes explains:

> [If you] hire somebody to set things up and then and pay them a couple of thousand dollars and never hear from that person again . . . before you know it you've lost your website entirely because that person was hacked or that person doesn't care or that person drops the ball. . . . In the case of abuse like a DoS attack on your site . . . you're going to go

down, and then you're going to get kicked off your platform, and then you're not going to know where to go.

In Security, Size *Really* Doesn't Matter

Running a small newsroom on a similarly small budget doesn't mean you need to compromise on information security. While you might not be able to hire a security consultant, the tools you have at your disposal are actually no different from those relied upon by the largest organizations. As the *New York Times'* Jason Reich puts it: "Ultimately, the tools that we use at the *New York Times* are pretty much the same tools that anyone can use—and they're cheap. [Whether it's] a VPN, or Signal, or the actual computer that you use . . . the Chromebook that the *New York Times* is going to use is that same Chromebook that you're going to use."

Moreover, Reich says, it's the *Times'* large size that demands more expensive equipment and expertise; such measures aren't necessary for smaller newsrooms: "The reason [we] have to spend all this money on more advanced things is because we have to do it for 1,600 journalists. . . . [If] you have a newsroom of ten people, don't even think about it. Just train them [and] . . . create policies that are that adaptable, that define principles and guidelines and objectives."

SETTING POLICIES AND PRIORITIES

Journalists who work creatively and independently are any news organization's greatest asset, so it's understandable that organizations are often reluctant to impose too many restrictions on how they go about their reporting.[11] At the same time, journalists do look to their organizations for cues on ethics and security issues,[12] meaning that even the smallest news organization can benefit from developing a key set of information security policies and practices.

THE BASICS AND BEYOND

Small news organizations can start by implementing the basics outlined in chapter 4, taking care to clearly tie each new technology or policy choice to the organization's articulated values. This will help ensure that plans to shift toward account compartmentalization or the use of password managers, for example, are embraced as quickly as possible by your colleagues.

At the same time, you can also start developing a broader set of programs and policies that build on those basics in an organic way. For example, articulating a clear policy on social media use is a natural outgrowth of asking employees to compartmentalize their feeds, and documenting the process of adopting a password manager or enabling MFA will give you the resources you need to make that transition a part of new employees' onboarding process. By treating these as organizational processes and not as individual requirements, you can smooth the transition to new ways of doing things while building out your institutional knowledge at the same time.

ENCOURAGE SECURITY SPILLOVER

Clearly, there is a limit to what any employer can—or should—mandate about employees' activities. At the same time, newsrooms have always recognized that journalists' activities outside the newsroom can have an impact on both their work and the organization.

So while you may not feel comfortable requiring your staff to, for example, enable MFA on all their personal accounts, that doesn't mean you cannot encourage such steps—which should, after all, be easier for them to take once they have grown accustomed to having those settings on their professional accounts. By encouraging them to adopt these practices across all aspects of their online lives, you will not only be protecting your workplace and its product but employees' personal security and well-being as well.

PREPARING FOR THE WORST TO PERFORM AT YOUR BEST

A lawsuit. A subpoena. A ransomware attack. Not all of these are things that you can prevent, but being prepared can mean the difference between a bad week and an existential crisis for your organization. Even if you don't have a dollar to spare for new technology, taking the time to learn about the legal and technical resources available to your organization is a worthwhile investment. For small news organizations in particular, says Harlo Holmes,

> One thing that is worth thinking about is your relationship to law enforcement. . . . Not only knowing your rights and knowing which

organizations might provide pro bono help should something happen but also thinking about how to protect—physically protect data in the event of somebody literally kicking down your door. . . . What to do in the case of a subpoena. What your data retention policy is—or rather that see-saw balance between responsible data retention in order to tell a story in perpetuity versus the fact that the material that you're holding onto might need to be as ephemeral as possible.

Consider a Data Retention Policy

For small news organizations in particular, a data retention policy—more intuitively described as a data *deletion* policy—can be a valuable tool for resisting subpoenas for information while minimizing legal expenses. While common in the legal and financial fields, data retention policies are only just gaining ground for news organizations that need to protect their reported information but cannot afford to wage a lengthy court battle to do so.

Put simply, a data retention policy is a written document that outlines how long particular types of materials are retained by the organization—and how and when they are deleted. By outlining and adhering to such a policy in consultation with a lawyer, your organization may be able to resist subpoenas for your reporting materials, on the basis that you no longer have them. Since deleting or removing such materials *after* receiving such a subpoena would be an obstruction of justice, an explicit data retention policy may allow you to publish controversial material with greater confidence. It also helps you avoid the time and effort required to comply with the subpoena and prevents unrelated materials from being swept up in the subpoena process.

Setting aside time to regularly review information security issues with employees reinforces security as a priority for the organization and provides a natural setting for identifying new issues, introducing new policies or programs, and checking in on the progress toward existing goals. You can use these meetings to complete specific tasks, like conducting online checkups and social media scrubbing,[13] and you can also use them as an opportunity to conduct hypothetical tabletop exercises, where you sketch out how your organization can or should respond to different scenarios.

In so doing, security concerns are normalized, and you condition your staff to be able to respond effectively if something goes wrong. As the *Markup*'s Adrianne Jeffries puts it: "You have to have . . . a plan for when something happens, and train the staff and say . . . 'Here's the fire drill/emergency exit plan.' So that you don't panic if something happens."

CHAPTER 11

Managing Risk for a Midsized Newsroom

On a Tuesday late in the summer of 2017, the *ProPublica* reporter Julia Angwin decided to take a midmorning yoga break. A few days earlier, Angwin and her colleagues Lauren Kirchner, Jeff Larson, and Madeline Varner had published a story about how extremist websites were able to monetize their views by using the services of companies like PayPal and Stripe.[1] When Angwin took her phone off "do not disturb" an hour later, she saw a text message from Kirchner: "I am under some kind of email attack."[2]

Kirchner was not alone. Angwin's and Larson's email boxes were also being flooded with messages, mostly by sign-up confirmation emails for sites and services they had never visited. Varner, who had no published email address on *ProPublica*'s website, was spared. As thousands of emails streamed into the team's inboxes over the next few hours, however, the publication's email system was overwhelmed entirely; no one in the newsroom could send or receive email. Eventually, the technology team suspended the original reporters' email addresses altogether in order to keep the rest of the office's email online.[3] Angwin, Kirchner, and Larson operated from temporary, unpublished email addresses for days.

While *ProPublica* had always taken security seriously, the software developer Mike Tigas and *ProPublica*'s deputy managing editor Scott Klein really "started getting buy in and resources behind security" after the email attack. There was "a tipping point when that happened," adds Klein, "and I think it opened a lot of eyes."

Klein and Tigas are emblematic of the type of security resources that many midsized news organizations are likely to have: people with security-relevant skills and expertise, even though "security" doesn't appear in their job title. "We are not big enough to have [information security] be a person's full-time job," says Klein. At the same time, *ProPublica* is large enough to have full-time IT and legal staff, as well as dozens of reporters, editors, and administrators. According to Jason Reich, vice president of corporate security at the *New York Times*, this is precisely the point at which news organizations need to move from a "relationship" model of information security to a more professionalized approach. In the former, "You don't have roles, you have people," says Reich. Though "the relationship model works, and it works really well," Reich continues, "the thing that props it up is going away. People don't work in companies for years and years anymore . . . so, broadly speaking, there's a need to professionalize a whole series of functions that, up until this point, were essentially buoyed up by a wealth of institutional and cultural knowledge."

Today, *ProPublica*'s "security" team—a group that include Tigas, members of the IT staff, and an attorney, among others—has formalized its efforts via monthly meetings and is empowered to conduct or commission security audits, makes recommendations on capital or service purchases, and shares responsibility for implementing security-based changes throughout the company. As a result, Klein and Tigas feel the company is well positioned to address "the things that we consider highest stakes" while also making sure that the organization as a whole is "very aware of where our information is and where we're talking about our stories."

While smaller organizations can use all-staff events to share and work through new security tools and policies, midsized news organizations— despite greater in-house expertise—can often have more difficulty reaching the entire company with their needs and decisions. As a result, effectively managing information security risk in a midsized news organization rests on leveraging expertise from across the organization, ensuring cross-departmental knowledge sharing and problem solving, and creating robust documentation and communication strategies so that staff both understand existing policies and seek out help if they need it. This way, midsized news organizations can ensure that their information security systems scale to meet the increasing complexity of the challenges they may face.

BUILDING AND TASKING YOUR SECURITY TEAM

Building an effective information security team means drawing on expertise from across the organization and earmarking both time and financial resources for information security needs. While the specific composition of your organization's team may vary, ensuring that it effectively represents the IT, legal, financial, and editorial concerns of the organization is essential to developing an holistic view of—and approach to—information security concerns.

ENGAGING IT

Given that so much of information security involves the use of information technologies, it is easy to assume that the primary responsibility for information security should reside with your organization's IT personnel. The reason that this is not the case, however, is perhaps best summed up by *ProPublica*'s Scott Klein: "IT culture and newsroom culture from time immemorial has been, 'Leave me the fuck alone,'" he says. "It's a bit 'IT is my enemy.'"

Klein's sense of the skepticism—if not outright mistrust—between newsrooms and IT departments is reinforced by my own research across dozens of news organizations, which found that an "us vs. them" mentality often dominates the relationship between newsroom and IT staff. This means that even though the IT department has essential expertise about digital communication systems, they are often poorly positioned to understand what journalists need from those systems in the newsroom or in the field. "Working with journalists in the field is something that I had to learn about," says Ankur Ahluwalia, vice president of technology solutions at the Associated Press. "The challenges they have are very different than protecting websites or systems and services."

Ahluwalia's comment also illustrates a larger point about contemporary information security: as much as the technology changes of recent decades have transformed the news industry, they have transformed IT information security as well. Traditionally, digital information security essentially sought to replicate physical boundaries in digital space, an approach that has been upended by the advent of mobile computing and bring-your-own-device newsrooms. Today, protecting against common hardware attacks has become more straightforward, and the frontlines of security have moved closer to users: "The architecture has shifted from the days of 'Here's my perimeter. Here's the big firewall, and everything inside is mine and you live outside of it,'" says Ahluwalia. "That doesn't work anymore. Most [data breaches] aren't somebody breaking into the system or by exploiting software . . . it's primarily somebody clicking on a link and giving up their credentials, right? That human element is hard to protect against."

As a result, your IT personnel can only be one part of a successful information security team; their expertise must be complemented by the perspectives of other key risk and resource groups within the company.

REPRESENTING THE NEWSROOM

Naturally, the most crucial stakeholders on any news organization's security team will be the editorial team: without the work of the company's journalists, there is no business or work to protect. That said, active newsroom participation in defining and designing information security objectives is also essential because the newsroom often represents the organization's largest constituency; to be effective at all, information security practices must work effectively for editorial staff.

Choosing your security team's newsroom representative(s) will depend on a number of factors. A journalist with a coverage area related to information security or a well-respected developer who has an independent interest in the subject can be invaluable for interpreting newsroom requirements into technical terms and vice versa. At the same time, editorial team members must have credibility as journalists within the newsroom, so that their support for security decisions will carry weight with the reporters and editors who will have to adopt them.

BUDGETING FOR RISK

Because information security is, at the organizational level, a form of business continuity, it's essential to have personnel with budgetary insight—if not authority—on your security team. Without this, it's virtually impossible to make meaningful decisions, even for the "simpler" problems that can be solved technologically. For example, one information security specialist at a midsized news organization described the futility of preparing for a denial-of-service (DoS) attack without sufficient budgetary and editorial input: "I can't make those decisions, about whether or not we take down content because it costs us $100,000 [to keep it online] over a two-day period, right? That's something that [the editorial leaders] will have to decide. So, I want their input on that kind of stuff. I mean, if we're coming out with a new application tomorrow, we could spend a lot of money securing it. We can make it a hardened target. But do we need to do that?"

Similarly, understanding the financial management style of the organization is crucial to choosing even among solutions with similar explicit costs. For example, many technology-based security "solutions" imply a significant level of overhead for personnel, and deciding where the cost-benefit lies between two potential solutions requires significant budget insight. As the AP's Ankur Ahluwalia illustrates: "For example, if you put in a great endpoint security system that tracks and flags all these things and all these alerts pop out, who is the person responsible for looking at all these desktop notifications coming in now and saying, 'That one's valid' and 'That one's not'?"

INVOLVING THE LAW

Most media organizations are familiar enough with libel risks that they have a well-formulated mechanism for managing them. As discussed in chapter 3, however, the legal vulnerabilities inherent in digital communication and storage tools make legal considerations an essential component of information security decisions as well.

As such, well-designed legal instruments—from data retention policies to customized vendor contracts—can go a long way toward mitigating more insidious information security risks, especially those associated with third-party services. At *ProPublica*, for example, legal concerns had long kept information systems in-house, which limited the technical sophistication and security of their systems. Through detailed conversations with third-party technology vendors, however, the newsroom has been able to take advantage of the more robust functionality *and* security offered by outside services providers. As *ProPublica*'s Scott Klein put it:

> There was a time when we started where the real directive to IT was to put everything in the building . . . [but] after consulting with a security consultant and after spending a lot of time thinking about it we kind of realized that if the threat is state hackers or even just very sophisticated private operatives, we would much rather have them go against security teams from Microsoft or security teams at Google—all of whom get a free lunch and have no concerns in life except keeping our email secure. . . . Whatever the legal tradeoffs are [around third-party services] can be mitigated. We have understandings with the people who host [technology solutions] for us, and the tradeoff has been worth it because we are now far, far more secure.

TASKING YOUR SECURITY TEAM

Successfully engaging the diverse range of stakeholders described in the previous section requires clear agenda setting. Whether you're bringing the team together in response to a security incident or to proactively address threats that have faced similar organizations, a clearly articulated set of security values (as discussed in chapter 9) and a focus on one or two top priorities will be crucial to the team's early success. Over time, the group will need less and less specific direction, as their ongoing efforts and regular check-ins with the organization's leadership matures the understanding of the information security needs and values of the company.

SITTING DOWN AT THE TABLETOP

If you don't already have a motivating incident or concern to task them with, there is great value in designing a handful of "tabletop" exercises for your security team. A strategy drawn from emergency preparedness, these scenario-based discussions give your information security group the opportunity to think through the implications of an incident and collectively identify ways to prevent or mitigate it. As such, the exercise becomes a method for identifying concrete information security steps for each part of the organization to take, and it requires little more than scheduling a monthly meeting in terms of upfront investment. As Mike Christie, general manager of global logistics and security at Reuters, says: "It could be as simple as 'A Twitter feed is hacked.' What are the implications? What are the defenses that we have? What's missing? [The team members] just have a conversation . . . [and] they walk out of every one of these meetings with three or four things that they have to do."

Depending on the size and focus of your newsroom, this type of effort might feel familiar: it's not dissimilar to the type of integrated editorial planning that may already take place around national elections or large-scale sporting events like the Olympics or World Cup. Instead of editorial planning, however, these tabletop exercises should be conducted on a regular schedule as a form of information security planning. While acculturating your security team—and the rest of your organization—to this approach may take time, it can help you actually achieve the "ounce of prevention" needed to avoid large-scale problems. As the AP's Ankur Ahluwalia put it: "[We do] a lot of dry runs around incident response . . . that's something we continually refine. That was another culture change for the organization: we have traditionally not done it all the time. . . . So that's been something we had to sort of train on. Like, 'Why we're doing it now? It's August, everybody's on vacation!' And it's like, 'No, this is a good time to do it.'"

DOCUMENT AND AUDIT

For tabletop exercises to be more than thought experiments, of course, your security team must be empowered to pursue the objectives they generate—and be held accountable for following through on them. To this end, you, as an organizational leader, will need to determine the mechanism and schedule for these efforts. If you are not able to participate directly in information security team meetings, then you can assign a deputy to take minutes, facilitate discussions, clarify timelines, and flag items for your review and approval. Whatever method you choose, timeliness is key: if your team's work gets hung up waiting for executive approval, then everyone will quickly become frustrated and abandon the effort.

Just as important as reviewing new initiatives promptly, however, is auditing their outcomes: understanding where time and resources are being spent and how effective they are in helping your organization meet its information security goals. Whether it's a new policy rollout or a new tool for reporting, outlining at the start of each initiative how the process and its effectiveness will be documented and evaluated is essential, since preventative measures will often have no other tangible outcomes. Equally important is recognizing that not all interventions will be successful, so finding ways to pivot if something isn't working is also essential. "You, as a leader in the organization . . . should have a meaningful way of doing the testing [of information security initiatives], with a view to improving," says organizational security expert Angela Sasse. "You're doing the testing in order to figure out: How well is it working? And if it's not working, what needs to change?"

EVALUATING INCIDENT RESPONSE

Just as initiatives begun by your security team need to be tracked and measured, so should your organization's work in response to particular reporting problems or issues. Flagging and escalating reporting-related information security concerns as they arise is key, but postmortems should also be an integral part of the incident response process, so that the information security team's work stays responsive to the newsgathering needs of the organization. As Reuters's Reg Chua says:

> I want to know, "How many times are we dealing with leaked documents that have value? How have we dealt with them? How many times are we dealing with source protection for somebody who's being serious?" . . . So that at some point I just pull together a report and say, "You know last year we intervened fifty times on source protection and ten times on document protection. This is what worked and this is what didn't work. And this is how we need to think about it."

Depending on the project, postmortems might include informal exit interviews with the journalists and editors on the story or a review of server log data following a malware incident. Whatever the specifics, your best learning opportunity comes from reflecting on the process and its outcomes; an honest evaluation of what worked and what didn't is precisely how you can generate ideas about how to improve results the next time. Documenting the risk assessment/recommendation and response design/postmortem process is also a crucial aspect of successfully "professionalizing" your organization's information security work. Only an understanding of what has happened before will let you make evidence-based decisions about future efforts and ensure that crucial institutional knowledge is preserved even as roles and personnel shift and evolve over time. And of course, preparing for one type of risk often helps protect you better against another: when one of NPR's largest member stations, KQED, was hit with a major ransomware attack in the summer of 2017, they learned a number of things the hard way. Allowing employees to install their own software—a byproduct of their already understaffed IT department—made their heavily networked systems vulnerable. Following the attack, they spent *months* recovering and were forced to do a system-wide security reckoning. While they largely managed to stay on the air, it was often at the expense of employees' health and well-being. KQED's director of IT John Reilly did find a silver lining, however: "In some ways I view this as a dress rehearsal. Because we're in an earthquake zone."[4]

Mandates for Risk Management

In the news business, adaptability is an essential characteristic for both reporting and information security practices, in order to ensure that neither undermines the other. As the *New York Times'* Jason Reich puts it, the goal for information security teams in news organizations is "to create a structure that is flexible enough to adapt to the really, really rapid and demanding needs of newsgathering."

At the same time, not all information security measures should be optional. Some of the most challenging questions your information security team will be about when it's appropriate to require certain information security measures, especially of the newsroom. Choose poorly, and journalists, in particular, will adopt workarounds. Fail to enforce essential measures, however, and you may expose your organization to brand-damaging security incidents, or worse.

As a newsroom leader, choosing whether and when to enforce security measures will necessarily be more art than science. At the same time, there are a few key questions you can use to help determine when something should be made mandatory.

Is This Approach Standard-Issue Outside the Newsroom?

As security breaches and privacy concerns become more commonplace across every industry, so are security and privacy technologies. Where MFA and encrypted messaging services were once niche security applications, today they are commonplace in consumer products and services. As a result, there's no reason to avoid mandating these baseline practices for reporting tools and processes. As *ProPublica's* Scott Klein says: "I think [journalists are] sort of hearing from the wider culture that two-factor is important. They all have two-factor on their Facebook and two-factor on their Gmail, and so when they came into work and they were getting two-factor here . . . I think the level of acceptance was much higher."

Is This Required for a Particular Journalist's Daily Work, or Do They Have Access to More Tools Than They Need?

Part of what made KQED's 2017 ransomware attack so devastating was that they had grouped together access to so many of their systems, meaning that malware could easily run rampant across all of them. So while breaking down knowledge silos is excellent, infrastructure silos can be valuable. Making sure that employees have access to all—and *only*—the systems that they need to do their daily work, and double-checking otherwise, is another essential security measure. As the AP's Ankur Ahluwalia says:

> It should not be the case once you're in you're "in" and you have access to everything. You really need to have access to only the things you need to get your job done. If it takes an extra hop of authentication to make sure you really should have access—that is an inherent architectural shift in the way we've gone about rolling out systems. So not every journalist has access to all editorial tools.

This is not to say that you shouldn't strive for your organization to be ahead of the curve when it comes to security; if your institutional culture can support stronger security practices, then it will only be to your advantage. Just keep in mind that you will need to be honest about auditing journalists' practices in the wild: a newsroom full of workarounds has the greatest security risks of all.

ENGAGING THE ORGANIZATION

Ultimately, your information security team's work can only be as robust as the engagement they have from the broader organization. Without sufficient visibility and flexibility, even the best-conceived plans and processes are unlikely to gain the traction required to be truly effective. While staffing your security team with representatives from key departments is essential, it is only the first step; you must think strategically about how you will raise awareness of—and help generate buy-in for—the work of your information security team. While your organization's specific culture will influence the precise methods you use to achieve this, remember that you're ultimately offering employees additional support and resources and that this will almost certainly be welcome news. As Destiny Montague of *Vice* reflects, "People are always pleasantly surprised when they find out that there are people who can help."

CONSOLIDATE POINTS OF CONTACT

When New York City adopted its 311 service system in 2003, the three-digit shortcode replaced an eleven-page directory of opaquely named departments that governed everything from overgrown trees to faulty sewer lines.[5] By the time the system logged its 100 millionth call less than a decade later, it had done more than streamline a byzantine and frustrating reporting process for individuals—it had become a valuable source of intelligence about the problems that New Yorkers encountered most often and felt most strongly about.[6]

Even if you don't have a fully staffed help desk, you can support similar efficiencies and insights around security by configuring all-purpose communication channels within your organization. Whether that's a Slack channel, an email alias, a VOIP number, or all three, having convenient, catch-all contact points for employees to ask questions and get feedback about information security will help them engage with your team *and* provide a natural data source for identifying your organization's top security issues.

Supporting Reporting in Multiple Ways

While dedicated communication channels for security can help your employees get security assistance when they need it, there can be editorial benefits to these systems as well. For example, the Tech + News Working Group at *BuzzFeed* evolved from an informal collaboration to become a valuable technical resource that has allowed the newsroom to expand its investigative efforts.[7] Through the group's Slack channel, reporters can request everything from basic help with terminology to support for actual tool building. By leveraging these synergies, *BuzzFeed* has been able to investigate algorithmic and "artificial intelligence" systems much more efficiently than would have otherwise been possible—making the group not just a way to streamline dealing with technology problems in the newsroom but also a way to leverage the organization's existing talent to support new forms of newsgathering.

DON'T BE AFRAID TO ADVERTISE

While most news organizations have invested heavily in audience engagement, few have put even a fraction of that effort into developing effective
internal communications. As a result, simply raising awareness about the
existence and activities of your information security team can go a long
way toward securing and protecting the work of your organization more
broadly.

IN THE OFFICE

While it may seem almost campy, using shared physical spaces to disseminate information is an extremely effective and low-overhead way to raise
awareness about available resources and best practices. Physical signs posted
in common workspaces and eating areas can offer small reminders about
available resources and best practices; locations where staffers are likely to
have some idle time—for example, near the office microwave, a shared coat
closet, or in an elevator waiting area—are ideal. For an even more captive
audience, take a cue from Google, which has chronicled best practices for
programming via their "Code on the Commode" inserts: printed reminders housed in plastic document holders and mounted inside bathroom
stalls. Some larger news organizations even print security contact information on the back of employee ID cards, ensuring that no matter the situation, security expertise is always close at hand.

OFFSITE AND ON THE ROAD

Whether they're in the field, temporarily working from home, or are a one-
person bureau in another region, offsite employees won't see the witty
posters you've put up by the coffee machine, but there are still plenty of
ways to give them little reminders about security resources and practices.
Email signatures, Slack reminders, and even the occasional online "brown
bag" can all be ways to encourage offsite employees to connect with security resources.

For the most part, however, the needs of offsite employees will not differ greatly from those in a dedicated office space. As *ProPublica*'s Scott
Klein puts it: "One of the great effects of moving infrastructure to the cloud
is that if you do it right, your remote users are no different than your head-
quarter users." The one exception to this may be their method of getting

online: reporters or employees on the road or in shared office spaces will need more support in securing their internet connections. These situations offer a perfect opportunity for your information security team to proactively contact offsite employees and give them an overview of how they can support their work.

DEVELOP ON-DEMAND MATERIALS

Although ensuring that employees know how to access human security expertise is essential, well-structured on-demand resources, like written guides and how-to videos, can help staffers help themselves. By letting the development of these materials grow out of existing information security work, institutional knowledge is captured and made accessible beyond that team. As the AP's Ankur Ahluwalia explains: "[We] put our heads together and realized we should at least come up with some kind of toolkit—just some known vetted tools that are out there. . . . We can explain what they do and how they could help a journalist address some of their most common use cases, whether it's file sharing or email. . . . And then, if you have something very very special you can come talk to us."

While creating quality resources will take time, of course, reviewing data about security interventions and questions sent to your dedicated communication channels will help clarify what should take priority when building out these materials. If employees have reported multiple doxxing incidents, for example, that's a good indicator that it's time to develop some on-demand instructional materials, as the *New York Times* did in early 2020.[8] Similarly, basic screencasts demonstrating how to lock down a social media profile or enable MFA on specific platforms are a fast and effective way to scale the work of your information security team to better meet the needs of the entire organization.

Even without the full-time information security specialists available to large newsrooms, midsized newsrooms can create simple organizational structures that leverage their existing expertise to effectively reduce risk. As noted in chapter 10, robust information security is not a matter of expensive technology solutions or even expertise—it is largely about creating well-managed communication and review processes that leverage your organization's existing resources. Through interdisciplinary collaboration, planning, and documentation, your information security team can both reduce your organization's security risks and augment its reporting efforts and sophistication in the process.

Case Study: Creating a "Golden Image" for Field Reporting

Despite its danger-courting reputation, Vice Media's ongoing reporting from places like North Korea and Iran has helped spur collaboration across the organization to create solutions that can withstand some of the most challenging information security contexts. Through close cooperation among multiple infrastructure and reporting teams, including information technology, physical security, digital security, and news production, the organization was able to build what Destiny Montague describes as a "golden image"—a fully loaded travel laptop that has all the reporting tools a team might need, but without any of the digital or physical traces that could jeopardize their safety. "If there is even a sticker on the bottom of the laptop that says *Vice*, or a barcode if they open up a laptop," says Montague, "it could be a problem in certain places."

To address this, the team ensures that software licenses and even destination URLs for uploading content can't be linked back to *Vice*, while also making sure that the machine has all the tools that reporters will need when they're on the road. For example, says Montague, "It would contain VPN software and some backup VPN options, because they may not work in every country." Likewise, the team will confirm that "all the software is updated and make sure that [the reporters] have secure chat options."

Understanding all the requirements for the building the ultimate travel laptop, however, was an iterative process that required multiple rounds of review and development. "A big part of it was getting all of the teams to agree on the process, and documenting that process, and then actually getting people to abide by that workflow," says Montague.

Since this "golden image" was created, however, it has helped streamline and secure high-risk reporting assignments. Now, Montague says, the production team can simply say, "All right, this person is going out next week—can we please get them a laptop that has this golden image on it? And that's ready to go."

CHAPTER 12

Security Strategies for Large Newsrooms

Most large news organizations are already rich in security expertise: from the operational security folks who identify and secure workspaces, to the infrastructure teams that secure networks and data centers, to the "physical security" specialists who create risk assessments for journalists reporting in conflict environments, large media companies are awash in highly specialized security knowledge.

Most of these newsrooms, however, still face a significant challenge in integrating, orienting, and growing that expertise to address modern information security threats. In today's reporting contexts, for example, a journalist's risk may stem not from the geography they're reporting from but from the community they're reporting on, and the severity of that risk might depend more on the size and virulence of that community's membership than its financial resources or technical sophistication.

Likewise, today's infrastructure threats are more likely to take the shape of a successful phishing campaign than a port-scanning attack on the company's firewall devices. As a result, the need to preserve and secure the efficiency, integrity, and independence of the newsgathering and publication process—in all its forms and across all its distribution channels and markets—means rethinking how large news organizations' existing teams interface and collaborate, as well as how threats are identified, escalated, and mitigated.

DISCARD THE "DIGITAL VERSUS PHYSICAL" DICHOTOMY

Many news organizations' security resources today are still organized around a physical/digital dichotomy that simply no longer exists. Decades of changes in the process of reporting, producing, and publishing news—through the rise of mobile computing, the global reach of digital publishing, and the explosive growth of social media—have dramatically increased new organizations' "attack surface": the number of ways their work can be compromised or exploited. Where once traditional computer network security might have been all the "digital" security a company needed, today every email, every account login, and every social media post can constitute a security risk. As such, large organizations need to change how they conceptualize protecting their information assets accordingly. As *Vice*'s Destiny Montague points out: "All aspects of security are tied together at this point in your life: digital security impacts what you do physically, and vice versa." "Digital security is just as important in today's journalism as physical security," says Reuters's Mike Christie. "You just have to integrate everything into your decision making and your risk assessment process from the ground up."

At a large organization, moving away from a siloed approach to security is easier said than done, however. The separation of responsibilities is already enshrined in org charts and budget lines, and the question of where information security should sit within the organization is controversial: editorial will want to ensure that security concerns do not curtail aggressive—and inherently risky—newsgathering efforts, while an "anything for the story" approach can distort business and organizational risks. In other words, information security must draw on understandings of both editorial's needs and priorities as well as the organization's bottom line.

Fortunately, achieving this combination of goals is not as far-fetched as it may seem. Despite differences in background knowledge, the concepts that underpin digital and physical security are well aligned. As the *New York Times*' Jason Reich puts it: "There is no distinction to me between the idea of how you keep someone from getting kidnapped or stepping on a landmine and getting harassed or hacked—the principles are completely intertwined."

The key to achieving this type of integrated approach to information security is to create one or more dedicated information security roles and ensure that they are properly staffed and privileged within the wider organization.

Should We Hire a CISO?

Recently, more large news organizations have begun hiring into chief information security officer (CISO) roles,[1] signaling a greater understanding of the need for high-level staff positions focused on information security issues.

More important than the specific title, however, is the nature of the role and the resources and visibility it commands: just as midsized news organizations will need to rally the expertise of disparate departments—from legal to IT—in order to generate useful information security insights and efforts, a C-level title is only as good as the respect commands in key departments—news being perhaps the most crucial. If calling your key information security person a CISO will be too corporate-speak for the newsroom to take seriously, choose something else instead. What matters is you hire someone with the latitude and resources to coordinate security activities across the company as a whole.

IDENTIFYING AND RECRUITING TALENT

Just as news organizations are not companies that have traditional missions or workforces, individuals with "traditional" security backgrounds are not necessarily the best qualified to lead their information security efforts. Yes, some technical expertise is essential. But finding information security personnel is not a matter of feeding a list of certifications to a consultancy, and current media-focused security expertise is too scarce to rely on poaching talent from other organizations. So where do you begin?

Wading into an untested talent pool can be especially difficult at large organizations, where leaders may feel more comfortable hiring any stripe of "veteran," even when a better-suited—if less familiar—candidate is available. With a moderate effort, however, it is possible to identify original talent—both inside and outside your organization—that can help you build out the information security expertise you need.

KEY CHARACTERISTICS

News organizations need information security specialists who can actually improve security, not just serve as a liability shield for the company in the event of a data breach or other security incident. Even if a candidate doesn't specifically have a news background, they need to really be interested in learning about the business of news: its values, priorities, and operational requirements. As the organizational security expert Angela Sasse puts it:

> When you're hiring a person, [you need] to make sure you get somebody who is very willing to learn about the business and is willing to learn how to bring their security skills to the business. To have an attitude of, "I'm here to help you do your job securely," not "I'm here to tell everybody what to do so we deliver security by some abstract set of rules." And also somebody who's willing to be visible, to be approachable. Somebody who's willing to learn how to communicate and negotiate and to convince people, rather than sort of take a "command and control" approach to security.

That a candidate may not have a résumé full of traditional security jobs should not be a deterrent; like many of the best reporters, many excellent security personnel are essentially self-taught. And when it comes to working with journalists, a more traditional security mindset can actually be a liability. As Jason Reich says, "It's easier to teach a reporter how to do security than it is to teach a cop how to work with reporters." So while basic technology and security knowledge is essential, the ability to work and communicate across departments—and especially within the newsroom—is probably an information security hire's most important trait. "When staffing information security teams," says Ankur Ahluwalia, vice president of technology solutions at the Associated Press, "my mantra is more of a personality fit. Will this person be able to support—be able to sit down and talk to—some of the journalists? Or are they better off hiding in a cubicle?"

"[Information security] is still inherently a tech job," Ahluwalia continues, "but it doesn't mean that you've been working for the NSA for five years. You have to understand technology at the basic level of, you know, what the internet is, and working knowledge of the cloud." In other words, ensuring that your information security personnel can work collaboratively, accessibly, and transparently across the organization is a much more important qualification than particular degrees, certifications, or even official prior experience. This makes conducting an information security search broadly, including within your own organization, that much more important.

Avoid the "Operators"

Whether through hostile environment and emergency first aid training (HEFAT) courses or work in conflict zones, many large news organizations already have contact with personnel who have a traditional (often military) security background. While some of these individuals—such as the *New York Times'* Jason Reich—have cultivated significant expertise in digital issues and integrated information security, many of them do not offer the strategic approach to security that most large newsrooms really need today. Dow Jones's director of news risk, Nathan Puffer—who is also ex-military—says the worst of these "operators" constitute a "plague" on the industry: "Operators take up resources and headcount, which then is *not* applied to people that can think about the needs and requirements of the organization from a kind of strategic policy/procedure/resourcing/mechanism perspective. . . . Operators tend to create a world in which they are increasingly needed because they apply a human heartbeat to every problem."

Puffer contrasts this one-to-one approach with a more integrated approach to information security, which he acknowledges can be more expensive up front but that "can create an ecosystem of mutually reinforcing behaviors that are documented, which creates a culture that's more aware."

This is not to say that there isn't a time and a place for specialized physical security services, but they are far from the only security professionals that news organizations should consider. "The security industry attempts to make itself like a gatekeeper," says Reich. "But it's wrong and it's incorrect. And it's also operationally incorrect . . . security is a very DIY industry and it really benefits from common sense in most cases."

DEFINING THE ROLE

Even with careful recruiting and a participatory hiring process, any new information security personnel are likely to encounter pushback if the scope—and limits—of their authority are not clearly defined from the outset. Obviously, information security personnel need to be allocated sufficient budget resources and reporting lines to independently evaluate existing policies and practices across the organization, develop risk assessments, and deliver training where needed. At the same time, none of these activities should be confused with the ability to "approve" or "reject" individual stories, projects, or coverage areas. The role of the information security department should principally be advisory, with the understanding that—just like reporting and publishing activities—information security concerns have a fundamental relationship to the integrity and efficacy of the organization's news products. As Chaz Repak, senior vice president for global real estate, facilities, and security at Dow Jones, puts it: "It's not [the security team's] business to say, 'You can't do this,'" he says. "That's why the approval process doesn't come through us. . . . It's our job to try to de-risk something as much as we can, and then it's up to the business to decide whether they want to move forward."

While information security concerns alone cannot and should not drive editorial priorities, however, editorial approval processes should be designed to solicit input from information security, as well as engage constructively in information security policy building, review, and implementation. Having these different parts of the organization work together on a regular basis will help improve security outcomes and realize broader security efficiencies across the organization.

ENGAGING OUTSIDE EXPERTS

Even with internal information security expertise, working with outside vendors to provide specialized training and consultations will sometimes be necessary, and your head of information security is a crucial liaison to these providers. A growing number of vendors can offer specialized information security products and training services that complement your in-house programs, such as simulated phishing campaigns or large-scale security audits.

Just as important, however, is your information security personnel's willingness and ability to build a network of relationships with information security experts at other media organizations and relevant nongovernmental organizations, especially given the dearth of third-party resources for understanding digital risk.

"It's easy to find something like International SOS that tells you the high physical risk locations around the world," says Repak. "Cyber risk? That's not so easy. It's not like there are a whole lot of lists out there that are up to date or not classified." Instead, he suggests, the best information about technical risks and online threats will come from researchers at universities, NGOs, and information security personnel at other media organizations.

Your head of information security will also need to work closely with vendors and personnel in other departments in order to coordinate and assess systems recovery and incident response and ensure that product and services agreements are kept up to date as new vulnerabilities are revealed.

REACHING THE ORGANIZATION

While core information security practices should be a basic literacy requirement for news professionals today, shifts in journalistic practice—especially the loss of more junior "apprentice"-type roles at news organizations—means that developing this literacy across a large organization will require training both experienced journalists and recent hires to support your specific information security culture.

Fortunately, many large news organizations already have robust training and professional development programs, but these probably have a structure and approach different from what is needed to introduce new information and practices. By building on and elaborating these approaches, however, information security priorities can be successfully integrated into your organization's operational fabric without reinventing the wheel.

MAKE THE MOST OF ONBOARDING

Hands down the most efficient—and effective—ways to begin improving your organization's information security is to integrate key principles and practices into your employee onboarding process. New hires are already prepared to learn new systems and take on new ways of working, so including information security–related tasks and policies is a simple way to reach employees effectively. Adding information security to the onboarding process also sends a clear signal about its importance to the organization. "If [information security] appears from the beginning in the induction training and so on," says Angela Sasse, "then people take seriously that it's actually something that the organization cares about."

The specifics of what appears in these onboarding modules will depend, of course, on your organizations' existing processes. For example, if newsroom employees are already given onboarding training beyond employee benefits and financial practices, newsroom-specific guidelines can be integrated into those modules. If all employees will receive the same training, then onboarding materials might focus more on "universal" best practices, like account security and password management. Ideally, says *Vice*'s security specialist Destiny Montague: "Any new employees would at least get some sort of training or documentation that would say: 'In order to do your job here we need you to read this document, go through steps to secure your accounts, make sure that you're brushed up on X, Y, and Z, and also understand that our team exists for you in case you ever come across anything where you might need help.'"

Newsroom employees' first days on the job are also an excellent opportunity to engage them in some of the longer-term tasks that are important to securing journalists' work. For Mike Christie of Reuters, these tasks would include social media "scrubbing" and general account separation, with an emphasis on how these practices protect both reporters *and* the integrity of their reporting. "Onboarding I think should be about, 'Let's figure out all your online vulnerabilities: Here's photos of your bedroom . . . here are pictures of you at a drunken party,'" says Christie. "If you're going to go into Iraq, you might have to go to a meeting with a Shiite militia leader, and guess what? They're going to do research."

In fact, says the security expert Matt Mitchell, news organizations should consider making basic information security practices a part of both onboarding and employees' annual disclosure agreement—at least in the newsroom, if not company-wide. Beyond disclosing conflicts of interest, for example, Mitchell suggests that every employee should sign a compact in which they commit to key information security practices. "And you are agreeing when you sign on that you will do those things or you can get fired," says Mitchell.

DEVELOP A RANGE OF TRAINING RESOURCES

Even if information security is a robust part of your onboarding program, on-demand references and self-directed assessments are invaluable in large organizations. As policies and platforms change, providing employees with real-time instruction on how to lock down their social media profiles, for example, is neither reasonable nor efficient. Instead, develop a library of how-to documents and follow-along videos that can provide employees with the knowledge they need on their own schedule and at their own pace. Of course, creating these materials is not enough; supervisors throughout the organization will still need to set aside time on a regular basis for employees to complete these tasks.

Given the scale and geographic spread of most large newsrooms, real-time, in-person training events should be reserved specifically for the type of complex, policy-oriented material that particularly benefits from group discussion and reflection. For example, determining which story pitches should be flagged and escalated for security review is a nuanced-enough process that collaborative, facilitated discussions will be one of the only meaningful ways to really get buy in from newsroom employees. Likewise, material that depends on specialized technology will need to be introduced in a context where newsroom employees, in particular, have the opportunity to ask questions and raise concerns. As a news editor once explained: "Having people that are journalists and actually want to know everything, they're like, 'Wait, I don't understand. I need to understand how this functions before I start to use it.' Which is also a thing of 'I need to understand how it functions so I feel comfortable using it.' "[2]

CULTIVATE SECURITY "CHAMPIONS"

Real-time trainings and awareness events are also excellent opportunities to identify people across the news organization who can be cultivated as security "champions" within their respective teams and departments. At Reuters, for example, this strategy has helped ensure that information security awareness reaches the global organization's many bureaus. As *Reuters's* global managing editor Reg Chua explains: "Our latest [approach] is to get a bunch of information security champions around the organization. . . . We hope that by having enough of them at enough bureaus, then they'll be the person on the ground who knows about [security]. And then hopefully when they hear about stuff, [they] can flag it up to us."

Engaging interested employees is especially for bootstrapping a high-contact approach to information security during the early rollout stages of new practices and policies. As the security expert Runa Sandvik points out: "More often than not, the security team is going to have a hard time scaling to the newsroom. But what you can do is identify people that will champion your message when you're not able to be that high-touch."

Likewise, security champions can share insights around how to best engage and motivate certain teams or departments and how to encourage those teams to share pain points that might not otherwise surface. As such, identifying and supporting security champions can grow your information security team's institutional knowledge in addition to increasing security expertise across the organization.

Most large news organizations have one or more help desk services that are staffed 24/7 in order to address common employee needs—and there is no reason that information security can't be among them. Preparing your help desk staff to answer common questions about security-related measures—whether it's how to configure MFA or turn on whole-disk encryption—is just another way to provide staff with as many entry points as possible for information security support. As Ahluwalia observes: "Bringing [the help desk] team along on the tools we're implementing or the challenges we're facing—keeping them up to date—that's good. It has been a good partnership with our team to have them answer some of these sort of easier questions, like 'I need a tool that helps me secure a video conference' or something."

BUILDING INSTITUTIONAL TRUST

Ultimately, the success of your organization's information security efforts will depend on your team's ability to cultivate a sense of trust and shared purpose—especially with the newsroom. Without this, the work of your specialists won't carry weight with reporters and editors, and their recommendations will be ignored at best—and actively undermined at worst. To allay fears that the information security team will curtail editorial freedoms, however, you'll need to publicly and transparently outline how your security team will report its findings and who is responsible for final decisions when they are involved.

IDENTIFY THE DECISION MAKERS

At *Reuters*, for example, general managers must approve any stories that may involve a significant security risk. While most of those managers are former journalists, decision making about high-risk stories has been intentionally moved one step away from the reporters and editors involved. As Chua explains:

> The goal of having the general managers make these decisions and having veto power is the rule of thumb that you are too invested in your own story to be able to make a reasonable decision about it. . . . The GM is not as invested in the story, and so they can take a broader view. So you might think it's perfectly safe for you to walk into this [situation],

but we are the ones that have to extract you. So you don't get to make that choice until we're comfortable that that would not put anybody else at risk.

Similarly, at the *Wall Street Journal*, editors handling high-risk stories seek out security assessments, and depending on the risk determination, says Repak, it will be passed up the editorial food chain for further approval. "If it's something high risk, then the regional editor-in-chief is going to have to approve it, not just the bureau chief," Repak explains. "And if it's extreme risk, then the editor-in-chief or the managing editor is going to have to approve it. . . . We want to make sure headquarters knows what kind of risk we're asking people to take."

While these additional measures can sometimes be met with skepticism, "reporters have really learned that this [process] is in their best interests," says Kate Ortega, assistant managing editor for operations at the *Wall Street Journal*. In part, this is because regular engagement with the security team improves reporting outcomes, making higher-risk stories more accessible the next time around. "We want to make sure that [editorial leaders] believe that the benefit that they're going to get from the reportage is worth the risk," says Repak. "And it almost always is, for a couple of reasons. One, because the job's inherently risky, and we accept a certain degree of risk. And two, because we're preparing them better than they would be prepared otherwise."

Building Trust with the Newsroom: What Security Professionals Should Know

Journalism is an inherently risky business, which means that certain security issues are a necessary part of doing business. Of course, the role of an information security professional is to minimize risk as much as possible, which will usually involve reporters and editors doing things differently than they have in the past. Proactively learning about the norms and practices of journalism will help you encourage secure behaviors that don't impinge on necessary newsgathering and publishing activities. In addition to attending journalism conferences, joining professional organizations, and reviewing public codes of ethics (such as those hosted by the Associated Press and the Society of Professional Journalists), just paying attention to the conversations happening in the

CONTINUED

newsroom and seeking advice from editorial peers can help you better understand the particular culture of your own organization.

At the same time, if you are just beginning your work with news organizations, you may need to adjust some of your expectations about how security considerations will (and will not) fit into the operations of editorial teams. For example, while knowing all the details of a particular story or reporting process might be useful, a certain degree of secrecy on the part of reporters and editors is normal. Information security teams "have to respect that news has to have its privacy," says *Dow Jones'* Chaz Repak. "It cannot be influenced by other areas of the company, and other areas of the company can't hear what news is up to."

In many security cultures, the idea of giving users this level of independence and discretion is anathema because users themselves are seen as the primary source of risk. While that *can* be true in news organizations, of course, so can the opposite: projects like the Panama Papers demonstrate that editorial staff who are deeply and constructively engaged around security issues can truly enhance an organization's security, rather than compromise it.

As such, viewing news staff as partners in the process of securing the organization is essential, even if they sometimes make choices that you're uncomfortable with. "You're working with a group of people whom you need to be seeing as an asset, not as a liability," says the *New York Times'* Jason Reich. "The security team does not approve or reject assignments, or get an editor or approve or reject assignments: the security team assists in making sure things are done safely."

The fact that achieving editorial priorities will supersede certain security concerns means you may need to respond to security incidents that were, on some level, preventable. Saying "I told you so," however, will only alienate the editorial partners you need to be effective. Instead, take on board the values of the newsroom as much as possible. "Our work on the security side has always been about building the capacity of the news organization to do more—and that is the question I am always challenging myself with," says *BuzzFeed*'s head of high-risk Eliot Stempf. "Am I getting in the way of something happening, or am I facilitating it?"

"The most important thing you can do from the security side is accept that a journalist's job is risky," says Repak. "Journalists have a job to do, and we are here to support them to do it in the safest way possible—if the business decides yes we want to go forward with [a story], then we support it 100 percent."

DEFINE YOUR RESPONSE STRATEGIES

Even with a well-informed and responsible staff, information security incidents will happen. Internet trolls will get angry, nation-states and hackers will go after your data, and software vulnerabilities will arise: it's simply not possible to prevent 100 percent of security incidents.

While prevention can go a long way, then, your organization needs to be prepared to respond when a security incident does, inevitably, happen. Of course, the two are not unconnected: A doxxing attack against a journalist who has carefully compartmentalized his online life, for example, will be much less dangerous than an attack directed at someone who hasn't taken those precautions. Still, how such an attack should be handled—who should be contacted and how; what documentation should be collected, if any; and how the target should respond, if at all—needs to be clearly outlined and communicated to staff at all levels: not just journalists and their editors but also folks like the help desk, technical support, security personnel, and human resources—all of whom may be called upon either during or following such an incident.

A thorough and actionable escalation plan helps ensure that your organization can respond quickly, appropriately, and efficiently to incidents as they arise; it also sets expectations and provides measurable benchmarks for evaluating that response. Incident response plans also should not be created and filed away but should be used to rehearse how crises will be handled. For example, Ahluwalia describes one such exercise:

We go through a simulation of a massive DDoS attack and how we react to it. What would the customer support desk do? What are the backup systems that we have in place that need to come online, are already online, that are separate and different that need to get triggered?. . . That's documented and rehearsed. And the assumption is in fifteen to twenty minutes the [backup system] should be up and online while you're going through the process of figuring out what is going on with [the primary system].

Beyond the direct practical value of escalation plans and dress rehearsals, active preparation for security incidents sends a reassuring signal to employees at all levels that the organization is equipped to deal with them effectively. Particularly in cases of doxxing or harassment, an escalation plan makes clear to employees that they have the support of the organization in the face of what can otherwise be an extraordinarily isolating and intimidating experience. By setting—and meeting—expectations about how security incidents will be handled, you also strengthen the positive rapport between your information security team and employees at every level of the organization.

INVEST, ASSESS, REPEAT

Improving your organization's information security obviously requires investment, but it may not be clear from the outset how much to invest or what the return on it should be. If your organization has not had dedicated information security resources before, "there are going to be lots of things to do," says Sasse, "and you won't be able to do everything at once." As a result, "You should have a plan, particularly in terms of having some outline of commitment of resources. If you're trying to make your organization secure . . . have a two-year plan, but with quarterly review of the things you've profiled."

Just as important is identifying how you will measure success and then budgeting in time and money for conducting those evaluations. "You need to start to develop some measurements," says Sasse. "You know, 'What are meaningful indicators of how well we are doing?' "

The initial cost of establishing your organization's information security work may seem daunting: you are essentially staffing and budgeting for an entirely new department. At the same time, good information security, like good editing, provides invaluable support for a news organization's bottom line. "It's not just 'You're spending money on security,'" says Sasse. "It's an investment in the resilience of the organization, of the ability to keep going when things go wrong . . . information security and business continuity . . . they're really all part of one activity."

Case Study: Transforming Information Security at the Associated Press

When Gianluca D'Aniello joined the Associated Press as CTO in 2016, one of the first moves he made was to begin transforming the company's approach to information security. Vice President of Technology Solutions Ankur Ahluwalia describes how the company's approach to information security has changed in the years since: "[Previously], this group was buried under some networking group, under the infrastructure team, with infosec sort of hiding away. And that was one of the things [D'Aniello] changed, saying, 'That may have worked in the past, but things have changed quite a bit. This needs to be more visible: it needs to work with end users [like] editorial staff and product teams of journalists in the field.'"

Part of making that change, of course, required reorienting several teams' activities to make security a part of their work from the start. Before this shift, says Ahluwalia, "security was something you layered on top, after the fact."

The first step was shifting the approach of the internal systems teams, in order to ensure that "when you're writing the software you're integrating the security principles." The second step, says Ahluwalia, was "working with a slew of third parties around services." As he explains: "Whether it's monitoring services or DDOS protection and things like that. . . . Industry experts help supplement our team in getting those things right: getting them configured, knowing how that works and how that would work on the day when we really need it."

The final step, of course, was working with journalists and editorial teams. Success in that arena "started with having a good partner in editorial," says Ahluwalia. It also meant reassessing the meaning of security, especially in the context of mobile computing: "We found as we moved from traditional desktops to now, you know, everybody's taking their work on the field and they want data and resources to be available from wherever they are . . . that's sort of inherently opened up a new slew of challenges about protecting stuff. People lose devices. People are in various parts of the world—they necessarily don't control how they're accessing the internet."

This shift required Ahluwalia and his team to think more creatively about how to engage end users—and especially journalists—on security topics: "Looking at, 'OK, is there a simple toolkit we can go create for people traveling to not-so-friendly parts of the world?' Or, generally, addressing the needs of journalists that need to make contact with sources and need data that they don't necessarily want available for everybody to snoop on. So we've come up with a simple toolkit, so that when in doubt you can look at this. And then, if you have something very very special you can come talk to us."

While each of these layers is important to the AP's overall information security strategy, connecting effectively with the people across the newsroom is the most essential. According to Ahluwalia and his information security architect Daniel Peluso, the lynchpin in an effective information security strategy is "establishing that relationship with journalists, to let them know that we're here for you, and we want to be able to provide you what you need."

CHAPTER 13

———

Facing Threats to the Profession

On August 9, 2014, just six hours after Michael Brown, a Black teenager, was shot to death by a white police officer in Ferguson, Missouri, Antonio French—then an alderman for St. Louis's Twenty-First Ward—began live-tweeting coverage of the protests that would engulf the area for months to come.[1] While the intensity and duration of those protests would help catalyze a moment of national and international reckoning around racism,[2] the events in Ferguson were also one of the first times that social media activity managed to drive mainstream news coverage. In successfully drawing attention to the police brutality that had often been downplayed through news organizations' tendency to rely on "official" police narratives,[3] social media coverage of the Ferguson protests was something of a turning point for news organizations, which soon began looking to social media trends as potential indicators of newsworthy events. At almost the same moment, however, evidence was mounting that social media platforms were increasingly being exploited to manipulate the perceptions of both the public and the press, through the misinformation and disinformation that would soon be known as "fake news."[4]

Today, the term "fake news" has been both politicized and weaponized in order to broadly discredit professional journalism.[5] But while the "info-demic" of misinformation accompanying global health crises like COVID-19 have highlighted just how devastating bad information can be, misinformation and disinformation are only two of the existential crises facing professional journalism today. The proliferation of online harassment, abysmal staff diversity at media organizations, and a lack of critical technical infrastructure are among the threats to journalists and journalism that also put at risk the democratic values that the press is meant to support.

MANAGING MISINFORMATION

By 2019, Americans identified "fake news" as the fifth most pressing issue facing the country, with more than half of those surveyed believing that it is a problem up to journalists to "fix."[6] While resources like the *Verification Handbook* and organizations like First Draft News have been instrumental in educating and empowering journalists on how to verify social media content, the news industry as a whole has yet to grapple effectively with the degree to which misinformation and disinformation are transforming the basic processes and expectations of reporting.[7]

"Most journalists who are breaking news stories don't necessarily assess that they might be part of a larger pool of targets," says Joan Donovan, who leads key research efforts on misinformation and disinformation at Harvard's Shorenstein Center. While professional reporters are trained to be skeptical of sources who may wish to manipulate them for personal gain, "journalists aren't always equipped to understand that there are people who are maybe potentially just interested in the hoax," she says.

"There are all these ways in which [journalists] get taught about different actors and what their interests might be," Donovan explains. What's missing, she says, is the understanding that "there's a group of people emerging online that see breaking news events as opportunities just to mess with journalists." While such groups may be relatively informal, their efforts are highly coordinated. Message boards are used to develop—and even name—particular strategies for targeting journalists with false information, just for the LOLs of seeing them humiliated when they must later retract their work. "It's not just that this stuff is happenstance," says Donovan. "It's that [online groups] talk about the techniques in these message boards, and they *name* those techniques. And then when the opportunity arises, they know they can kick into action because they've already dealt with some of the tactical maneuvering and organization and presorted what they're going to do, when they're going to do it, and how they're going to do it."

Donovan has published several reports detailing the strategies that online groups use to target journalists. In their 2019 report on "source hacking," Donovan and her coauthor Brian Friedberg describe some of the methods used to manipulate journalists' attention and coverage, such as "viral sloganeering," leak forgery, evidence collages, and "keyword squatting."[8] Some, like leak forgery and evidence collages, manipulate verified information by poisoning genuine document sets or cherry-picking data points in order to plant false information or generate persuasive—and misleading—narratives around breaking events. Viral sloganeering and keyword squatting, on the other hand, leverage memes and hashtags to obfuscate the origin of certain ideas that then make their way into news coverage. Keyword squatting, for example, uses the popularity of certain hashtags or terms to create digital artifacts—including social media profiles and pages—that are used to effectively impersonate members of well-known but decentralized movements like Black Lives Matter and Antifa. In viral sloganeering, verbal and visual memes (like 2018's "Jobs not Mobs") are carefully crafted and fed into the publishing ecosystem as a means to shape the rhetoric of both politicians and the press. This is often accomplished through yet another tactic known as "news spamming," which Donovan describes as using a "trading up the chain" model in order to drive coverage of a particular issue, idea, or event: "You get some smaller blog with no standards to cover something, then you get someone newsworthy to tweet that low-standard blog. . . . Other blogs or online news organizations then will cover that newsworthy individual either to debunk it or to say, 'Oh, how outrageous.' And then that might turn into mainstream coverage and/or cable news." While many of these misinformation threats are already on journalists' minds, how to deal with them is not always well understood. Leak forgery already occupies the thoughts of Reuters' Reg Chua, for example. "What's the chance somebody comes in and starts modifying documents?" he wonders. "How am I going to know?"

While leak forgery and keyword squatting can largely be addressed through rigorous verification practices, Donovan believes that addressing more sophisticated threats will require dedicated resources.[9] In their source hacking report, for example, Donovan and Friedberg call on news organizations to invest specifically in information security.[10] "Information security as a lens to understand this makes sense to us," says Donovan, because "this is about the information environment and how [malicious actors] can use essentially social engineering tactics to be believable enough as sources of information. Then journalists fall into those traps because they align very well with known tropes in that moment."

In her view, an information security desk would, among other things, "Keep track of . . . some of these known spaces of misinformation. Just so that [journalists] have someone to go to to say, 'Hey, is this thing real?'" Cultivating this type of intelligence will require committing new resources specifically to information security, even at large media companies with sophisticated security expertise. As *Dow Jones*'s Chaz Repak says, "We can't ask our cyber team to come up with a list of cyber risk locations and keep it updated."

Such a "cyber risk" resource would better equip newsrooms to detect and defend against the misinformation strategies that are frequently used to manipulate journalists' coverage. By identifying trolling campaigns and media-training strategies designed in advance of major events,[11] an information security desk could help inoculate journalists against those tactics. Likewise, developing robust editorial plans around the type of periodic breaking news events would help prevent journalists' being exploited by online "chaos actors" who, Donovan says, "are actively trying to sow disinformation in that moment." She adds, "There are ways you can plan to deal with school shooters. There are ways you can plan to deal with misogynistic violence. . . . Think through those scenarios, and know who it is that you will contact that you trust."

RESPONDING TO HARASSMENT

In recent years, harassment has arguably become the most pervasive threat facing professional journalists. Fueled by a combination of political antagonism, shifting editorial practices, and increased competition, journalists today are constantly at risk of being targeted by both high-profile individuals and anonymous trolls who want to intimidate, embarrass, or endanger them. In general, journalists globally face greater physical threats than ever;[12] online, the situation is even more dire. "People are shocked by how well [online harassment] scales," says the Freedom of the Press Foundation's newsroom security director Harlo Holmes. "Even people whose job it is to work with these topics specifically are shocked by how fast it evolves as a tactic."

At news organizations with more robust security programs, the tangible costs of the worst online harassment are already very apparent, as threats spill over from the digital realm to the physical. This is especially common in more industrialized regions, according to *Dow Jones'* Chaz Repak:

> In the more developed parts of the world . . . that's where the physical risk and the cyber risk are even more intertwined. When we do coverage of certain areas of the interwebs that people don't like, they tend to get touchy about it and do things like doxx our people and make threats. And so it's a real intertwining of physical and cybersecurity because all of a sudden you have our staff being attacked online, [malicious actors]

trying to get information about us and posting pictures of people's homes . . . and you know we're giving people bodyguards and moving them out of their homes.

Often hidden from newsrooms—and the industry—are the less tangible costs of online harassment, like reduced productivity, increased self-censorship, and a general outflow of talent from the industry. A 2018 research report from the International Women's Media Foundation (IWMF), for example, found that almost 30 percent of the women journalists surveyed had considered leaving the profession because of harassment, while 37 percent reported avoiding certain stories as a result. More than a third reported one or more symptoms of trauma, while nearly one-quarter reported harassment had interfered with or limited their productivity or interfered with their career advancement.[13]

At the same time, research indicates that news organizations and the broader industry can help reduce both the prevalence of online harassment and its impact on reporters. For example, while one-quarter of those surveyed in the 2018 IWMF research did not report incidents of online harassment to management because they did not know how, of those that *did* report such incidents, almost 60 percent were at least somewhat satisfied with management's response.[14] This suggests that robust, integrated information security strategies that include mitigating and responding to all levels of online harassment can help news organizations reduce the negative impact of these experiences on both individual reporters and their own bottom line. As Reuters's Mike Christie puts it:

> In most cases, we'll hear about the really serious stuff, but we won't hear about the routine stuff that just builds up from that. I mean, if the female White House correspondent keeps on getting marriage proposals every time she appears on CNN right now, she just kind of dismisses it. But that easily leads to other stuff you kind of want to keep an eye on, because it might actually be quite menacing. . . . [And] when you've got a thousand of these things, you might just say, "OK, I won't cover [the White House] again. I'm just going to do Congress."

REDUCING THE EFFECTS OF ONLINE HARASSMENT

News organizations invest heavily in developing the skills and talents of their journalists; reducing the harm done by online harassment is a simple way to protect the value of that investment. Many of the most important measures, moreover, are practically free to implement. For example, research from PEN America suggests that simply acknowledging, at the highest levels, that online harassment exists can be one of the most crucial steps for news organizations to take;[15] through simple surveys, organizations can also collect valuable data about the type and frequency of harassment experienced. This data can then be used to inform relevant policies—from social media usage and comment moderation guidelines to wellness strategies—and to persuade social media platforms to intervene where appropriate. As Joan Donovan puts it:

> In terms of information security, if you had someone that did even some basic network modeling to look at who in your organization is being targeted online for harassment . . . you can find generally the hubs of that harassment and go after the hubs rather than the spokes. And presenting that information over to the platform companies can be very useful.

REDUCING THE PREVALENCE OF ONLINE HARASSMENT

Many of the fundamental information security practices that have already been addressed in this book (especially in chapter 4) are also instrumental in reducing some of the harms associated with online harassment: strong password practices, robust compartmentalization of social media accounts, and regular scrubbing of employees' digital footprints helps reduce the quantity of raw material available for doxxing attacks and makes successful hacks of online accounts less likely. At the same time, there are fundamental aspects of today's journalism culture that increase the risks faced by all journalists, but especially those experienced by women, LGBTQ, and BIPOC reporters.

CURB SOCIAL MEDIA EXPECTATIONS

While social media can be a valuable forum for engaging with audiences, the fact that journalists even are often expected to build and maintain a personal brand via social media means that they will also personally bear the brunt of the online attacks and trolling. "In the media we tend to be a little bit too accepting of the fact that journalists are their brand," says Christie. "And it's a problem because all this bad stuff happens in [reporters'] DMs [Twitter direct messages], and you have no control over it. And I [as a Reuters security professional] can't do anything about it."

Joan Donovan points out that the pressure for individual journalists to be, in effect, their own news distributors via social media also increases their susceptibility to misinformation, as it creates a difficult confluence of personal and professional demands:

> I think we should start to move away from . . . individual reporters being the ones who are relied upon to distribute their articles. . . . I think that this is putting too much pressure on individual journalists to find the story, create the story, distribute the story, and then be responsible for how that story lands in the world . . . [because it] makes them very susceptible to picking up either bad sources or to jumping on a story too quickly.

REVIEWING HEADLINE PRACTICES

While online headlines are often optimized for search engine and social media trends, few news readers appreciate that they are rarely written by the author of an article. Yet as PEN America's "Online Harassment Field Manual" points out: "When headlines are written to be deliberately inflammatory or divisive, it's the writer of the article—not the editor who selected the headline—who becomes the target of vicious online harassment."[16] News organizations should monitor the relationship between provocative headlines and online harassment, to make sure that a brief spike in traffic isn't coming at the cost of days or weeks of ongoing harassment.

INCREASING INCLUSION

As a global pandemic, record joblessness, and waves of protests against racial violence converged, 2020 became a year of global reckoning on many levels. The news industry was no exception, as both high-profile reporters and entire newsrooms began publicly and privately airing long-held grievances about the abysmal state of newsroom diversity and the deleterious effects of homogenous staffing on news coverage.[17] Unsurprisingly, poor staff diversity has negative consequences for newsrooms' security along a number of axes: it jeopardizes the safety of those BIPOC, LGBTQ, and other minority reporters who have managed to succeed in the newsroom already, and it makes the newsroom as a whole more susceptible to the kind of groupthink that fails to recognize the misinformation, harassment, and outright mistakes that undermine the credibility of the professional press.

For example, poor diversity undermines the threat modeling process, which requires that journalists feel comfortable with centering their identity in order to be effective. As the *New York Times'* Jason Reich points out, threat modeling "won't work in an adversarial relationship—which is to say that in a place where a freelancer or a reporter has concerns about their identity in their workplace and they see it as a liability instead of as an asset." Unfortunately, the limits of the *Times'* own diversity were put on full display in June 2020, when the paper ran an error-riddled op-ed by the Republican senator from Arkansas, Tom Cotton, that called for "an overwhelming show of force" against civilian protesters, just days after running an article that detailed the threats facing journalists reporting on protests in response to the death of George Floyd. In response, *Times* journalists were forced to speak out publicly, tweeting "Running this [piece] put Black @nytimes staff in danger."[18] Multiple journalists also reported losing sources as a result of the op-ed, putting future reporting at risk as well.[19]

A lack of diversity in the newsroom can also create sourcing problems that make the entire organization more susceptible to misinformation. In the run-up to the 2016 U.S. election, for example, dozens of prominent media figures and organizations interacted with or embedded tweets from social media accounts like @blacktivists, which were later identified as Russian sock-puppet accounts posing as racial justice organizations.[20] Yet while many media organizations were taken in, multiple activist groups recognized these accounts as inauthentic,[21] as had the Black feminist activists and scholars Shafiqah Hudson and I'Nasah Crockett when divisive social media campaigns targeting Black women emerged in 2014; those efforts were almost certainly a dry run for the 2016 election interference.[22] As Joan Donovan puts it:

> The imposter Black Lives Matter is a really good thing to draw out here, because also we know that there's a lot of astroturfing that goes on within quote unquote Black Twitter. And the way in which journalists decide to represent Black issues should be rooted in sources that they trust and that they've cultivated themselves, not sources that have kind of shown up and thrown something into their DMs that seems provocative.

The absence of diverse reporters with deeply cultivated sources makes newsrooms more vulnerable to misinformation, and it also severely limits the type of coverage they can provide. As Crockett said at a SRCCON journalism conference in 2018: "The lack of nuanced, compassionate, and historically grounded coverage of Black lives is a direct result of exclusionary policies, both formal and informal, that have kept Black folks out of newsrooms, or has limited our involvement."[23]

A more inclusive newsroom can also help reduce the negative impact of harassment by ensuring that internal policies and practices are informed by a wide range of experiences and ideas. PEN America, for example, finds that the "perspectives of women, people of color, and members of the LGBTQ+ community are especially valuable" in these discussions.[24]

A truly diverse newsroom will also be less likely to make the kinds of mistakes that can alienate readers and embarrass publications. In 2018, for example, NPR's Twitter handle posted a tweet referring to "el ano de la mujer" in connection with a story about a record number of women running for office in Mexico. As the photojournalist Melissa Lyttle pointed out on Twitter: "ano = anus, año = year. Tildes matter. So does diversity in a newsroom."[25]

CHAPTER 14

Looking Ahead

In 2012, *This American Life* ran a piece on a company called Journatic, which was producing local news pieces with fake bylines written by remote freelancers, many of whom were thousands of miles away from the communities they were "covering."[1] In his interview with *This American Life*, Brian Timpone, an executive at Journatic, was unrepentant about his company's practices. "I personally think we're saving journalism," Timpone told the show's host Sarah Koenig.[2] Although the Journatic name disappeared in 2013, its founder and his practices remained, rebranded as Locality Labs. Over the following years, Timpone's network of "pink slime" websites grew, numbering in the hundreds by 2019 and ballooning to over 1,200 by the following year.[3]

In the lead-up to the 2016 presidential election, Americans' trust in the mass media hit an all-time low: only 32 percent of Gallup poll respondents had even "a fair amount" of trust that the mass media would "report the news fully, accurately and fairly."[4] "Made-up news or information" was one of Americans' top concerns in 2019, just barely behind "the U.S. political system" and "the gap between rich and poor." Concerns about the information ecosystem were also substantially greater than those about terrorism.[5] Historically, local news outlets have enjoyed more trust than their national counterparts, a trend that was buoyed in 2020 as Americans turned to local news outlets for information related to the COVID-19 pandemic.[6] As divisive national issues come home to smaller communities and as "pink slime" websites proliferate, however, even the privileged trust that local news outlets enjoy could easily slip away.[7]

While groups as varied as social media platforms, nonprofit foundations, and even government agencies have announced technological efforts to help defend against misinformation, news organizations need to examine how they can help improve trust within an increasingly uncertain publishing climate.[8] After decades of allowing technology companies and social media platforms to dictate the tools used to gather and disseminate the news, it's time for journalistic organizations to outline what types of technology are needed to sustain, preserve, and scale reputable journalism in the twenty-first century. Successfully threading the needle between technological capacity and human effort in developing these solutions will require a proactive approach to news technology design and development, in order to ensure that new publishing tools and standards truly support the needs of both the industry and the public.

THE CASE FOR AUTHENTICATION

"As deep fake technology becomes more advanced and more accessible, it could pose a threat to United States public discourse and national security," three members of Congress wrote to Director of National Intelligence Dan Coats in 2018. "By blurring the line between fact and fiction," the letter states, "deep fake technology could undermine public trust in recorded images and videos as objective depictions of reality."[9]

The rise of deepfakes—convincing synthetic audio and video media, which now can be generated in close to real time—has been described by both the press and lawmakers as dangerous to the information ecosystem and even to democracy.[10] Compounding concern over the risk these tools pose is the acknowledgment by computer scientists that detecting manipulated audiovisual materials computationally amounts to an arms race: every time researchers find a weakness in the tools for generating deepfakes, those tools will be improved to address the shortcoming.[11]

At the same time, deepfakes are really just a new milestone in the long history of "cheap fakes," contend Britt Paris and Joan Donovan in their 2019 report on the subject. "News coverage claims that deepfakes are poised to assault commonly-held standards of evidence, that they are the harbingers of a coming 'information apocalypse,'" they write. "But what coverage of this deepfake phenomenon often misses is that the 'truth' of audiovisual content has never been stable—truth is socially, politically, and culturally determined."[12]

Given the degree to which accusations of "fake news" have been used to undermine legitimate journalistic efforts,[13] many news organizations are already alert to the threat posed by deepfakes and are wrestling with the extent to which detecting them can be automated away. "Do you have the tools, the technology to vet [media] at scale?" asks the Associated Press's Ankur Ahluwalia. "Is that the job of individual journalists working on the story to make sure that's right? Or does information security have a role in saying, 'Here are some tools that I can give you'?"

Even if robust tools for deepfake detection are built,[14] however, they cannot protect against what misinformation experts like Paris, Donovan, and First Draft's Claire Wardle describe as "the liar's dividend," that is, "the lies and actions people will get away with by exploiting widespread skepticism to their own advantage."[15] Whether or not media organizations actually fall prey to deepfakes, in other words, the very fact that deepfakes exist can be exploited to undermine the credibility of legitimate journalism.

For media companies, reducing the liar's dividend is not about developing better technical mechanisms for detecting deepfakes—technology companies and academics are better positioned and incentivized to take on that challenge. Instead, media companies need to invest in technical standards and mechanisms that will allow their own digitally published media to be robustly and efficiently authenticated, as a defense against efforts to "denounce the authentic as being fake."[16]

Specifically, reputable media publishers should apply cryptographic signatures to each piece of digital content they publish and include a record of that signature in a publicly available blockchain ledger. By doing so, these news organizations would be extending their commitment to transparency and accountability to their publishing technology: these cryptographic signatures could be used to efficiently confirm the provenance of a piece of digital media and attest to its contents at a specific point in time.

Digitally signing articles in this way would short-circuit the liar's dividend in a number of ways. First, content from reputable news organizations would be nearly impossible to forge, reducing the effectiveness of phishing-based disinformation campaigns like "Project Mayfly," where adversaries duplicate the look and feel of legitimate news websites like the *Atlantic* and the *Guardian* to lend credibility to their disinformation. With a system of digital signatures in place, any reader who had previously visited the genuine websites of these publications would be instantly alerted to the deception without any additional effort.

Cryptographically signed news content could also help mitigate another major risk facing news publishers and the public at large: the loss of the "first draft of history" to digital decay. As Sharon Ringel and Angela Woodall detail in their 2019 report "A Public Record at Risk: The Dire State of News Archiving in the Digital Age," of the more than twenty news organizations they surveyed, "not one was properly saving a holistic record of what it produces."[17] While many journalists may believe (or hope) that organizations like the Internet Archive are filling the gap, the reality is that such efforts are simply not robust enough to act as an indisputable record of what has—or hasn't—been published online.[18] Though digitally signing content would not, in and of itself, guarantee the creation of robust digital news archives, it could pave the way by providing potential archiving institutions with useful guarantees about *what* they were archiving. This would help make distributing digital collection efforts among libraries, nonprofits, and universities—which have already developed significant collaborations around sharing physical reference materials—more feasible. User-facing signatures would even allow individuals to participate, allowing a digital copy of a news article, for example, to be authenticated at a later date just as effectively as an old printed copy of *Life* magazine.

Perhaps most importantly, however, a commitment by reputable publishers to cryptographically sign their digital content would establish the practice as a mark of credibility with readers, by making it not just possible but *efficient* to hold media companies accountable for the material they publish. For most news publishers, this would simply be a technical codification of existing practice, but one that would make the high standards of the industry transparent to readers and provide a benchmark for distinguishing trustworthy media in the digital space. While researchers at news organizations and universities (including myself) have already begun developing prototypes of such technologies,[19] buy-in from the journalism industry at large, along with the cooperation of browser makers, social media platforms, and search engines, will be crucial to providing digital media with the integrity guarantees that readers both need and deserve.

MAKING DIGITAL PUBLISHING INTERNET INDEPENDENT

On the morning of October 21, 2016, internet users on the East Coast began having trouble accessing popular websites like Reddit, Spotify, the *New York Times*, and *Wired*.[20] Though it took several hours, eventually the source of the problem it became clear: a massive DDoS attack targeting a small Domain Name Service (DNS) operator called Dyn had made it impossible for millions of browsers to complete the lookups necessary to connect well-known domains to their underlying IP addresses. As a result, while the affected websites and news organizations were online and technically available, they remained inaccessible to large numbers of users.

This was not the first time that U.S. news organizations had been effectively taken offline. Just a few years before, Superstorm Sandy had ravaged the East Coast, temporarily knocking offline the servers of websites like *BuzzFeed* and *Gawker*.[21] As the storm took out electrical transformers and wireless towers around the city, entire neighborhoods were left without power or internet connections—and the news access they usually provide.[22]

Today, more than one-third of Americans prefer to get their news—whether local or national—online.[23] Yet the dependence of digital publishing on the internet can be a weakness: in times of emergency, uncertainty, or upheaval, internet access is often reduced, restricted, or eliminated. While the idea that digital publishing and distribution could continue without the internet may seem absurd, the development of low-power microcomputers has dramatically lowered the requirements for creating digital distribution points: essentially, highly localized Wi-Fi networks where readers can download digital news—whether or not the internet at large is available.[24] While similar systems have been deployed in classrooms, protests, and libraries, there have been only limited experiments with their use for news.[25] Though the idea of a "digital newsstand" might seem quaint, creating such "hotspots" for downloading news content would help provide twenty-first-century news publishers with the same type of distribution control in the digital space that they have long enjoyed in the print realm. Especially given that private companies control the infrastructure on which so many publishers rely,[26] it's crucial that news organizations remain viable and independent—even in the face of changing algorithms and allegiances.

UPDATING JOURNALISM EDUCATION

Ultimately, improving the information security landscape for journalism as a whole will require the effort and participation of everyone in the industry—from novice reporters to the top leadership of the world's largest newswires. It will, however, also require the participation of the educators who—whether they are introducing a new generation to the profession or helping established journalists improve their craft—must truly engage with information security as a means to protect, preserve, and further journalists' work.

Like the rest of the industry, of course, journalism programs at all levels have had to contend with the industry's massive transformation over the past twenty years. There is a persistent sense that there are not enough class hours available to sufficiently prepare students for their roles in the modern newsroom. To many journalism educators, no doubt, information security expertise will seem like just another competency to try to squeeze into an overloaded curriculum. Such concerns, of course, misapprehend information security as an "add-on" to contemporary reporting processes instead of as essential to their robustness and integrity. Since failing to take reasonable precautions around one's reporting materials or professional accounts would constitute both a significant ethical lapse and a blow to any reporter's credibility, upgrading journalism education to include information security is essential preparation for students at all levels.

Integrating information security concerns into journalism curricula, of course, requires both access to expertise and a commitment from academic leaders and existing faculty. As a 2016 report by the Knight Foundation into data journalism education found, however, finding faculty qualified to address digitally mediated reporting methods can be difficult,[27] and existing faculty are not always enthusiastic about integrating contemporary practices into their existing courses.

Unsurprisingly, one goal of this book is to provide interested educators—as well as newsroom professionals—with a useful foundation for understanding the principles of information security for journalists, in the hope that it can support earnest efforts to secure the present—and future—of journalistic practice. While there is still much work to be done, there is already much we can do—if we choose to invest in the idea that the work of journalism is to provide the public with the most comprehensive and credible understanding of the events that shape their worlds and to do so with integrity, accountability, and transparency.

NOTES

INTRODUCTION

1. Matthew Cole et al., "Top-Secret NSA Report Details Russian Hacking Effort Days Before 2016 Election," *The Intercept*, June 2017, https://theintercept.com/2017/06/05/top-secret-nsa-report-details-russian-hacking-effort-days-before-2016-election/.

2. Office of Public Affairs, "Federal Government Contractor in Georgia Charged with Removing and Mailing Classified Materials to a News Outlet," U.S. Department of Justice, June 2017, https://www.justice.gov/opa/pr/federal-government-contractor-georgia-charged-removing-and-mailing-classified-materials-news.

3. Justin C. Garrick, "Affidavit in Support of Application for Arrest Warrant," Federal Bureau of Investigation, June 2017, https://www.justice.gov/opa/press-release/file/971331/download.

4. Matt Ford, "The Feds Arrest an Alleged Leaker," *The Atlantic*, June 2017, https://www.theatlantic.com/politics/archive/2017/06/the-feds-arrest-a-alleged-leaker/529248/.

5. Micah Lee, "Ed Snowden Taught Me to Smuggle Secrets Past Incredible Danger. Now I Teach You," *The Intercept*, October 28, 2014, https://theintercept.com/2014/10/28/smuggling-snowden-secrets/.

6. Lorenzo Franceschi-Biccherai, "Meet the Man Hired to Make Sure the Snowden Docs Aren't Hacked," *Mashable*, May 27, 2014, https://mashable.com/2014/05/27/micah-lee-greenwald-snowden/#i7AOWSgVMsqj.

7. Andy Greenberg, "The Ex-Google Hacker Taking on the World's Spy Agencies," *Wired*, July 7, 2014, https://www.wired.com/2014/07/morgan-marquis-boire-first-look-media/.

8. Ben Smith, "The Intercept Promised to Reveal Everything. Then Its Own Scandal Hit," *New York Times*, September 3, 2020, updated September 4, 2020, https://www.nytimes.com/2020/09/13/business/media/the-intercept-source-reality-winner.html.

9. Garrick, "Affidavit."

10. Robert Graham, "How the Intercept Outed Reality Winner," *Errata Security*, June 6, 2017, https://blog.erratasec.com/2017/06/how-intercept-outed-reality-winner.html#.W7e-tehKiHt.

11. Joe Uchill, "WikiLeaks Offers $10,000 to Get Intercept Report Fired," *The Hill*, June 6, 2017, https://thehill.com/policy/cybersecurity/336518-wikileaks-offering -10000-to-get-intercept-reporter-fired.

12. Smith, "The Intercept Promised to Reveal Everything."

13. National Security Agency, "NSA Report on Russia Spearphishing," *The Intercept*, June 2017, https://www.documentcloud.org/documents/3766950-NSA-Report -on-Russia-Spearphishing.html#document/p1.

1. THE ESSENTIALS OF DIGITAL COMMUNICATIONS

1. Paul Baran, "On Distributed Communications Networks," *IEEE* CS-12, no. 1 (1964): http://www.cs.ucla.edu/classes/cs217/Baran64.pdf.

2. Elisa Shearer, "Social Media Outpaces Print Newspapers in the U.S. as a News Source," Pew Research Center, December 10, 2018, https://www.pewresearch.org/fact -tank/2018/12/10/social-media-outpaces-print-newspapers-in-the-u-s-as-a-news -source/.

3. Richard R. John, *Spreading the News: The American Postal System from Franklin to Morse* (Cambridge, MA: Harvard University Press, 1995).

4. John, *Spreading the News.*

5. Baran, "On Distributed Communications Networks."

6. Joseph Goldstein, "New York Police Are Using Covert Cell Phone Trackers, Civil Liberties Group Says," *New York Times*, February 11, 2016, https://www.nytimes .com/2016/02/12/nyregion/new-york-police-dept-cellphone-tracking-stingrays.html; Ali Winston, "Did the Police Spy on Black Lives Matter Protesters? The Answer May Soon Come Out," *New York Times*, January 14, 2019, https://www.nytimes.com/2019 /01/14/nyregion/nypd-black-lives-matter-surveillance.html.

7. Gabrielle Lim et al., "Burned After Reading: Endless Mayfly's Ephemeral Disinformation Campaign," *Citizen Lab*, 2019, https://citizenlab.ca/2019/05/burned-after -reading-endless-mayflys-ephemeral-disinformation-campaign/.

8. "SVETONI TRANQVILII VITA DIVI IVLI," http://thelatinlibrary.com /suetonius/suet.caesar.html#56.

9. Whitfield Diffie and Martin E. Hellman, "New Directions in Cryptography," invited paper, Stanford University, 1976, vol. IT-22.

10. Alma Whitten and J. D. Tygar, "Why Johnny Can't Encrypt: A Usability Evaluation of PGP 5.0," *Proceedings of the Eighth Conference on USENIX Security Symposium*, vol. 8 (Washington, DC: USENIX Association, 1999), 14.

11. Larry Greenemeier, "NSA Efforts to Evade Encryption Technology Damaged U.S. Cryptography Standard," *Scientific American*, September 18, 2013, https:// www.scientificamerican.com/article/nsa-nist-encryption-scandal/; Timothy B. Lee, "The Heartbleed Bug, Explained," *Vox*, May 14, 2015, https://www.vox.com/2014/6 /19/18076318/heartbleed.

12. Matt Fowler, "Armouring up Online: Duncan Campbell's Chief Techie Talks Crypto with El Reg," *The Register*, December 19, 2014, https://www.theregister.co.uk /2014/12/19/crypto_toolkit_1/?page=3.

2. DIGITAL DATA IN A LEGAL FRAME

1. Richard R. John, *Spreading the News: The American Postal System from Franklin to Morse* (Cambridge, MA: Harvard University Press, 1995).

2. Berger v. New York, 388 U.S. 41 (1967).

3. Justice John Marshall Harlan II, "Katz v. United States, Concurring," *Cornell Law School*, December 18, 1967, http://www.law.cornell.edu/supremecourt/text/389/347.

4. Justice Stewart, "Katz v. United States, Opinion of the Court," *Cornell Law School*, 1967, http://www.law.cornell.edu/supremecourt/text/389/347.

5. Justice Powell, "United States v. Miller," *Cornell Law School*, April 21, 1976, http://www.law.cornell.edu/supremecourt/text/425/435.

6. Justice Blackmun, "Smith v. Maryland," *Cornell Law School*, June 20, 1979, http://www.law.cornell.edu/supremecourt/text/442/735.

7. "Carpenter v. United States," *Oyez*, https://www.oyez.org/cases/2017/16-402.

8. Nathaniel Sobel, "Do Geofence Warrants Violate the Fourth Amendment?", *Lawfare*, February 2020, https://www.lawfareblog.com/do-geofence-warrants -violate-fourth-amendment; United States Code, part 1, chap. 121, Legal Information Institute, Cornell Law School, http://www.law.cornell.edu/uscode/text/18/part -I/chapter-121.

9. United States Code, part 1, chap. 119, Legal Information Institute, Cornell Law School, http://www.law.cornell.edu/uscode/text/18/part-I/chapter-119.

10. Josh Gerstein, "Obama Defends Leak Prosecutions," *Politico*, May 12, 2016, https://www.politico.com/blogs/under-the-radar/2016/05/obama-defends-leak -prosecutions-first-amendment-223134.

11. Avi Asher-Schapiro, "Leak Prosecutions Under Trump Chill National Security Beat," *Committee to Protect Journalists*, March 6, 2019, https://cpj.org/blog/2019 /03/leak-prosecutions-trump-national-security-beat.php.

12. Katie Benner, "Pentagon Analyst Is Charged in Leaks of Classified Reports," *New York Times*, October 9, 2019, updated October 14, 2019, https://www.nytimes .com/2019/10/09/us/politics/kyle-frese-classified-leaks.html; Peter Maass, "Jeffery Sterling, Convicted of Leaking About Botched CIA Program, Has Been Released from Prison," *The Intercept*, January 19, 2018, https://theintercept.com/2018/01/19/jeffrey -sterling-cia-leaking-prison/.

13. Matt Apuzzo, "Times Reporter Will Not Be Called to Testify in Leak Case," *New York Times*, January 12, 2015, https://www.nytimes.com/2015/01/13 /us/times-reporter-james-risen-will-not-be-called-to-testify-in-leak-case-lawyers -say.html.

14. Maass, "Jeffery Sterling."

15. Kathleen Ann Ruane, "Journalists' Privilege: Overview of the Law and Legislation in Recent Congresses," *Congressional Research Service*, January 19, 2011, http://www.fas.org/sgp/crs/secrecy/RL34193.pdf; India McKinney and Andrew Crocker, "Yes, Section 2015 Expired. Now What?," Electronic Frontier Foundation, April 16, 2020, https://www.eff.org/deeplinks/2020/04/yes-section-215-expired -now-what.

16. Adam Liptak, "A High-Tech War on Leaks," *New York Times*, February 11, 2012, http://www.nytimes.com/2012/02/12/sunday-review/a-high-tech-war-on-leaks.html.

17. United States Code, Legal Information Institute, Cornell Law School, http://www.law.cornell.edu/uscode/text/50/1861.

18. Charlie Savage and Leslie Kaufman, "Phone Records of Journalists Seized by U.S," *New York Times*, May 13, 2013, https://www.nytimes.com/2013/05/14/us/phone-records-of-journalists-of-the-associated-press-seized-by-us.html.

19. Charlie Savage, "Holder Tightens Rules on Getting Reporters' Data," *New York Times*, July 12, 2013, http://www.nytimes.com/2013/07/13/us/holder-to-tighten-rules-for-obtaining-reporters-data.html.

20. "Court Halts Police Subpoena for Media's Protest Images," Associated Press, August 20, 2020, https://apnews.com/article/4a725836de71e123c1437fc68f02948f.

21. Susan McGregor, "AP Phone Records Seizure Reveals Telecom's Risks for Journalists," *Columbia Journalism Review*, 2013, http://www.cjr.org/cloud_control/ap_phone_records_seizure_revea.php.

22. Department of Justice, *Searching and Seizing Computers and Obtaining Electronic Evidence in Criminal Investigations* (Washington, D.C.: Office of Legal Education Executive Office for United States Attorneys, 2009), 115–19, https://www.justice.gov/sites/default/files/criminal-ccips/legacy/2015/01/14/ssmanual2009.pdf; Guy Taylor, "Armed Agents Seize Records of Reporter, *Washington Times* Prepares Legal Action," *Washington Times*, October 25, 2013, http://www.washingtontimes.com/news/2013/oct/25/armed-agents-seize-records-reporter-washington-tim/.

23. Chimel v. California, 395 U.S. 752 (1969).

24. Riley v. California, 573 U.S. 373 (2014).

25. Sophia Cope and Adam Schwartz, "Ninth Circuit Goes a Step Further to Protect Privacy in Border Device Searches," Electronic Frontier Foundation, August 22, 2019, https://www.eff.org/deeplinks/2019/08/ninth-circuit-goes-step-further-protect-privacy-border-device-searches.

26. Mike Masnick, "Judge Says Giving Up Your Password May Be a 5th Amendment Violation," *Tech Dirt*, 2013, https://www.techdirt.com/articles/20130425/08171522834/judge-says-giving-up-your-password-may-be-5th-amendment-violation.shtml.

27. Marcia Hoffman, "Apple's Fingerprint ID May Mean You Can't 'Take the Fifth,'" *Wired*, September 12, 2013, http://www.wired.com/2013/09/the-unexpected-result-of-fingerprint-authentication-that-you-cant-take-the-fifth/; Lee Rainie, "Americans' Complicated Feelings About Social Media in an Era of Privacy Concerns," Pew Research Center, March 27, 2018, https://www.pewresearch.org/fact-tank/2018/03/27/americans-complicated-feelings-about-social-media-in-an-era-of-privacy-concerns/.

28. Issie Lapowsky, "New York's Privacy Bill Is Even Bolder Than California's," *Wired*, June 4, 2019 https://www.wired.com/story/new-york-privacy-act-bolder/.

29. Andrea Peterson, "The Government Can (Still) Read Most of Your Emails Without a Warrant," *Think Progress*, March 20, 2013, https://thinkprogress.org/the-government-can-still-read-most-of-your-emails-without-a-warrant-322fe6defc7b/.

30. David Ruiz, "Email Privacy Act Comes Back, Hopefully to Stay," Electronic Frontier Foundation, May 29, 2018, https://www.eff.org/deeplinks/2018/05/email -privacy-act-comes-back-hopefully-stay.

3. ASSESSING RISKS AND THREATS

1. Jillian Kramer, "Millennials May Be the Least Safe Generation Online," *Glamour*, November 23, 2015, https://www.glamour.com/story/safety-online-millennials.

4. EVERYDAY ESSENTIALS

1. "The Stanford Integrated Digital Library Project," National Science Foundation, https://www.nsf.gov/awardsearch/showAward?AWD_ID=9411306.
2. "Information Finding Projects in the Stanford Digital Library," Stanford Digital Libraries Technologies, http://ilpubs.stanford.edu:8091/diglib/pub/infofinding.html.
3. Sergey Brin and Lawrence Page, "The Anatomy of a Large-Scale Hypertextual Web Search Engine," *Computer Networks and ISDN Systems* 30 (1998): 107–17.
4. "Plan to Straighten Out Entire Life During Weeklong Vacation Yields Mixed Results," *The Onion*, July 18, 2001, https://www.theonion.com/plan-to-straighten-out -entire-life-during-weeklong-vaca-1819566088.
5. "Neo-Nazi SWATters Target Dozens of Journalists," *Krebson Security*, July 19, 2019, https://krebsonsecurity.com/2019/07/neo-nazi-swatters-target-dozens-of -journalists/; NYT Open Team, "How to Dox Yourself on the Internet," *NYT Open*, February 27, 2020, https://open.nytimes.com/how-to-dox-yourself-on-the-internet -d2892b4c5954.
6. Dan Goodin, "Bypassing TouchID Was 'No Challenge at All' Hacker Tells *Ars*," *Ars Technica*, September 24, 2013, https://arstechnica.com/information-technology /2013/09/touchid-hack-was-no-challenge-at-all-hacker-tells-ars/.
7. Marcia Hoffman, "Apple's Fingerprint ID May Mean You Can't 'Take the Fifth,'" *Wired*, September 12, 2013, http://www.wired.com/2013/09/the-unexpected -result-of-fingerprint-authentication-that-you-cant-take-the-fifth/.
8. Aaron Smith, "Password Management and Mobile Security," Pew Research Center, January 26, 2017, https://www.pewinternet.org/2017/01/26/2-password -management-and-mobile-security/; Alex Hern, "Google Aims to Kill Passwords by the End of This Year," *The Guardian*, May 24, 2016, https://www.theguardian.com /technology/2016/may/24/google-passwords-android.
9. Joseph Bonneau et al., "The Quest to Replace Passwords: A Framework for Comparative Evaluation of Web Authentication Schemes," IEEE, 2012, https://ieeexplore .ieee.org/abstract/document/6234436.
10. Lorenzo Franceschi-Bicchierai, "The SIM Hackers," *Vice*, July 17, 2018, https:// www.vice.com/en_us/article/vbqax3/hackers-sim-swapping-steal-phone-numbers -instagram-bitcoin; Brian Barrett, "How Even the FTC's Lead Technologist Can Get Hacked," *Wired*, June 9, 2016, https://www.wired.com/2016/06/even-ftcs-lead-tech nologist-can-get-hacked/.

11. Andy Greenberg, "How the Syrian Electronic Army Hacked Us: A Detailed Timeline," *Forbes*, February 20, 2014, https://www.forbes.com/sites/andygreenberg/2014/02/20/how-the-syrian-electronic-army-hacked-us-a-detailed-timeline/.

12. Mike Butcher, "UK Health Service Hit by Ransomware, Amid Possible Global Attack on Systems," *TechCrunch*, May 12, 2017, https://techcrunch.com/2017/05/12/uk-health-service-hit-by-ransomware-amid-possible-global-attack-on-systems/; Zack Whittaker, "Two Years After WannaCry, a Million Computers Remain at Risk," *TechCrunch*, May 12, 2019, https://techcrunch.com/2019/05/12/wannacry-two-years-on/; "NotPetya Cyber-Attack Cost TNT at Least $300m," *BBC News*, September 20, 2017, https://www.bbc.com/news/technology-41336086; Andy Greenberg, "The Untold Story of NotPetya, the Most Devastating Cyberattack in History," *Wired*, August 22, 2018, https://www.wired.com/story/notpetya-cyberattack-ukraine-russia-code-crashed-the-world/.

13. Elissa Redmiles, "Why Installing Software Updates Makes Us Wanna Cry," *Scientific American*, May 16, 2017, https://www.scientificamerican.com/article/why-installing-software-updates-makes-us-wannacry/.

14. Michael Fagan, Mohammad Maifi Hasan Khan, and Ross Buck, "A Study of Users' Experiences and Beliefs About Software Update Messages," *Computers in Human Behavior* 51, part A (2015): 504–19, https://doi.org/10.1016/j.chb.2015.04.075.

5. FUNDAMENTALS FOR FIELD REPORTING

1. Wesley Lowery, "In Ferguson, Washington Post Reporter Wesley Lowery Gives Account of His Arrest," *Washington Post*, August 13, 2014, https://www.washingtonpost.com/politics/in-ferguson-washington-post-reporter-wesley-lowery-gives-account-of-his-arrest/2014/08/13/0fe25c0e-2359-11e4-86ca-6f03cbd15c1a_story.html; Wesley Lowery, "Wesley Lowery's Arrest," Facing History and Ourselves & the News Literacy Project, https://www.facinghistory.org/resource-library/video/wesley-lowerys-arrest.

2. "Washington Post Journalist Chased by Looters in Chicago," U.S. Press Freedom Tracker, August 10, 2010, https://pressfreedomtracker.us/all-incidents/.

3. "Public Relations Department," Freedom of the Press Foundation, December 14, 2016, https://www.documentcloud.org/documents/3238288-Camera-Encryption-Letter.html; Zack Whittaker, "Camera Makers Resist Encryption, Despite Warnings from Photographers," *ZD Net*, January 31, 2018, https://www.zdnet.com/article/a-year-later-camera-makers-still-resist-encryption/.

4. Irwin Reyes et al., " 'Won't Somebody Think of the Children?' Examining COPPA Compliance at Scale," Pet Symposium, 2018, https://petsymposium.org/2018/files/papers/issue3/popets-2018-0021.pdf.

6. REPORTING ABROAD

1. CBP cannot legally deny entry to U.S. citizens.

2. Seth Harp, "I'm a Journalist but I Didn't Fully Realize the Terrible Power of U.S. Border Officials Until They Violated My Rights and Privacy" *The Intercept*, June 22, 2019, https://theintercept.com/2019/06/22/cbp-border-searches-journalists/.

3. Sophia Cope and Adam Schwartz, "Ninth Circuit Goes a Step Further to Protect Privacy in Border Device Searches," Electronic Frontier Foundation, August 22, 2019, https://www.eff.org/deeplinks/2019/08/ninth-circuit-goes-step-further-protect-privacy-border-device-searches.

4. Patrick T. Fallon, "Nothing to Declare: Why U.S. Border Agency's Vast Stop and Search Powers Undermine Press Freedom," Committee to Protect Journalists, October 22, 2018, https://cpj.org/reports/2018/10/nothing-to-declare-us-border-search-phone-press-freedom-cbp.php.

5. Kyllo v. United States, *Oyez*, https://www.oyez.org/cases/2000/99-8508.

6. Lorenzo Franceschi-Bicchierai, "No, You Don't Need a Burner Phone at a Hacking Conference," *Vice*, July 18, 2019, https://www.vice.com/en_us/article/bj9qbw/no-you-dont-need-a-burner-phone-at-a-hacking-conference.

7. Craig Wigginton, "Global Mobile Consumer Trends, 2nd Edition," Deloitte & Touche, LLP, 2017, https://www2.deloitte.com/content/dam/Deloitte/us/Documents/technology-media-telecommunications/us-global-mobile-consumer-survey-second-edition.pdf; Stephen J. Blumberg and Julian V. Luke, "Wireless Substitution: Early Release of Estimates from the National Health Interview Survey, July–December 2016," National Center for Health Statistics, July–December 2016, https://www.cdc.gov/nchs/data/nhis/earlyrelease/wireless201705.pdf.

8. Wigginton, "Global Mobile Consumer Trends."

9. Mike Masnick, "The Ultimate Bad Take: Bloomberg's Leonid Bershidsky Thinks a WhatsApp Vulnerability Proves End to End Encryption Is Useless," *Tech Dirt*, May 14, 2019, https://www.techdirt.com/articles/20190514/11481042210/ultimate-bad-take-bloombergs-leonid-bershidsky-thinks-whatsapp-vulnerability-proves-end-to-end-encryption-is-useless.shtml.

10. WhatsApp, "Privacy Notice," WhatsApp, July 7, 2012, https://www.whatsapp.com/legal?doc=privacy-policy&version=20120707.

11. Timothy B. Lee, "The Heartbleed Bug, Explained," *Vox*, May 14, 2015, https://www.vox.com/2014/6/19/18076318/heartbleed; Jon Brodkin, "Tech Giants, Chastened by Heartbleed, Finally Agree to Fund Open SSL," *Ars Technica*, April 24, 2014, http://arstechnica.com/information-technology/2014/04/tech-giants-chastened-by-heartbleed-finally-agree-to-fund-openssl/.

12. Bambuser (@bambuser), "We just got this: 'secret police arrested a person because he had bambuser application on his mobile' Disgusting to hear! #Assad #Syria," Twitter, September 16, 2012, https://twitter.com/bambuser/status/247397258918776834.

7. CREATING A CULTURE OF SECURITY

1. Jesse Holcomb, "Investigative Journalists and Digital Security," Pew Research Center, February 5, 2015, https://www.journalism.org/wp-content/uploads/sites/8/2015/02/PJ_InvestigativeJournalists_0205152.pdf.

2. Susan E. McGregor, Franziska Roesner, and Kelly Caine, "Individual Versus Organiztional Computer Security and Privacy Concerns in Journalism," *Sciendo*, July 14, 2016, https://content.sciendo.com/view/journals/popets/2016/4/article-p418.xml.

3. Atul Gawande, "Slow Ideas," *New Yorker*, July 22, 2013, https://www.newyorker .com/magazine/2013/07/29/slow-ideas.

4. Atul Gawande, "On Washing Hands," *Counter Punch*, March 24, 2007, https:// www.counterpunch.org/2007/03/24/on-washing-hands/; Atul Gawande, "Hand Washing: A Deadly Dilemma," Association for Psychological Science, November 29, 2011, https://www.psychologicalscience.org/news/full-frontal-psychology/hand -washing-a-deadly-dilemma.html.

5. P. Dolan et al., "Influencing Behavior Through Public Policy," Institute for Government, Cabinet Office, 2010, http://www.instituteforgovernment.org.uk/sites /default/files/publications/MINDSPACE.pdf.

6. Adam Grant and David Hoffman, "It's Not All About Me: Motivating Hand Hygiene Among Health Care Professionals by Focusing on Patients," *Psychological Science* 22 (2011): 1494–99.

7. P. Wesley Schulz et al., "The Constructive, Destructive, and Reconstructive Power of Social Norms," *Psychological Science* 18, no. 5 (May 2007): 429–34.

8. Harry Brignull and Alexander Darlington, "What Are Dark Patterns?," https:// www.darkpatterns.org/.

9. Grant and Hoffman, "It's Not All About Me."

10. Maria Bada, Angela M. Sasse, and Jason R. C. Nurse, "Cyber Security Awareness Campaigns: Why Do They Fail to Change Behavior?" CoRR, 2019, http://arxiv .org/abs/1901.02672.

8. SECURITY STRATEGIES FOR TEAMS

1. Ethan Chiel, "The *Gawker*–Hulk Hogan Trial and the Horror of Work Chats That Stick Around Forever," *Splinter*, March 9, 2016, https://splinternews.com/the -gawker-hulk-hogan-trial-and-the-horror-of-work-chat-1793855252.

2. Samuel Greengard, "Getting Rid of the Paper Chase," *Workforce*, November 1999, https://www.questia.com/read/1P3-46378607/getting-rid-of-the-paper -chase.

3. William Turton, "Dear Slack, Please Add OTR," *Vice*, December 2, 2015, 8, https://www.vice.com/en_us/article/8q89ba/dear-slack-please-add-otr; Joseph Cox, "Why Slack Doesn't Have End-to End Encryption Because Your Boss Doesn't Want It," *Vice*, October 16, 2018, https://www.vice.com/en_us/article/kzj5xn/why-slack -doesnt-have-end-to-end-encryption-boss.

4. Adrianne Jeffries, "We're Taking a Break from Slack," *Vice*, May 16, 2016, https:// www.vice.com/en_us/article/aekk85/were-taking-a-break-from-slack-heres-why.

5. Adrianne Jeffries, "An Oral History of Our Week Without Slack," *Vice*, May 20, 2016, https://www.vice.com/en/article/gv5jpy/an-oral-history-of-our-week-without -slack.

6. Susan E. McGregor, Franziska Roesner, and Kelly Caine, "Individual Versus Organizational Computer Security and Privacy Concerns in Journalism," *Sciendo*, July 14, 2016, https://content.sciendo.com/view/journals/popets/2016/4/article-p418 .xml.

7. Mike Issac, "WhatsApp Introduces End-to-End Encryption," *New York Times*, April 5, 2016, https://www.nytimes.com/2016/04/06/technology/whatsapp-messaging -service-introduces-full-encryption.html; Natalie Gagliordi, "Slack Launches Enterprise Key Management, a Tool That Gives Admins Control Over Encryption Keys," *ZD Net*, March 18, 2019, https://www.zdnet.com/article/slack-launches-enterprise-key -management-a-tool-that-gives-admins-control-over-encryption-keys/.

8. Steve Lohr, "A 10-Digit Key to Your Private Life: Your Cell Phone Number," *New York Times*, November 12, 2016, https://www.nytimes.com/2016/11/13/business /cellphone-number-social-security-number-10-digit-key-code-to-private-life.html.

9. Susan E. McGregor, Elizabeth Anne Watkins, and Kelly Caine, "Would You Slack That? The Impact of Security and Privacy on Cooperative Newsroom Work," *Proceedings of the ACM on Human-Computer Interaction*, December 2017, http://doi .acm.org/10.1145/3134710.

10. Micah Lee, "Ed Snowden Taught Me to Smuggle Secrets Past Incredible Danger. Now I Teach You," *The Intercept*, October 28, 2014, https://theintercept.com/2014 /10/28/smuggling-snowden-secrets/.

11. Alma Whitten and J. D. Tygar, "Why Johnny Can't Encrypt: A Usability Evaluation of PGP 5.0," *Proceedings of the Eighth Conference on USENIX Security Symposium*, vol. 8 (Washington, DC: USENIX Association, 1999); Steve Sheng et al., "Why Johnny Still Can't Encrypt: Evaluating the Usability of Email Encryption Software," Symposium on Usable Privacy and Security, 2006, 3–4; Scott Ruoti et al., "Why Johnny Still, Still Can't Encrypt: Evaluating the Usability of a Modern PGP Client," *arXiv* preprint (2015): 1510.08555.

12. Lorenzo Franceschi-Bicchierai, "People Are Freaking Out That PGP Is 'Broken'—but You Shouldn't Be Using It Anyway," *Vice*, May 14, 2018, https://www .vice.com/en_us/article/3k4nd9/pgp-gpg-efail-vulnerability.

13. Ken Reese et al., "A Usability Study of Five Two-Factor Authentication Methods," Usenix, August 12–13, 2019, https://www.usenix.org/system/files/soups2019 -reese.pdf.

14. Michael Fagan et al., "An Investigation Into Users' Considerations Towards Using Password Managers," *Springer Open*, March 15, 2017, https://hcis-journal .springeropen.com/articles/10.1186/s13673-017-0093-6.

15. Alma Whitten and J. D. Tygar, *Proceedings of the 8th Conference on USENIX Security Symposium*, vol. 8 (Washington, DC: USENIX Association, 1999), 14; Sheng et al., "Why Johnny Still Can't Encrypt"; Ruoti et al., "Why Johnny Still, Still Can't Encrypt."

9. WORKING WITH FREELANCERS AND COMMUNITY CONTRIBUTORS

1. Matthew S. Weber and Allie Kosterich, "Managing a 21st-Century Newsroom Workforce: A Case Study of NYC News Media," TOW Center for Digital Journalism, March 22, 2018, https://www.cjr.org/tow_center_reports/managing-a-newsroom -workforce-nyc-case-study.php.

2. ACOS Alliance, "We Must Embed a Culture of Safety in Our Profession," ACOS Alliance, 2016, https://www.acosalliance.org/the-principles.

3. "Anonymous Sources," Associated Press, https://www.ap.org/about/news-values -and-principles/telling-the-story/anonymous-sources.

4. "Why the *Times* Published Details of the Whistle-Blower's Identity," *New York Times*, September 26, 2019, https://www.nytimes.com/2019/09/26/reader-center /whistle-blower-identity.html; Julian E. Barnes et al., "White House Knew of Whistle-Blower's Allegations Soon After Trump's Call with Ukraine Leader," *New York Times*, September 26, 2019, updated November 26, 2019, https://www.nytimes.com /2019/09/26/us/politics/who-is-whistleblower.html.

5. Eliana Miller and Nicole Asbury, "Photographers Are Being Called On to Stop Showing Protesters' Faces. Should They?," *Poynter*, June 2020, https://www.poynter .org/ethics-trust/2020/should-journalists-show-protesters-faces/; Kelly McBride, "Should Images of Protesters Be Blurred to Protect Them from Retribution?," NPR, June 18, 2020, https://www.npr.org/sections/publiceditor/2020/06/18/879223467 /should-images-of-protesters-be-blurred-to-protect-them-from-retribution; Mark Morales and Laura Ly, "Released NYPD Emails Show Extensive Surveillance of Black Lives Matter Protesters," CNN, January 18, 2019, https://www.cnn.com/2019/01/18 /us/nypd-black-lives-matter-surveillance/index.html; George Joseph and Murtaza Hussain, "FBI Tracked an Activist with Black Lives Matter as They Traveled Across the U.S., Documents Show," *The Intercept*, March 19, 2018, https://theintercept.com /2018/03/19/black-lives-matter-fbi-surveillance/.

6. ACOS Alliance, "We Must Embed a Culture of Safety."

7. Fergus Bell, in Craig Silverman, ed., *Verification Handbook for Investigative Reporting* (2015), chap. 8, http://verificationhandbook.com/.

8. Josh Sanburn, "One Year After Filming Eric Garner's Fatal Confrontation with Police, Ramsey Orta's Life Has Been Upended," *Time*, https://time.com/ramsey-orta -eric-garner-video/.

9. Chloe Cooper Jones, "Fearing for His Life," *The Verge*, March 13, 2019, https:// www.theverge.com/2019/3/13/18253848/eric-garner-footage-ramsey-orta-police -brutality-killing-safety; Sanburn, "One Year After."

10. Associated Press, "Witness Regrets 'Stupid' Decision to Publish Film of Paris Policeman's Murder," *The Guardian*, January 12, 2015, https://www.theguardian.com /world/2015/jan/12/man-regrets-stupid-decision-to-publish-shocking-film-of-paris -policemans.

10. ESSENTIALS FOR SMALL NEWSROOMS

1. Sarah Holder, "When Local Newsrooms Shrink, Fewer Candidates Run for Mayor," *Bloomberg City Lab*, April 11, 2019, https://www.citylab.com/life/2019/04 /local-news-decline-journalist-news-desert-california-data/586759/; Elizabeth Grieco, "U.S. Newspapers Have Shed Half of Their Newsroom Employees Since 2008," Pew Research Center, April 20, 2020, https://www.pewresearch.org/fact-tank/2020/04/20 /u-s-newsroom-employment-has-dropped-by-a-quarter-since-2008; Christopher Ali

and Damian Radcliffe, "Life at Small-Market Newspapers: A Survey of Over 400 Journalists," Tow Center for Digital Journalism, May 10, 2017, https://www.cjr.org /tow_center_reports/local-journalism-survey.php; Sara Fischer, "Newsroom Layoffs Will Be Brutal in 2020," *Axios*, July 21, 2020, https://www.axios.com/newsroom -layoffs-2020-c509fb2d-ef58–4fcf-bcdd-3d40022a7a39.html.

2. Steve Lohr, "A 10-Digit Key to Your Private Life: Your Cell Phone Number," *New York Times*, November 12, 2016, https://www.nytimes.com/2016/11/13/business /cellphone-number-social-security-number-10-digit-key-code-to-private-life.html; Brian X. Chan, "I Shared My Phone Number. I Learned I Shouldn't Have," *New York Times*, August 15, 2019, https://www.nytimes.com/2019/08/15/technology /personaltech/i-shared-my-phone-number-i-learned-i-shouldnt-have.html; Joseph Cox, "T-Mobile 'Put My Life in Danger' Says Woman Stalked with Black Market Location Data," *Vice*, August 21, 2019, https://www.vice.com/amp/en_us/article /8xwngb/t-mobile-put-my-life-in-danger-says-victim-of-black-market-location-data; Brian Barrett, "How Even the FTC's Lead Technologist Can Get Hacked," *Wired*, June 9, 2016, https://www.wired.com/2016/06/even-ftcs-lead-technologist-can-get -hacked/; Lorenzo Franceschi-Bicchierai, "The SIM Hackers," *Vice*, July 17, 2018, https://www.vice.com/en_us/article/vbqax3/hackers-sim-swapping-steal-phone -numbers-instagram-bitcoin.

3. Susan McGregor, "Legalized Sale of Browser Histories Should Worry Journalists," *Columbia Journalism Review*, April 12, 2017, https://www.cjr.org/politics/browser -history-privacy-trump.php; Jon Brodkin, "FTC Investigates Whether ISPs Sell Your Browsing History and Location Data," *Ars Technica*, March 27, 2019, https:// arstechnica.com/tech-policy/2019/03/ftc-investigates-whether-isps-sell-your -browsing-history-and-location-data/.

4. Alan Henry, "Five Best VPN Service Providers," *Life Hacker*, March 23, 2014, http://lifehacker.com/5935863/five-best-vpn-service-providers; Liam Tung, "Google Parent's Free DIY VPN: Alphabet's Outline Keeps Out Web Snoops," *ZD Net*, March 21, 2018, https://www.zdnet.com/article/google-parents-free-diy-vpn-alphabets -outline-keeps-out-web-snoops/.

5. Susan E. McGregor, Elizabeth Anne Watkins, and Kelly Caine, "Would You Slack That? The Impact of Security and Privacy on Cooperative Newsroom Work," *Proceedings of the ACM on Human-Computer Interaction*, December 2017, http://doi .acm.org/10.1145/3134710.

6. "With Another Ransomware Attack, Time for Stations to Protect Themselves," *Inside Radio*, July 23, 2019, http://www.insideradio.com/free/with-another-ransom ware-attack-time-for-stations-to-protect-themselves/article_47d43ff6-ad29-11e9 -9457-4b7b575e0247.html; Jon Brooks, "The Crippling Ransomware Attack on a San Francisco NPR Member Station," KQED, October 31, 2017, updated January 8, 2018, https://www.kqed.org/futureofyou/436414/the-crippling-ransomware-attack-on -kqed-the-inside-story.

7. Sharon Ringel and Angela Woodall, "A Public Record at Risk: The Dire State of News Archiving in the Digital Age," TOW Center for Digital Journalism, March 28, 2019, https://www.cjr.org/tow_center_reports/the-dire-state-of-news -archiving-in-the-digital-age.php.

8. Shan Wang, "We're Getting Closer to the Day When News Apps and Interactives Can Be Easily Preserved in Perpetuity," Nieman Lab, August 22, 2018, https://www.niemanlab.org/2018/08/were-getting-closer-to-the-day-when-news-apps-and-interactives-can-be-easily-preserved-in-perpetuity/.

9. Andy Greenberg, "How the Syrian Electronic Army Hacked Us: A Detailed Timeline," *Forbes*, February 20, 2014, https://www.forbes.com/sites/andygreenberg/2014/02/20/how-the-syrian-electronic-army-hacked-us-a-detailed-timeline/; Julia Angwin, "Cheap Tricks: The Low Cost of Internet Harassment," *ProPublica*, November 9, 2017, https://www.propublica.org/article/cheap-tricks-the-low-cost-of-internet-harassment.

10. Rani Molla, "These Publications Have the Most to Lose from Facebook's New Algorithm Changes," *Vox*, January 25, 2018, https://www.vox.com/2018/1/25/16927676/facebook-algorithm-change-publisher-traffic-lose-advertising-reach-distribution.

11. Susan McGregor et al., "Creative and Set in Their Ways: Challenges of Security Sensemaking in Newsrooms," USENIX, 2017, https://www.usenix.org/conference/foci17/workshop-program/presentation/watkins; Susan E. McGregor et al., *Investigating the Computer Security Practices and Needs of Journalists* (Washington, DC: USENIX, 2015), 399–414.

12. McGregor, *Investigating the Computer Security Practices and Needs of Journalists*.

13. Kate Cox, "It's Creepy, but Not Illegal, for This Website to Provide All Your Public Info to Anyone," *Consumer Reports*, 2018, https://www.consumerreports.org/consumerist/its-creepy-but-not-illegal-for-this-website-to-provide-all-your-public-info-to-anyone/.

11. MANAGING RISK FOR A MIDSIZED NEWSROOM

1. Julia Angwin et al., "Despite Disavowals, Leading Tech Companies Help Extremist Sites Monetize Hate," *ProPublica*, August 19, 2017, https://www.propublica.org/article/leading-tech-companies-help-extremist-sites-monetize-hate.

2. Julia Angwin, "Cheap Tricks: The Low Cost of Internet Harassment," *ProPublica*, November 9, 2017, https://www.propublica.org/article/cheap-tricks-the-low-cost-of-internet-harassment.

3. Angwin, "Cheap Tricks."

4. Jon Brooks, "The Crippling Ransomware Attack on a San Francisco NPR Member Station," KQED, October 31, 2017, updated January 8, 2018, https://www.kqed.org/futureofyou/436414/the-crippling-ransomware-attack-on-kqed-the-inside-story.

5. "New York Launches 311 Citizen Service System," *Government Technology*, May 20, 2003, https://www.govtech.com/public-safety/New-York-Launches-311-Citizen-Service.html.

6. Steven Johnson, "What a Hundred Million Calls to 311 Reveal About New York," *Wired*, November 1, 2010, https://www.wired.com/2010/11/ff_311_new_york/.

7. Logan McDonald, "How Buzzfeed's Tech Team Helps Journalists Report on Technology with Authority," *BuzzFeed*, September 4, 2019, https://tech.buzzfeed.com /tech-and-news-working-group-7dabaaa38e45.

8. NYT Open Team, "How to Dox Yourself on the Internet," *NYT Open*, February 27, 2020, https://open.nytimes.com/how-to-dox-yourself-on-the-internet -d2892b4c5954.

12. SECURITY STRATEGIES FOR LARGE NEWSROOMS

1. "Erinmichelle Perri Joins the *Times* as Chief Information Security Officer," New York Times Company, August 12, 2019, https://www.nytco.com/press/erinmichelle -perri-joins-the-times-as-chief-information-security-officer/.

2. Susan E. McGregor, Franziska Roesner, and Kelly Caine, "Individual Versus Organizational Computer Security and Privacy Concerns in Journalism," *Proceedings on Privacy Enhancing Technologies* 4 (2016): 418–35, https://doi.org/10.1515/popets -2016-0048.

13. FACING THREATS TO THE PROFESSION

1. Beth O'Malley, "Antonio French's Tweets Chronicled Ferguson Protests," *St. Louis Post-Dispatch*, August 29, 2014, https://www.stltoday.com/news/multimedia /special/antonio-french-s-tweets-chronicled-ferguson-protests/article_ffabdcf0-405c -5ce3-82bb-e32560915ed4.html; Shannon Luibrand, "How a Death in Ferguson Sparked a Movement in America," *CBS News*, August 7, 2015, https://www.cbsnews .com/news/how-the-black-lives-matter-movement-changed-america-one-year-later/.

2. Lowery, "In Ferguson"; Camille Drouet, "Michael Brown Murder: Understand Everything About the Affair Shaking the United States," *Le Monde*, August 14, 2014, updated August 21, 2014, https://www.lemonde.fr/ameriques/article/2014/08/14 /meurtre-de-michael-brown-tout-comprendre-de-l-affaire-qui-secoue-l-amerique _4471464_3222.html.

3. Keya Vakil, "The News Media Whitewashed Police Brutality for Decades. Here's Why We Believed Them," *Courier*, July 7, 2020, https://couriernewsroom.com/2020 /07/07/the-news-media-whitewashed-police-brutality-for-decades-heres-why-we -believed-them/.

4. Craig Silverman, "I Helped Popularize the Term 'Fake News' and Now I Cringe Every Time I Hear it," *BuzzFeed News*, December 31, 2017, https://www.buzzfeednews .com/article/craigsilverman/i-helped-popularize-the-term-fake-news-and-now-i -cringe.

5. A. G. Sulzberger, "The Growing Threat to Journalism Around the World," *New York Times*, September 23, 2019, https://www.nytimes.com/2019/09/23/opinion/press -freedom-arthur-sulzberger.html.

6. Amy Mitchell et al., "Many Americans Say Made-Up News Is a Critical Problem That Needs to Be Fixed," Pew Research Center, June 5, 2019, https://www

.journalism.org/2019/06/05/many-americans-say-made-up-news-is-a-critical -problem-that-needs-to-be-fixed/.

7. Fergus Bell, in Craig Silverman, ed., *Verification Handbook for Investigative Reporting* (2015), chap. 8, http://verificationhandbook.com/; "Misinformation Is Damaging Communities Around the World," *First Draft*, https://firstdraftnews.org/.

8. Joan Donovan and Brian Friedberg, "Source Hacking: Media Manipulation in Practice," *Data and Society*, https://datasociety.net/wp-content/uploads/2019/09 /Source-Hacking_Hi-res.pdf.

9. Bell, *Verification Handbook*.

10. Donovan and Friedberg, "Source Hacking."

11. Allie Conti, "Neo-Nazi to Troll Army: 'We Have to Be Sexy' at the Big Alt-Right Rally," *Vice*, August 9, 2017, https://www.vice.com/en_us/article/599zmx/neo -nazi-to-troll-army-we-have-to-be-sexy-at-the-big-alt-right-rally; Andrew Anglin, "PSA: When the Alt-Right Hits the Street, You Wanna Be Ready," *Daily Stormer*, August 9, 2017, https://dailystormer.name/psa-when-the-internet-becomes-real-life-and-the-alt-right-hits-the-street-you-wanna-be-ready/.

12. "Washington Post Journalist Chased by Looters in Chicago," U.S. Press Freedom Tracker, August 10, 2010, https://pressfreedomtracker.us/all-incidents/; "Explore CPJ's Database of Attacks on the Press," Committee to Protect Journalists, https:// cpj.org/data.

13. Michelle Ferrier, "Attacks and Harassment: The Impact on Female Journalists and Their Reporting," International Women's Media Foundation, September 2018, https://www.iwmf.org/wp-content/uploads/2018/09/Attacks-and-Harassment.pdf.

14. Ferrier, "Attacks and Harassment."

15. "Online Harrassment Field Manual," PEN America, https://online0p6.75ha rassmentfieldmanual.pen.org/best-practices-for-employers/.

16. "Online Harrassment Field Manual."

17. "On Combating Racism and Discrimination at the *Post*," *New York Times*, 2020, https://int.nyt.com/data/documenthelper/7022-letter-from-washington-post-un /1501aa1ca97145b26b2d/optimized/full.pdf#page=1; Ben Smith, "Inside the Revolts Erupting in America's Big Newsrooms," *New York Times*, June 7, 2020, updated June 9, 2020, https://www.nytimes.com/2020/06/07/business/media/new-york-times -washington-post-protests.html; Wesley Lowery, "A Reckoning Over Objectivity, Led by Black Journalists," *New York Times*, June 23, 2020, https://www.nytimes.com/2020 /06/23/opinion/objectivity-black-journalists-coronavirus.html; Khadeeja Safdar, Jeffrey A. Trachtenberg, and Benjamin Mullin, "America's Newsrooms Face a Reckoning on Race After Floyd Protests," *Wall Street Journal*, June 15, 2020, https://www .wsj.com/articles/americas-newsrooms-face-a-reckoning-on-race-after-floyd-protests -11592256570; David Folkenflik, "Rancor Erupts In *LA Times* Newsroom Over Race, Equity, and Protest Coverage," NPR, June 15, 2020, https://www.npr.org/2020/06 /15/874530954/rancor-erupts-in-la-times-newsroom-over-race-equity-and-protest -coverage.

18. Marc Tracy and Rachel Abrams, "Police Target Journalists as Trump Blames 'Lamestream Media' for Protests," *New York Times*, June 1, 2020, updated June 12, 2020, https://www.nytimes.com/2020/06/01/business/media/reporters-protests-geo

rge-floyd.html; Laura Hazard Owen, "'This Puts Black *NY Times* Staff In Danger': *New York Times* Staffers Band Together to Protest Tom Cotton's Anti-Protest Op-Ed," Nieman Lab, June 4, 2020, https://www.niemanlab.org/2020/06/this-puts-black -people-in-danger-new-york-times-staffers-band-together-to-protest-tom-cottons-anti -protest-editorial/.

19. Marc Tracy, "Senator's 'Send In the Troops' Op-Ed in the *Times* Draws Online Ire," *New York Times*, June 3, 2020, https://www.nytimes.com/2020/06/03/business /tom-cotton-op-ed.html.

20. Ben Popken, "Russian Trolls Duped Global Media and Nearly 40 Celebrities," *NBC News*, November 3, 2017, https://www.nbcnews.com/tech/social-media/trump -other-politicians-celebs-shared-boosted-russian-troll-tweets-n817036.

21. Georgia Wells and Deepa Seetharaman, "Facebook Users Were Unwitting Targets of Russia-Backed Scheme," *Wall Street Journal*, October 13, 2017, https://www .wsj.com/articles/facebook-users-were-unwitting-targets-of-russia-backed-scheme -1507918659.

22. Rachelle Hampton, "The Black Feminists Who Saw the Alt-Right Threat Coming," *Slate*, April 23, 2019, https://slate.com/technology/2019/04/black-feminists -alt-right-twitter-gamergate.html.

23. I'Nasah Crockett, "Power Talks: I'Nasah Crockett on Black Women and Representation in Media," interview by Kim Power, *Srccon Power*, December 13, 2018, article, 10:15, https://power.srccon.org/transcripts/SRCCONPOWER2018-talks -inasah/.

24. "Online Harassment Field Manual."

25. Melissa Lyttle (melissalyttle), "Ano = anus, año = year. Tildes matter. So does diversity in a newsroom," Twitter, June 30, 2018, https://twitter.com/melissalyttle /status/1013184166916059136.

14. LOOKING AHEAD

1. Dan Kennedy, "Exposing the 'Pink Slime' Journalism of Journatic," *Media Nation*, July 5, 2012, https://dankennedy.net/2012/07/05/exposing-pink-slime -journalism/.

2. "Switcheroo: Forgive Us Our Press Passes," narr. Sarah Koenig, *This American Life*, June 29, 2012, https://www.thisamericanlife.org/468/transcript.

3. Carol Thompson, "Dozens of New Websites Appear to Be Michigan Local News Outlets, but with Political Bent," *Lansing State Journal*, October 20, 2019, updated October 22, 2019, https://www.lansingstatejournal.com/story/news/local/2019/10/21 /lansing-sun-new-sites-michigan-local-news-outlets/3984689002/; Priyanjana Bengani, "As Election Looms, a Network of Mysterious 'Pink Slime' Local News Outlets Nearly Triples in Size," *Columbia Journalism Review*, August 4, 2020, https://www.cjr .org/analysis/as-election-looms-a-network-of-mysterious-pink-slime-local-news -outlets-nearly-triples-in-size.php.

4. Art Swift, "Americans' Trust in Mass Media Sinks to New Low," *Gallup*, September 14, 2016, https://news.gallup.com/poll/195542/americans-trust-mass-media -sinks-new-low.aspx.

5. Mitchell, "Many Americans."

6. Elisa Shearer, "Local News Is Playing an Important Role for Americans During COVID-19 Outbreak," Pew Research Center Fact Tank, July 2, 2020, https://www.pewresearch.org/fact-tank/2020/07/02/local-news-is-playing-an-important-role-for-americans-during-covid-19-outbreak/.

7. John Sands, "Local News Is More Trusted Than National News—but That Could Change," Knight Foundation, October 29, 2019, https://knightfoundation.org/articles/local-news-is-more-trusted-than-national-news-but-that-could-change/.

8. Emily Dreyfuss and Issie Lapowsky, "Facebook Is Changing News Feed (Again) to Stop Fake News," *Wired*, April 10, 2019, https://www.wired.com/story/facebook-click-gap-news-feed-changes/; AI Initiative, "Press Release: Artificial Intelligence and the News—Seven Ideas Receive Funding to Ensure AI Is Used in Public Interest," *AI Initiative*, March 12, 2019, https://aiethicsinitiative.org/news/2019/3/12/artificial-intelligence-and-the-news-seven-ideas-receive-funding-to-ensure-ai-is-used-in-the-public-interest; DARPA, "Semantic Forensics (SemaFor)," August, 2019, https://www.grants.gov/web/grants/view-opportunity.html?oppId=319894.

9. Adam B. Schiff, Stephanie Murphy, and Carlos Curbelo, Office of the Director of National Intelligence Deep Fakes Letter, September 18, 2020, https://schiff.house.gov/imo/media/doc/2018-09%20ODNI%20Deep%20Fakes%20letter.pdf.

10. Editorial Board, "Deepfakes Are Dangerous—and They Target a Huge Weakness," *Washington Post*, June 16, 2019, https://www.washingtonpost.com/opinions/deepfakes-are-dangerous--and-they-target-a-huge-weakness/2019/06/16/d3bdbf08-8ed2-11e9-b08e-cfd89bd36d4e_story.html; Oscar Schwartz, "You Thought Fake News Was Bad? Deep Fakes Are Where Truth Goes to Die," *Guardian*, November 12, 2018, https://www.theguardian.com/technology/2018/nov/12/deep-fakes-fake-news-truth; Donie O'Sullivan, "Lawmakers Warn of 'Deepfake' Videos Ahead of 2020 Election," *CNN Business*, January 28, 2019, https://www.cnn.com/2019/01/28/tech/deepfake-lawmakers/index.html; Simon Parkin, "The Rise of the Deepfake and the Threat to Democracy," *Guardian*, June 22, 2019, https://www.theguardian.com/technology/ng-interactive/2019/jun/22/the-rise-of-the-deepfake-and-the-threat-to-democracy.

11. James Vincent, "Deepfake Detection Algorithms Will Never Be Enough," *The Verge*, June 27, 2019, https://www.theverge.com/2019/6/27/18715235/deepfake-detection-ai-algorithms-accuracy-will-they-ever-work.

12. Britt Paris and Joan Donavan, "Deepfakes and Cheap Fakes: The Manipulation of Audio and Video Evidence," *Data and Society*, September 18, 2019, https://datasociety.net/wp-content/uploads/2019/09/DS_Deepfakes_Cheap_FakesFinal-1.pdf.

13. A. G. Sulzberger, "The Growing Threat to Journalism Around the World," *New York Times*, September 23, 2019, https://www.nytimes.com/2019/09/23/opinion/press-freedom-arthur-sulzberger.html.

14. Luisa Verdoliva, "Media Forensics and DeepFakes: An Overview," *IEEE Journal of Selected Topics in Signal Processing* 14, no. 5 (August 2020): 910–32.

15. Claire Wardle, "This Video May Not Be Real," *New York Times*, August 14, 2019, https://www.nytimes.com/2019/08/14/opinion/deepfakes-adele-disinformation.html.

16. Paul Chadwick, "The Liar's Dividend, and Other Challenges of Deep-Fake News," *Guardian*, July 22, 2018, https://www.theguardian.com/commentisfree/2018/jul/22/deep-fake-news-donald-trump-vladimir-putin.

17. Sharon Ringel and Angela Woodall, "A Public Record at Risk: The Dire State of News Archiving in the Digital Age," TOW Center for Digital Journalism, March 28, 2019, https://www.cjr.org/tow_center_reports/the-dire-state-of-news-archiving-in-the-digital-age.php.

18. Adrienne LaFrance, "Raiders of the Lost Web," *The Atlantic*, October 14, 2015, https://www.theatlantic.com/technology/archive/2015/10/raiders-of-the-lost-web/409210/.

19. "SaTC: CORE: Medium: Collaborative: Cryptographic Provenance for Digital Publishing," *National Science Foundation*, https://www.nsf.gov/awardsearch/showAward?AWD_ID=1940670; Sasha Koren, "Introducing the News Provenance Project," *NYT Open*, July 23, 2019, https://open.nytimes.com/introducing-the-news-provenance-project-723dbaf07c44.

20. Lily Hay Newman, "What We Know About Friday's Massive East Coast Internet Outage," *Wired*, October 21, 2016, https://www.wired.com/2016/10/internet-outage-ddos-dns-dyn/.

21. "Hurricane Sandy: Elderly People Trapped, Gas Shortages, and Gridlock," *Mother Jones*, October 25, 2012, https://www.motherjones.com/politics/2012/10/hurricane-sandy/.

22. Susan E. McGregor, "You Are Here: Site-Specific Storytelling Using Offline Networks," Tow Center for Digital Journalism, August 25, 2017, https://www.cjr.org/tow_center_reports/storytelling-offline-networks.php.

23. A. W. Gieger, "Key Findings About the Online News Landscape in America," Pew Research Center, September 11, 2019, https://www.pewresearch.org/fact-tank/2019/09/11/key-findings-about-the-online-news-landscape-in-america/.

24. McGregor, "You Are Here."

25. Nate Anderson, "PirateBox: An 'Artistic Provocation' in Lunchbox Form," *Ars Technica*, January 2011, http://arstechnica.com/tech-policy/2011/01/piratebox-an-artistic-provocation-in-lunchbox-form/; Dan Phiffer, "OccupyHere," 2016, https://github.com/occupyhere/occupy.here; Jason Griffey, "Library Box," Librarybox Project, 2012, http://librarybox.us/; Susan E. McGregor, "Can Mesh Networks and Offline Wireless Move from Protest Tools to News?" Nieman Lab, November 10, 2014, https://www.niemanlab.org/2014/11/can-mesh-networks-and-offline-wireless-move-from-protest-tools-to-news/; McGregor, "You Are Here."

26. Kelly Weill, "Will *Daily Stormer* Founder Andrew Anglin Lose His Website on the Lam?" *Daily Beast*, September 21, 2017, updated September 22, 2017, https://www.thedailybeast.com/will-daily-stormer-founder-andrew-anglin-lose-his-website-on-the-lam.

27. Joscelyn Jurich, "What's Missing from Journalism Education and How We Can Improve the Field," Knight Foundation, March 2016, https://knightfoundation.org/articles/whats-missing-data-journalism-education-and-how-we-can-improve-field1.